"This memoir was a complete pleasure, beginning to end, full of love and zaniness and tenderness and absolutely fascinating detail. Randy Fertel was blessed with an incredible wealth of anecdote, and his prose brings it all vividly to life. What a fine piece of writing this is."

– TIM O'BRIEN
National Book Award–winning author of *The Things They Carried*

"*The Gorilla Man and the Empress of Steak* is a one-of-a-kind real-life tale, as layered, rich, and full of surprises as a street map of New Orleans. Randy Fertel had the good fortune to be born to a pair of American originals, and his parents had the great fortune to live out their fascinating lives in front of a son who's a natural-born storyteller. This is one of my favorite books of the year."

– MARK CHILDRESS
New York Times bestselling author of *Georgia Bottoms* and *Crazy in Alabama*

"With unsparing honesty and love, Randy Fertel unravels the mystery of his eccentric, legendary parents. *The Gorilla Man and the Empress of Steak* is by turns wry and sad, hilarious and heartbreaking, but always, always delectable."

– STEWART O'NAN
award-winning author of *Emily, Alone*

"This wonderfully affecting family memoir is a well-told tale of personalized social history, a sentient evocation of the sights, sounds, tastes, smells and feel of New Orleans and its sprawling interface with the mighty river and gulf that are its hope and despair, its inescapable fate. Drawing from 200 years of his family's thrive-and-survive presence on the lip of a watery grave, Randy Fertel gives us a palpable sense of its essence—as close as you can get without living there yourself."

– JOHN EGERTON
author of *Southern Food: At Home, on the Road, in History*

"Fortune gave Randy Fertel this zany cast of characters: the shoplifting grandmother, the litigious, multimillionaire mother with a taste for the ponies, the father whose family made its money in pawn shops. But from this rich raw material he has added his own wit, meticulous research, and gift for telling a tale. Read this book for the joy of it. But be forewarned. If you're not careful, you'll laugh your way into a knowledge of running a steak house, collecting debts from the mafia, and taking the *family* out of a 'family business.'"

– LOLIS ELIE
Story editor HBO's *Treme*, co-producer PBS's *Faubourg Treme*

"*The Gorilla Man and the Empress of Steak* is that rare memoir that manages to be both intimately personal and yet of broad appeal. For it is truly the portrait of a generation, even as it brings vividly to life a panoply of individual characters in New Orleans. They may be black or white or Creole; they may be male or female. But all fill the reader with joy and wonder, and a fair share of tears as well. Beautifully written, affectionate, witty, this book tugs us from one cover to the other."

– DAVID H. LYNN
Editor, *The Kenyon Review*

"Who better to deliver the strange soul of New Orleans, a city we can't live without, than Randy Fertel? Ruth and Rodney's child, who suffered and gloried terribly at their hands, is New Orleans's latest beautiful family memoirist."

– PAUL HENDRICKSON
National Book Award finalist and author of *Looking for the Light: The Hidden Life and Art of Marion Post Wolcott*

THE GORILLA MAN
AND THE
EMPRESS OF STEAK

THE GORILLA MAN

AND THE

EMPRESS OF STEAK

A NEW ORLEANS FAMILY MEMOIR

RANDY FERTEL

UNIVERSITY PRESS OF MISSISSIPPI / JACKSON

WILLIE MORRIS BOOKS IN MEMOIR AND BIOGRAPHY

www.upress.state.ms.us

Designed by Peter D. Halverson

The University Press of Mississippi is a member of the Association of
American University Presses. ·

Illustrations are from the collection of the author except where otherwise noted.

Portions of this book appeared in different forms in *New Orleans Magazine, Corn Bread
Nation 2: The Best of Southern Food Writing, Kenyon Review, My New Orleans: Ballads to the
Big Easy*, ed. Rosemary James, *Intersection / New Orleans*, ed. Anne Gisleson, *Gastronomica,
Creative Nonfiction, Zenchilada*, and the play *Native Tongues*, directed by Carl Walker.

First printing 2011
∞
Library of Congress Cataloging-in-Publication Data

Fertel, Randy.
The Gorilla Man and the Empress of Steak : a New Orleans family memoir / Randy Fertel.
p. cm. — (Willie Morris books in memoir and biography)
Includes bibliographical references and index.
ISBN 978-1-61703-082-6 (cloth : alk. paper) — ISBN 978-1-61703-083-3 (ebook)
1. Fertel, Rodney. 2. Fertel, Ruth. 3. Fertel, Randy—Childhood and youth. 4. Fertel, Randy—
Family. 5. New Orleans (La.)—Biography. 6. Restaurateurs—Louisiana—New Orleans—
Biography. 7. Businesspeople—Louisiana—New Orleans—Biography. 8. New Orleans (La.)—
Social life and customs. I. Title.
F379.N553A227 2011
976.3'35—dc22   2011010691

British Library Cataloging-in-Publication Data available

for Matt and Owen

in an effort to turn the page

on the family legacies

Steak for all of us immigrants means America.
BETTY FUSSELL[1]

The image of a wild animal becomes a starting point for a daydream.
JOHN BERGER[2]

CONTENTS

THE GORILLA MAN
AND THE
EMPRESS OF STEAK

OVERTURE

THE OLYMPIA BRASS BAND PLAYED "DIDN'T SHE RAMBLE" AFTER MY mother's body had been "cut loose," as the saying goes in New Orleans, placed in the mausoleum she and her best friend had built together. As is customary in New Orleans, the band played a dirge, "A Closer Walk with Thee," on the way to the entombment. Then, turning from the grave, we celebrated the life:

> *Didn't she ramble . . . she rambled*
> *Rambled all around . . . in and out of town*
> *Didn't she ramble . . . didn't she ramble*
> *She rambled till the butcher cut her down.*

The mourners formed the second line behind the band and the family—what there was of it—marching or dancing to the syncopated rhythms, waving handkerchiefs and twirling umbrellas in the hot mid-April sun. Everyone knew this was the way it should be. Though she grew up in the Mississippi Delta south of New Orleans, Ruth Fertel was born in New Orleans and had thrived there, reigning as one of the great restaurateurs in a city of great restaurants.

The brass band celebrated the considerable rambling she had managed. I had just done the same in my eulogy. A good friend, who knew of my conflicts with my mother, told me later he had a moment of panic when I rose to give it. *I didn't know which speech you would give*, he laughed. *I knew either one could have been honest.*

Ramble she did indeed. And not often in ways most would count ordinary. One night at dinner, in the late 1990s, five or so years before, my mother announced that she and Lana Duke had purchased a plot at the prestigious Metairie Cemetery and would build a tomb together. For almost thirty years, Lana Duke had worked hand-in-hand with Mom to develop the advertising and the Ruth's Chris brand. As Mom's empire grew, Lana not only worked for the company but also became part of it, owning franchises in San Antonio and Toronto. But I was stunned. A Fertel-Duke tomb? *There goes Lana again.* She would be family for eternity, setting a new benchmark for BFFs everywhere.

My next thought, however, was, well, after all, it's the first indication Mom's given that she's mortal, so, hey, don't stand in the way.

Mom took me to see the cemetery grounds. As we walked among the tombs, Mom noted departed customers. *He liked his filet medium rare. She liked her martinis up.* We arrived at the twenty-seven-foot plot, under moss-draped cypress trees. Mom liked the nearby lagoon where the ducks' swimming let her imagine she might hunt her way through eternity. *Maybe you should bury me with the 12-gauge Beretta.* She hoped the spot's beauty would encourage visitors to linger. *I know you're all going to love visiting me here.* The cemetery was once the site of the Metairie Race Course founded in 1838; a century or so later, Mom became the first licensed woman Thoroughbred trainer in Louisiana's distinguished racing history and shared a stable of horses with my dad. *Maybe we could install a betting window?* she added.

I pretty much forgot about this *folie*, until a year later I got a call from a friend in the funeral business. His family had been burying mine for three generations. He had just passed by the Fertel-Duke Mausoleum. *It's the most elaborate tomb to be built in New Orleans in fifty years. Which is saying something*, he added unnecessarily. Outside, three colors of granite, bas-reliefs, pilasters, and granite benches. Inside, a stained glass window with an angel trumpeting Louis Armstrong's most famous line: "It's a Wonderful World." And space for three on each side. The art department at Lana's advertising firm, Duke Unlimited, had designed it.

No doubt it was Lana who conceived the "tomb picnic," too, soon after its completion. Lana's instincts as a publicist did not sleep. Two hundred guests were invited for the "blessing of the tomb." A large tent for the occasion was sited on the lagoon's bank. It was monsoon season and torrential rains began promptly as we settled into our greasy barbecue chicken and ribs. *If there's a tomb picnic for anyone on the planet that should not have bad food*, I grumbled to my friends, *it's my mom's tomb picnic*. The band was a sleazy white party band from Fats Domino's Ninth Ward that played all the favorites that Fats and Frank and Elvis made famous, lo, these many years ago—but I wish they had been walking *from* New Orleans! *If there's a city whose tomb picnic should not have bad music, it's New Orleans.*

As the torrents continued, the lagoon overflowed. Soon we were surrounded by a moat, shielding ourselves from the downpour as best we could, removing our shoes and socks and plashing around as the water encroached. Father Bob Masset, a Holy Name priest and bon vivant who had been enjoying Mom's steaks on his parishioners' dime since the sixties, parted the seas with his jokes and his benediction. *Father Bob liked his ribeyes rare*, she announced when she took the mic. Just then, lightning struck close. She jumped and the sound system crackled. *Have I offended Somebody?* she wondered. Her death in 2002 was still three years off.

Rumor had it, the tomb had cost $750,000, "the most expensive shotgun double in New Orleans history," a friend quipped. "Question is, Randy, will you be buried there? And who will be on top, you or Lana?" I begged him to stop conjuring such images. Lana's got heft.

The next day, beneath a banner headline, "Tomb Share," the New Orleans *Times-Picayune* covered the party for "Ruth Fertel's ultimate retirement spot." A large photograph showed Father Bob and Mr. Davis, who had been sculpting my mother's beehive hairdos since 1964, dancing a jig before the tomb with Ruth and Lana.

Since our cities of the dead are on the tourist beat, almost immediately tour busses added the Fertel-Duke tomb to their itineraries. But word got back to Mom that another rumor was making the rounds. Some New Orleanians took the double tomb to mean that Ruth Fertel was gay. For once, it was Mom who was stunned, almost to silence. Then simply, "Well, let them think what they want."

The tomb had preceded the cancer, though some wondered, *maybe she knew something*. Mom smoked heavily most of her life, Pall Malls, then L&Ms, ending with low-tar coffin nails. She quit a number of times. *Guess I smoked too long*, she quipped after her diagnosis, as if she had miscalculated how long she let her bet ride at the craps table.

Mom was given, on the outside, six months. The cancer had spread to her liver and lymph nodes. A fighter as always, she went into remission twice and lasted two years. During chemotherapy, Mom wore a Ruth's Chris ball cap to cover her baldness. During hospitalizations, no one held Mom's hand at her bedside. She had trained us all too well.

She missed her own tribute dinner by a week. Some friends had doubted the wisdom of my hosting such a dinner, planned for six months, that to do so was to deny my conflicted feelings. For me the challenge was to honor both feelings—both were real—and to honor my feelings about my mother's public persona publically and my private feelings privately. It would be good to reconcile those conflicts but in the meantime the challenge was to hold them both in suspension. This book is an effort to do both, to honor both sets of feelings and to reconcile their conflict.

After the dinner, attended by some five hundred guests, my aunt Helen said the one thing I longed to hear, *You done her proud.*

"Everything was Ruth Ann, Ruth Ann, Ruth Ann," Aunt Helen began. "Ruth Ann could do no wrong."

Deep in the Mississippi Delta, I sat a couple years after the funeral at Helen's kitchen table as she ladled a bowl of her seafood gumbo. I was trying to understand whence came the Empress of Steak's imperial sway. Helen had been married to Mom's brother, Sig. Sig had died ten years earlier but maybe Helen could explain. Why had it always been so hard for me to feel close to Mom?

Seventy miles below New Orleans, Helen's hometown, Buras, is a sliver of land surrounded by water, river on one side, bayous and marshland on the other. It is ten miles below Happy Jack, where Mom and Sig grew up. The crabs, shrimp, and oysters Helen spooned over rice had been taken the day before from the bayous, bays, and marshes that had been the family's larder for generations. The roux that made the gumbo so deep brown and rich came from my great-great-uncle Martin's recipe, a family treasure.

Helen grew up in a close-knit Croatian enclave in Buras. When she married Uncle Sig, she moved upriver to Happy Jack and learned the way the French cooked. The Croats based their cuisine on spaghetti, the French, on rice. Uncle Martin had learned his roux from his mother, Josephine Hingle, whom everyone called Gr'Mom. The Hingles had come from Alsace in the 1720s. They could cook, *I guarANtee, cher,* as they said in their

1. Paw-Paw with Ruth Ann and Sig, c. 1928.

Cajun-tinged accent. But ask if they were Cajun and *No, we are French French* and they expected you to understand the distinction.

Just outside Helen's kitchen window, ocean-going tankers, on their way to or from New Orleans, loomed above the tall levee that held back the Mississippi River. Around us, I noted a few familiar scraps from a lifetime of memories at Sig's Antique Restaurant. Helen's sideboard held family photographs and knick-knacks Sig had collected for the restaurant. He had built it with his own hands from huge cypress beams and old, soft red brick he scavenged from the foundations of crumbling plantations.

At Sig's Antique Restaurant in Happy Jack, Helen ruled as cook. Sig ruled as architect, mason, carpenter, and chief raconteur, a highball never far from reach. They flourished for a time in the sixties and seventies catering to the Freeport Sulphur Company—just a mile downriver—and Shell and Humble Oil and later Exxon, whose operations riddled the Delta. The oil crash in the early eighties put an end to their thriving. Still, weekend fishermen from New Orleans, driving back up from Empire and Venice with ice chests full of redfish and speckle' trout, stopped for Helen's famous gumbo and crab-stuffed flounder. Best of all, they stopped for the prime steaks that came through the back fence at the original Chris Steak House that would later become my mother's restaurant empire: Ruth's Chris Steak House.

Helen recalled, "Big Brother Sig couldn't get any attention. Your paw-paw was a good man, but . . . , well, for Paw-Paw, Ruth hung the moon." Helen paused. "Your grandmother Nan' Jo' tried to make it up to Sig, to make up for Paw-Paw's favoring Ruth."

During the Second World War Sig had served as a paratrooper, 82nd Airborne. Sig was the platoon's sole survivor after a drop beyond the Rhine. Demobbed, he learned that Paw-Paw had used his GI money to send Ruth to college when she started at fifteen.

"Sig was used to Ruth getting her way," Helen said sadly. "Sig always gave in." She remembered how, when both their restaurants were up and running, "In all those stories they did on Ruth, she never mentioned that her brother had a restaurant. It would have been so easy to say something nice."

Helen spooned more rice and gumbo into my bowl. Food was always our family's comfort, the closest thing we had to feeling close. She allowed herself a chuckle. "Ruth sure hit the roof when that Underground Gourmet fella gave Sig's restaurant a better review than hers. Collins said our steaks were as 'platonic' as Ruth's *used to be*, when all the time we were getting the meat out of her walk-in cooler. Boy, she was hot!" Helen has a great laugh. Gifted with great Croatian bones, now in her eighties she is still a beauty.

I asked Aunt Helen if Mom had always been so competitive. She reminded me of the story, long in family lore, when they were kids playing on the levee. Three years younger, Ruth Ann wanted to shoot Sig's new BB gun. They knew Paw-Paw's rule: *If you ever point that gun at anyone, I'll throw it in the river.* So Ruth Ann said, "If you don't let me shoot your BB gun, I'll tell Dad you pointed it at me." Which she did. Paw-Paw climbed the levee and into the river went the gun. Sig watched as it turned over and over, end over end, until the current swept it away.

I remembered Uncle Sig telling that tale at one of our huge Thanksgivings, with a bit too much of his homemade orange wine in him. He chuckled his way through the story but Mom cut it short, furious, saying, "That never happened. I never did that."

I had come to Aunt Helen with a need to know how my mother could have been so generous to those at a distance and so competitive with those who were close, like me. Aunt Helen offered another clue.

"Of course, she was competitive with your father, too, with the race-horses and all."

When I am introduced in New Orleans, locals are likely to hang on my name for a moment.

—*Fertel . . . Fertel . . .*

If the looks are bright and eager, as if a mouthwatering steak has just been set before them, then I know I'll hear, *Are you Ruth Fertel's son?* Or, as if I were the offspring of a restaurant, *Are you Ruth's Chris's son?*

If the look takes a decidedly wary turn, then I'm sure to hear, *Are you related to Rodney Fertel?* Or worse, *Are you the Gorilla Man's son?*

For many years, the wary looks outnumbered the eager ones. I was away at college during my father's Gorilla Man campaign, but his name and reputation have been hard to shake.

My parents had colorful and fascinating lives—but to live inside their worlds wasn't exactly nurturing. My father, Rodney Fertel, was odd, self-centered, and nuts. In New Orleans he will forever be known as the Gorilla Man, the local character who campaigned for mayor in a gorilla suit. My slight, feisty mother was determined to feed the world. Ruth Udstad Fertel won every accolade in the restaurant industry and became a female icon in the business world, "The First Lady of American Restaurants," according to the official corporate narrative. But the Empress of Steak reserved all the glory for herself. Her appetite for winning excluded everyone, even her offspring. Nearly all the key players in the global empire of Ruth's Chris Steak House ended up suing her, to get what they felt they deserved.

I must confess that I was among them.

CHAPTER ONE

HOT SPRINGS

IF WE COULD RETURN TO THE MOMENT CAPTURED IN A 1948 PHOTO, this couple, Mom and Dad, Ruth and Rodney, might catch our eye as they stride down Central Avenue in Hot Springs, Arkansas. In full sunlight, Ruth holds the crook of Rodney's right arm and gazes at the camera with self-assurance and an easy smile. While women behind her clutch their bags tight, she carries a handbag by its strap. She wears heels with bows.

That sunny day in Hot Springs, an unseen ornate gold barrette tooled in her initials—RUF—holds her hair swept back from her high brow. The barrette is a gift from her husband, whose family is in the trade—pawnshops.

His face in shadow and wearing sunglasses, not unaware of the camera himself, her husband gazes at her with fondness and regard. Rodney sports a tie with bold ovals and in his right hand he carries a folded paper, probably the Daily Racing Form. He wears his shirtsleeves rolled. His left arm swings forward with a watch on his wrist, the first of many gold Rolexes, and a cigarette in the tips of his fingers—he has yet to give them up. One can almost see the "insouciant challenge of his loping walk," as Terry Teachout, Louis Armstrong's recent biographer, paints it.[3] Dad shared with Pops the same neighborhood, New Orleans's South Rampart Street.

It is three years since the end of the Second World War in which Rodney Fertel (né Weinberg) did not serve (4-F for reasons that have always been obscure). It's two years since Ruth Fertel (née Udstad) graduated from Louisiana State University with honors in physics and chemistry. She is

1.1 Ruth and Rodney in Hot
Springs, Arkansas, c. 1948.

twenty-one, he is twenty-seven. In less than a year, their firstborn son, Jerry,
will enter the world. In two years, I will arrive.

They come from a watery world and they've found another here. In the
hills to their left and right are Hot Springs Mountain and West Mountain
where forty-seven underground springs spew a million gallons of water a
day, no matter the weather. Carbon dating shows that four thousand years
ago the water fell as rain upon the Ouachita Forest of central Arkansas.
Since then it has seeped slowly down through the earth's crust until, su-
perheated by the earth's core, it gushes rapidly to the surface, a constant
143 degrees Fahrenheit. Mountain Valley Water, Rodney's lifelong favorite
brand, was founded nearby. Since the dawn of time, spring floods have
coursed south, building with alluvial ooze the deep Mississippi Delta where
Ruth was born.

In this year, 1948, Hot Springs is a wide-open town, dominated by the
Southern Club, a gambling house in operation since 1893. In Las Vegas,

1.2 Ruth and Rodney cutting up in Hot Springs.

Bugsy Siegel's Flamingo Hotel is only two years old and "the Strip" still but a dream. The mineral baths and the gambling tables draw Rodney and Ruth here from their home in New Orleans for long stays. Rodney enjoys independent means inherited from his pawnbroker grandparents; no job pulls him home.

The horses bring them, too. In 1948, the Fair Grounds in New Orleans celebrates its Diamond Jubilee, seventy-five years of continuous Thoroughbred racing. Hot Springs's Oaklawn Park is almost as old. This very summer, Louisiana governor Earl Long, Huey's brother and an inveterate gambler, comes to Hot Springs "for his arthritis." Governor Long begins his day with the *Daily Racing Form* and the tout sheets. He helped the Mob install slots throughout Louisiana; they let him know when the fix is in. Ruth and Rodney Fertel share Governor Long's taste for racehorses. In a few years, Ruth will earn her Thoroughbred trainer's license.

Rodney and Ruth sometimes stay at the Hotel Arkansas, a spa and casino run by Owney Madden, a gangster from Liverpool by way of Manhattan's Hell's Kitchen. Owney Madden, or "Owney the Killer," as he was called, had turned the Cotton Club in Harlem into a success before going upriver to spend seven years in Sing-Sing—which didn't prevent his owning a casino in unregulated Hot Springs. To Mae West, fellow denizen of Hell's Kitchen whose career he bankrolled and whom he dated, Madden was "sweet, but oh so vicious." The Hotel Arkansas is favored by gangsters both Jewish and Italian: Louis Lepke, Lucky Luciano, Meyer Lansky, Joy Adonis, Frank Costello. Luciano fled the Waldorf-Astoria for Hot Springs in 1936 when Tom Dewey, district attorney of New York City and future governor of New York, indicted him for prostitution. It took twenty Arkansas Rangers to surround and take Luciano at the Hotel Arkansas.

Still in the honeymoon glow, Rodney this time splurges on a room at the Arlington Hotel, looming beyond the camera's sight at the head of Central Avenue. Al Capone at one time kept a fourth-floor corner suite overlooking the Southern Club, his favorite, just across the street. He played at a raised poker table in order to command a clear view of the entire room. When Capone strode down Bathhouse Row, his goons surrounded him, two in front, two behind, and one on either side. Hot Springs had America's largest treatment center for the syphilis that would later kill him.

The famous New Orleans madam Norma Wallace was known to vacation here with her boyfriend Sam Hunt, an affiliate of Al Capone. Norma's first whorehouse in New Orleans was half a block from the Fertel Loan Office, where Rodney's grandparents made the money that made him rich. Sam and Julia Fertel saved every nickel and dime to buy property on Canal Street, the main business district in New Orleans. They also purchased the wood-framed house at 359 Whittington Avenue in Hot Springs where Rodney will later live. There, I will first hear a woodpecker and there, thirty years later, Telemachus-like but only half-wanting reconciliation, I will seek my father and find the door ajar, the house empty, filled only with the rainwater that falls through the hole in the roof and the floor beneath it.

Over their shoulders the photo shows a sign for Hammons:

SEA FOOD STEAKS CHICKEN

Hammons, no apostrophe. *Sea Food*, two words. Inside a sign promises *One Day Out of the Ocean*, meaning one day up from the Louisiana bayous where Ruth was born. Rodney prefers Hammons to the Arlington's grand dining room with its organ and white-gloved black waiters and where, at age thirteen, I develop a taste for watercress salad and cornbread sticks slathered in butter and honey.

Rodney has not yet developed his taste for political clowning: his Gorilla Man campaign for New Orleans mayor, with its catchy slogan—*Don't vote for a monkey. Elect Fertel and get a Gorilla*—lies twenty years in the future.

Ruth has not yet read the classified ad that will, in 1965, lead her to borrow $22,000 to purchase a little steak house with seventeen tables near the Fair Grounds in New Orleans.

My parents were married just a few years, from 1947 to 1958. They each had a certain glamour. But it's a wonder that two such strong personalities ever shared the same coordinates. How had they come about, which is to say, how had I come about? I asked Mom once, long after their contentious divorce, "Why did you marry him?"

"He had horses." Her matter-of-factness tried to hide her own befuddlement and hardly cleared up mine. "I was a country girl and a tomboy. I was at LSU. Your dad owned a stable.

"When I first met him," she added with a caustic laugh, "I thought he was a stable boy. We ran off and got married, honeymooned in Hot Springs, then took a trip around the world. Though your dad cut it short."

Which means my first sibling rivals were racehorses. Later Dad would add two gorillas to the list and Mom a restaurant.

CHAPTER TWO

HOME MOVIES AND SNAPSHOTS

DAD ALWAYS HAD THE LATEST GADGET—LIKE OUR KODAK BROWNIE Hawkeye box camera and Super-8 movie camera and projector. Family photos and filmstrips found their way into a cardboard box, and I liked to explore its jumbled contents. I mastered the family's eight-millimeter projector and, darkening our front room on Seville Drive and putting a white sheet over the painting of the Arab and camels (bought in Paris on Mom and Dad's honeymoon), I'd thread the sprockets and adjust the frame. I'd watch dozens of cartoon reels that Dad brought home—and home movies, lots of home movies that I rescued from the cardboard box. Decades later I had them transferred to DVD, and I watch them still.

Reel after reel of these silent home movies show Dad's clown face, atop his athletic frame, mugging for the camera. On a dock littered with Spanish mackerel, his arms grow ever larger to measure the one that got away. Then a jump cut to Dad lowering the smallest fish, head first, into his clownish maw. In another reel, at the Audubon Zoo, Mom behind the camera, he makes like a chimpanzee—*chee-chee, chee-chee*—scratching his armpits, then his crotch. The screen goes suddenly dark.

Before a thatched *chikee* hut at Paradise Beach in the Bahamas, joking, he shakes a magnificent palm tree to get coconuts. Then Dad takes his turn behind the camera, following Mom, who glides, cigarette in hand, to the same palm and leans demurely, smiling.

2.1 Randy on Seville Drive.

Dad often manned the camera. Always glowing before the lens, Mom tosses her boys in the air, swings us, helps us with our first steps, and displays us in matching, starched outfits. In reel after reel, Mom is beautifully groomed—splashing into the waves toward the camera, target shooting with rifles and revolvers, deep sea fishing or casting from the dock, far and effortlessly. Mom was one of the boys, a diminutive Kate Hepburn, game for anything. And always, always outclassing Dad, his mugging no match for Mom's thousand-watt smile.

A family movie shows Paw-Paw and Grandma Jo's house in Happy Jack: we are all on the back porch, a cypress cistern to the left, a washing machine with its hand-cranked mangles sheltered on the porch to the right. I am two years old, and the camera follows my project: moving a litter of kittens from the yard, one by one up the steps, across the porch, and through the screen door. The camera pans across as Jerry, age three, follows me from behind and releases the kittens one by one back into the yard.

Another: it's the gentle surf at Grand Isle, Louisiana. Jerry enters the frame at a dead run. He runs right over me—*plop!*—then walks, triumphant, toward the camera, which shakes with laughter.

Another: Mardi Gras season had our complete attention. One home movie shows Dad mugging with me at his side on Grandma Annie's gallery overlooking Rampart Street. Below us, awaiting the Zulu parade, shoulder-to-shoulder, the crowd roils with anticipation of floats full of black men in black face and grass skirts. Everyone wants the hand-painted coconuts they throw from the floats. Louis Armstrong was King of the Zulus once, *the proudest day of his life.*

Another family movie records a costume party that may be Mardi Gras or my fourth birthday. I am a clown with a ruffled collar out to my shoulders.

One Mardi Gras, I am on the "neutral ground" on Canal Street, the wide median where the streetcars run. I am behind the stands that line Canal Street, scrambling for some beads on the streetcar tracks. The beads are glass—jewels to a five-year-old—with little tags that declare their origin in Czechoslovakia. A black boy about my age asks to see them. I am five, proud to show hard-won treasure. He grabs them and when I won't let go, he breaks them. Better broken than that I should possess them. I stand aghast, then run back crying to the stands.

Downtown at the Saenger, Dad can watch two or three movies in an afternoon. Or, as often happened, sleep through them, but not before buying popcorn with extra butter for Jerry and me.

Long before the Gorilla Man campaign, *King Kong* was Dad's favorite. Dad could watch it three times in a row. The Fox Theatre, near the racetrack, revived it one Saturday matinee. King Kong's first appearance sent me screaming up and down the aisle.

Jerry and I play pool in a place we call "Dad's bar." Dad is said never to have worked a day in his life but he holds court here, his building, his bar. The first toys that I remember playing with are a couple of magnets, black-and-white Scotties from Haig & Haig Scotch. I play endlessly with their attraction and repulsion, turning them to make them dance apart and jump together.

Too young to hold cues, Jerry and I roll the ivory balls around by hand. Not gently. Tender fingers unwilling to wait their turn, curled around ivory balls, get crunched.

—*Cheater!*

—*You're a cheater!!*

While Mom pours drinks behind the bar, cigarette in hand, and Dad talks to his cronies, Jerry hits me. The *faucets flow*—Mom's phrase—and she adds, *If you don't quit pouting, you'll trip over that bottom lip.*

• • •

Jerry's attacks come at the drop of a hat. I stare at him a certain way, and the next thing I know, I'm bloody. When I complain that Jerry has beaten me up, Mom says, *Well, you probably gave him one of your looks.*

The room I share with Jerry is a battleground divided by an imaginary line. Red drapes, red-and-white star quilts, red enameled bookcases filled with a set that includes *Black Beauty* and *Treasure Island* which I alone read. I covered my bedstead with college and university pennant decals I ordered from the inside back cover of a *Superman* comic. Our separate closets' floors are each a jumble of clothes, sports gear, and toys. I cross a dangerous no-man's-land to reach my bed on the far wall.

—*Mom, Jerry's on my side.*
—*Jerry, stay on your side.*
—*Randy stared at me.*
—*Randy, don't stare. Can't you boys get along?*

"Ruth, the way those boys fight, it's just not right. You should take them to see someone," said Gloria, Mom's one-time college roommate and best friend.

"Boys will be boys," Mom replied. "Remember how Jerry used to pull himself up to Randy's crib and bite his toes till he cried?"

It's February fifth, Mom's birthday. There is no birthday party. I'm standing in the yellow Formica kitchen alone with Mom. I've learned two songs in Mrs. Fleming's Cub Scout den, "M.O.T.H.E.R." and "Ka-Ka-Ka Katie." I've decided this will be part of my birthday gift. My face is red but my heart is full, and I stumble through the songs.

Mom leans on the yellow Formica counter in slacks and a blouse, her smile strained. Her nose is straight, her cheekbones high, and her hair shoulder length, brown with a shock of natural dark blond highlights pulled back from her brow by her monogrammed gold barrette. Freckles give her that country-girl look. I think she's beautiful, like the other song we learned, "Five-Foot-Two, Eyes of Blue." Which she is. Which she has.

She uncomfortably gives me a quick hug. I uncomfortably give Mom her other presents—a kitchen fork and spatula that I've bought on my own at Morgan and Lindsey, the five-and-dime in the Parkchester Shopping Center, an adventurous bike ride from home. I spent an hour deciding what to buy her with the money I saved. They will help turn pork chops and flip banana pancakes, residing in the utensil drawer for the rest of our stay on

2.2 Mom and Jerry on Seville Drive.

Seville Drive—two decades. Their cheap baked-on enamel paint will slowly chip away.

We are sitting around the kitchen table, yellow Formica counters nearby, the electric cooktop and oven. It's almost dinnertime. Red beans simmer on the electric stove. We play 500 Rummy.

"Sometimes I wonder if maybe we are being dreamed," I dream aloud in Mom's hearing.

"What?"

"Like we're people in someone else's dream. . . ."

"Randy, don't be stupid."

The jack of hearts I throw down is no match for my reddened face.

I've been sent to my room after a fight. Mom comes in and sits on the edge of my bed.

She loves me, she explains, but doesn't like me. . . . I should make myself more likeable.

Does Mom think that this will help me mend my ways? Mom doesn't say how. *Is Jerry someone she can like?* I wonder. *What makes Jerry so likable?*

Jerry suffers from migraines. When they come on, he darkens our room, takes to his bed and cries himself to sleep. Mom brings him a cold washcloth for his forehead. I give him his darkness and quiet and stay out of his way.

At home Mom's nickname for me is *Randy Pandy*, after the poor slob of a panda bear that is one of Woody Woodpecker's chief targets. My sympathies in the world of Woody and Andy Panda are simple but in the world of Tom and Jerry they are complicated. Both are tricksters, each targeting the other using different means. Tom the Cat relies on his brute strength to offset his opponent and Jerry the Mouse relies on his cunning to outwit his. Tom smirks while Jerry, in whose name I hear an echo of my brother's, wears a smile as puckish as his countertricks. I long for the power of Jerry the Mouse to dodge his larger enemy. And for once to get him back.

I see some home movies without the help of a projector.

I am standing on the porch, a white railing before me, the soft greens of early summer all around. A woodpecker taps. The soft liquid light is not the hammer and anvil sunshine of south Louisiana where we live most of the year. The Ozarks' gentle foothills are mountains to us who see Monkey Hill in Audubon Park as a vast peak, taller than the highest levee, built so local kids would have a place to roll downhill.

But suddenly I am aware of difference all around me. The woodpecker's resonant tapping seems to float not just on the air but also on the light. The air, too, is different, soft and liquid, though not with that oppressive saturation of the Delta air.

This front porch is my whole world. The woodpecker fills it up with its shudder and with the quiver of the me that watches and hears and feels the me listening. How many fingers am I? Three? Four? By myself, on the porch, listening to the air and light.

CHAPTER THREE

THOROUGHBREDS

IN 1955, EXCITEMENT SEIZED OUR HOUSEHOLD AS MOM PREPARED to take the test for her Thoroughbred trainer's license. Horse racing was a largely male world. Mom and Dad both loved horses, but only Mom had the confidence to master the book on which aspiring trainers were tested.

In the oral exam, the racing stewards tried to challenge her knowledge of horses. Mom was exultant: the first woman Thoroughbred trainer in Louisiana. The *Daily Racing Form* article—"Young Mom Outruns Stewards"—was made into a varnished plaque that hung between our baby pictures in the den on Seville Drive.

Mom and Dad stabled the horses at the backside of the track, just a few miles from where we lived in new Gentilly, out by Lake Pontchartrain. The oldest continuously running track in the nation, the Fair Grounds Racetrack was buoyed by the Frenchman's ingrained passions for horseflesh and for gambling.

Mornings at the barn were brisk. The Fair Grounds Racetrack had a winter season, Thanksgiving through Easter. Robins flocked in the infield, tens of thousands of them, "the harbingers of spring," a sight in the dead of winter that contradicted the lessons of kindergarten. But it was for me the only thing out of joint here. With enough going on to keep us occupied, even Jerry and I seemed to get along. Around the barns, a Weimaraner named Smoke could climb ladders and pick out by smell individual oyster shells that we took turns throwing into a whole pile of them, each a

3.1 Mom in the tackroom.

dead ringer for the rest. Goats, used to gentle edgy horses, would nudge me
when I fed them alfalfa, never fast enough.

Mom and Dad were in their glory. The horses were exercised and
clocked, then washed and curried, all rippling muscle and high spirits, high
stepping, prancing, champing at the bit as they shook their heads trying to
throw it. Their breath and wet backs turned to steam the wintry air. Then,
while they were hot-walked, wearing a path in front of the stalls, consulta-
tions ensued—*what regime the horse needed next, what tonic, what workout,
what race she was ready for*. They held high counsel, smoking and laughing.
Keep turning left was Dad's smug advice to me, when he'd let me hot-walk
one of the huge but reliable horses whose docility could be counted on. It
was important that horses cool down and dry out before being put up in
their stalls and he's happy to save the hot-walker's fifty-cent fee. Chico, the
groom, would pat their chests to see if they had cooled enough to be put
up. Other horses nickered at me from behind their Dutch doors, or, if I got
too close, might try to bite as I jumped out of the way. Dad provided sugar
cubes, apples, and carrots as horse treats. I stretched out my palm, arched
beyond flat, rubbing their hairy noses, nibbled by their fleshy lips, stroking
their strong glistening necks.

3.2 Dad with horse.

Mom or Dad would let me muck out the stalls with the big pitchfork that I could barely lift. Or I was put to saddle-soaping the tack, bridle and reins, and saddle, lathering the sponge with the big bar of clear brown soap, slathering on the oily suds that soaked into the glistening leather. I watched as Chico made up the oat mixture with the pungent rich additions of vitamins in molasses-like syrup. They'd let me hold the hose to fill the stall's bucket as Chico poured the oat mixture in the galvanized washtub that hung from a clip on the stall's planked wall.

With his Super-8, Dad filmed me astride a horse in the Fertel racing silks. I beamed, proud of my imagined mastery, as I desperately clung to the saddle horn. My western boots dangled high above the stirrups.

The morning workout done, we'd breakfast in the backside restaurant, the Horsemen's Cafeteria, with its smells of fried egg, bacon, and coffee—*you want pure or chicory?*—and, most pungent, horsemen of all shapes and sizes—owners, trainers, jockeys, exercise girls, hot-walkers, stall-muckers—most with leathery skin and the smell of cigarettes. More cigarettes, more laughing. Stories. *That nag. That boat race. Did you see that filly's quarter-mile workout? She's no Black Gold, but she can run. You bet, I like her in the Handicap.*

3.3 Mom with Chico.

The paddock before the race was tense with ritual pageantry. The horses paraded in. I smelled the rich urine-soaked straw and sensed the tension in the air. I watched the saddling, the consult amongst owner, trainer, and jockey, instructions given and received, the jockey handed up onto his mount wearing our colors, the horses prancing out to the famous rich alluvial sand of the Fair Grounds track. The horses had names like Speedy Jane, Skipper's Lady, Carrara Sue, and Squealing Star, a well-named gelding.

In the grandstands, we heard the bugles call, watched the horses break—*They're off!*—followed the pack as they circled the track, and listened to the announcer's rhythmic cadence. Horses and riders pounded down the stretch and crossed the wire. Jockeys saluted the grandstand with their whips before dismounting. Winning tickets were ballyhooed and curled in raised fists. Losing tickets were torn in disgust. Sometimes, the winner's circle photo featured Ruth and Rodney Fertel with the winning horse— Chico holding the reins and Little Joe mounted on high, the photo finish framed above.

Simplicio "Chico" Cosme, a Puerto Rican émigré who spoke little English, and the tiny Cajun jockey Joe Trahan, whose English wasn't a whole

Ruth Fertel Owner
R J Giardina Trainer Up
Eddie Delahoussaye Up
            Fair Grounds

FRISKIE FRAT

Shady Cross 2nd
Magic Deal 3rd
6 Furlongs 1:15:1
31 Jan 1979

3.4 Mom in the winner's circle.

lot better, were often around the house as well as the barn. Chico was *a good leg man* by my father's account. *A good leg man is hard to find.* He rubbed the acrid liniment on the horses' shanks and wrapped them tight and clean. Joe sat around the kitchen table, a country boy appreciative of Mom's cooking. But only nibbling: *Gotta watch my weight, cher.* Chico was a different story. His gratitude was destined for Dad.

As good as Mom's food was, Dad loved eating out.

This was the Fertel dining experience: Dad clowning; Jerry and Randy fighting; Mom rolling her eyes. At Tujague's, in the French Quarter since 1859, the five-course set menu was sure to include shrimp remoulade, then boiled beef brisket with Creole sauce. As we waited for its delivery, Dad made a show of eating as many crackers as appeared on the table, slathered in Heinz ketchup—he was master of the slow drip—or drenched in Lea & Perrins. If there were no crackers to amuse Dad, then our noses would serve. These he would "steal"—*got your nose*—and then "retrieve" from behind our ears: *Look what I found! Whataya gimme for it?* Our arms waving, delighted.

Or we would cross the Quarter to Turci's on Poydras, an Italian Galatoire's with its white-linen tables and mirror-lined walls, a place where finger bowls with lemon slices were delivered after the stuffed artichokes. I called the delicious pignoli nuts in the stuffing "artichoke seeds." While waiting for his spaghetti bordelaise, Dad catapulted spoons into his water glass or noisily missed. *Here, you try.* The one-armed lady who manned the register sent dark looks our way. She scared us, but she didn't faze Dad. Little fazed Dad, whose main goal was to get a rise out of you.

Tired of this game, Mom would perform her own trick, lighting a cigarette: *This works every time.* Sure enough, the waiter arrived. *Yep, here comes the food,* as she crushed it out. Then the meatballs and spaghetti in rich red gravy and Dad's spaghetti bordelaise with lots of garlic and parsley. When I turned up my nose, I'd hear, *Garlic is good for you, son.* Afterwards I would excavate one by one the layers of spumoni, brought from Angelo Brocato's in the Quarter, and relish each morsel of candied fruit.

We sometimes ate at Chris Steak House near the racetrack. Or more often up the street at Chris's one-time partner Johnny Vojkovich's Crescent City Steak House where the steaks swam in even more butter. Another gruff old Croatian, Mr. Johnny was friendlier with Dad than old man Chris Matulich. At Crescent City, Dad brought out nickels and quarters from his deep noisy pockets to feed the jukebox. What *CC Rider had done* and *how you spent all Fats's money* set the rhythms by which Jerry and I devoured the porterhouse pieces on our hot plates, spooned over with butter and steak drippings. We dipped hot crusty French bread into the residue, the platter tipped on a turned-over serving spoon in the center of the table. Jerry and I fought over the porterhouse bone: *It's my turn. You had it last time.* Our endless contretemps were only partly explained by Mom's family adage: *Closer the bone, sweeter the meat.* Almost weekly, we all wolfed down the steaks with abandon.

Dad loved any excuse to celebrate. Dressed in pajamas, Jerry and I were bundled up for the drive to the French Quarter. Speedy Jane won the feature race today.

Curbside service at the Morning Call delivered the excitement of beignets and chocolate milk. Mom and Dad had café au lait. Jerry and I blew powdered sugar on one another. Dad joined in.

3.5 Mom and Dad with Ike.

The situation quickly turned sour.
—*Jerry punched me!*
—*Randy, stop whining.*

Dad's support for Eisenhower in his second presidential campaign mobilized us all. Dad had Jerry and me carry I LIKE IKE posters to school on the bus. They were his gift to Sam Barthe, the private school we loved. I was six, a good age for campaigning. The posters sparked political fistfights on the bus with those commie Stevenson supporters. For once Jerry and I fought on the same side.

Dad's surprise birthday party for the president at the Shushan Lakefront Airport enlisted Mom, who appeared front-and-center at Ike's side. Mom wore a smart suit with an equestrian flair and dark gloves, perfectly at ease next to the man who saved Europe. Dad, marginalized even though it was his party, peered out in heavy glass frames from behind Mamie's striped hat, futilely trying to get the camera's attention. Looking at the photo now, I don't envy his having to compete with Mom. The footing was never equal.

The next year we flew to Miami and stayed at the Kingston Hotel. You could see the lights of Miami Beach across Biscayne Bay. One day, I tagged along as Dad retrieved a money transfer at the bank, to buy a pink Cadillac convertible. When Mom was a little girl, she and her cousin Audrey Jaco-mine—Uncle Nick's daughter and two years older—would tell one another of their dreams as they walked through the prairie in Happy Jack at the mouth of the Mississippi River. They would go to the back levee to roast fiddler crabs in an iron skillet purloined from Nan' Jo's kitchen along with a bottle of cooking oil. Mom, who cooked but would not eat the scavengers, dreamed of a pink convertible with a white top. Now she had it.

On the drive back to New Orleans in our new pink car, Elvis came on the radio. "Blue Suede Shoes" and "Hound Dog" inspired an excitement in me that was new and hard to know what to do with. Jerry and I bounced on the back seat. Our new car was worthy of Elvis.

At a roadside stand in Silver Springs, after the glass-bottom boats, the deer-petting zoo, and watching the cheetahs run at sixty miles per hour, just like in *Ramar of the Jungle*, I stood beside Dad, staring as he drank pitcher after pitcher of fresh-squeezed all-you-can-drink orange juice, ex-ultant, every glassful a victory.

—*Got to get your money's worth, son. Food is expensive. Here, they won't see. Have another glass.*

—*Rodney, did you have to bet on every single bowl game?*

—*How was I to know they'd let that black boy play for Pitt in the Sugar Bowl? Threw those Georgia boys for a loop and they couldn't score a point. Or that Maryland would beat the spread in the Orange Bowl?*

—*Dammit, Rodney, how can you bet our whole month's income! And Chi-co can handle the horses at Arlington. Chicago's a long way. When are you coming home?*

— . . .

—*Dammit, Rodney, you left me high and dry. There is no money in the account. How am I to feed the boys?*

— . . .

—*What do you mean, they need a diet anyway?*

Dad wasn't home.

Some nights I crawled into bed with Mom and warmed my feet under her legs. She never sent me back to my own bed in the room with Jerry.

In the morning she fussed: *Randy, don't come to my bed.*

For a while, we walked to Parkchester Shopping Center for groceries. Dad gave Chico Mom's pink Cadillac DeVille convertible, to haul hay, oats,

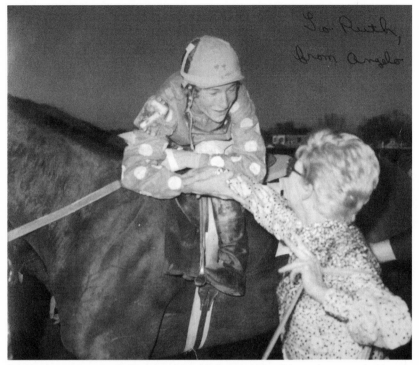

3.6 Mom congratulates Angelo Trosclair and Tudor Tambourine in New Orleans after winning the New Orleans Handicap.

and tack. Months later, Dad dumped the Cadillac—only a year old now but unfit to be driven—in front of our house, the unsightly heap shaming us before the neighbors.

Mom brought home a used 1956 black Ford Fairlane.

A storm blew in over Lake Pontchartrain from the north. My favorite sleeping weather. I stood on the bed to reach the high north window and slid it open. The cold wind tugged at the hooks and hardware of the red drapes that Mom made. I loved snuggling under the red-and-white star quilt. I liked forcing one leg between wall and mattress until I could get my right leg half under. The weight of the mattress made me feel embraced.

Shortly after Mom and Dad separated, I was scheduled to compete in my first swim meet. An all-state swimmer himself, Dad had early sent us to the best swim coach, a man with the great name Bill Christmas. Swim practice in the pool at City Park was as much fun as his name. Again and again we climbed on his shoulders to dive and do flips. I took not only to the swimming and diving but also to the competition. I was beginning to give Jerry a run for his money.

But determined to hurt Dad, Mom withdrew me from the meet. I lingered at the cast-iron fence in front of the enormous Audubon Park pool, gazing at the lanes where the meet would be held. At the pool's center, a fountain sprayed water.

A few years later, in the early 1960s, the city would close the pool, largest in the South, rather than integrate it. It never opened again.

Mom and Dad's legal drama took place behind drawn curtains. All I knew was that Dad, so long a troubling presence, was suddenly a troubling absence. While he lived with us, there was shouting and cursing: scenes. Then there was a loud silence that the drone of the TV did little to drown out.

After a couple years' absence, Dad appeared at the door on Seville Drive. He'd been to Havana. He had a moustache that surprised me. It scraped when he kissed me, the last kiss from him I remember. Another time, Dad visited me during school and took me out of class to go to the zoo. Then he disappeared again, and the money for Sam Barthe private school went with him. I returned to public school.

Mom didn't harp on Dad's faults and failings. Still, I overheard many stories in long coffee klatches as she worked out her anxiety and anger through a pall of smoke around the kitchen table. *Well, Audrey, we had a fight and I moved to the spare bedroom. He never invited me back. S'been downhill from there.* One part of their long, drawn-out legal battle was over the horses. Dad sold them for $1 apiece to a crony. *Out of spite. Anything to hurt me.*

When, twenty years later, Mom's horse Tudor Tambourine won the New Orleans Handicap—*the most exciting day of my life*—half her glee must have been that Dad finally got his comeuppance for the many horse-related offences he committed against her. Tudor Tambourine became an equine legend, paying $75, the longest shot ever to win Louisiana's most prestigious race, and now rumored to be buried in the Fair Grounds infield beside Black Gold. With a purse of $110,000, Dom Perignon flowed long into the night at Ruth's Chris Steak House. By then, my mother had become something of a legend herself.

CHAPTER FOUR

SOUTH RAMPART STREET

"THE MISSISSIPPI RIVER RAN OVER ITS BANK AND DROWNED ALL OUR cattle which we had driven on the levee for protection," my great-uncle Nick Jacomine wrote of the hurricane of September 1915 in his shakily handwritten memoir, *The Story of My Life: Things I Can Remember.* "The water was so rough that the cattle were swept so far that some of them were never found. Up to five feet of water . . . every thing was destroyed, rice ready to be threshed and all foods and small animals. The government sent a relief boat with food and all twice a week and that's what kept us going till the water receded."

If a horse stable brought my parents together from worlds apart—South Rampart Street and the furthest reaches of the Mississippi Delta—the hurricane unknowingly linked their families thirty years before. The ninth most intense storm in recorded history, the storm registered 140 miles per hour winds, a Category 4, when it made landfall twenty-five miles east of Plaquemines at Grand Isle in Barataria Bay where Jean Lafitte once hid his pirate empire. This put Plaquemines Parish in the storm's dangerous northeast quadrant.

A few hours after the Jacomines took to the levee, streetcars in New Orleans stopped operating. Over eight inches of rain were recorded in the next twenty-one hours. (Katrina would drop eight to ten inches.) But the levees held and the twelve-foot "screw pumps," invented by New Orleans engineer Albert Baldwin Wood and installed just that year, delivered as

4.1 The Fertel Building at Rampart and Common. Photo by Charles L. Franck Studios. The Historic New Orleans Collection, acc. no. 1979.325.659.

promised, removing over nine billion gallons of water from the city streets. The city was saved.

Flooding was minimal but the high winds tore the city apart. Uptown in Audubon Park winds flattened Horticultural Hall, built for the 1884 Cotton Exposition. Downtown, Jackson Square was in shambles. The clock on the St. Louis Cathedral stopped at 5:50 p.m. Nearby, on the Pontalba Buildings, ironwork and chimneys were ripped away. The Presbytere's cupola was demolished and the Cabildo, its sister building where the French transferred ownership of Louisiana to the Americans in 1803, lost most of its roof slates. The dome and the upper floors of the vacant St. Louis Hotel—once a thriving slave market—received heavy damage. The steeple of the First Presbyterian Church on Lafayette Square across Canal in the American Sector was hurled through the church roof and two adjoining rooming houses.

Two blocks away, the fortress-like structure of Chevra Thilim Orthodox Synagogue was left virtually untouched. My great-grandfather, Sam Fertel, was president of the congregation. He and his wife, Julia, held down their own fortress, a pawnshop on Rampart Street a few blocks away. Their three safes, filled with diamonds and deeds, were soon ready for another day of business.

"Was he an observant Jew?" I asked his grandson Stanley Fink three-quarters of a century later, trying to piece together the family story.

"Randy," he replied, surprised at the need to explain, "being president of the synagogue, that was just about money."

South Rampart Street is where my father's life on the margins began.

Born in 1900, Grandma Annie, my father's mother, lived on South Rampart Street above the one-time family pawnshop. Even as a boy, I sensed that "normal" people did not live downtown across Canal Street from the French Quarter—and certainly not on South Rampart Street, which, in the 1950s and 1960s, was, to my suburban eye, one step up from Skid Row. The Fertel Loan Office had long disappeared by then, but the Fertels still owned two corners at Rampart and Common and another at Rampart and Gravier, as well as property further up Rampart, and several more valuable locations nearby on Canal. However dilapidated the buildings, the Fertels made consistently smart buys of marginal real estate that later increased in value. Buildings labeled "Fertel Building" populated South Rampart Street on three key corners, Common, Gravier, and Perdido. They owned buildings at Canal and Rampart. One housed the prestigious Pickwick Club for a while, and another they leased for decades to W. T. Grant, a five-and-dime store. They also owned a seamen's flophouse hotel at Canal Street and the river.

Perhaps a few other merchants still lived above their stores, but most had moved to the suburbs. Grandma Annie stayed on amidst the downbeat pawnshops, haberdasheries, and milliners who catered to a black clientele who could *buy* clothes in the grand department stores on Canal Street—Maison Blanche, Krauss, Marks Isaacs—but couldn't try them on there. On Rampart Street, they could try them on. The Jewish merchants worked the sidewalks like the hawkers on nearby Bourbon Street, declaring to each passerby that just inside hung the perfect blue suit to make them look swell.

Grandma Annie's apartment featured a once-beautiful, now-rickety cast-iron gallery (what we call balconies in New Orleans) verging on collapse from rust and decay. My brother and I loved to go out and watch the streetcars rattle past. Her furnishings were sparse, pretty much limited to an iron bed. The room featured drop-cord lighting. She kept a Chrysler Imperial, with a driver who wore a chauffeur's hat and white shirt. One of my earliest memories: chuckling, the driver showed me how, if you pass

4.2 Annie joins us for Thanksgiving dinner.

your hand before the radio dial, the radio would dial itself, the red cursor moving from left to right and back as if by magic. On the floor unseen lay the actuator button.

Like her chauffeur, my grandmother had some playfulness in her, with a giggle and a belly laugh, each shaking her like jelly. One home movie shows Grandma Annie sweeping out the Cadillac, mugging broadly for the camera with energetic strokes of the broom—front seat, back seat, driver's side, passenger's side. Done, she hands the broom to her daughter-in-law, who doesn't look entirely amused.

Grandma Annie was said to have been a great beauty in her youth. One of the Werlein kids—they owned the music store on Canal Street that published the first sheet music in jazz history—fell in love with her. Descendants of antebellum immigrants, German Jews like the Werleins did not mix with East European Jews, whom they disdained as "Orientals." Leery of an alliance with the Fertels of Rampart Street and with Annie especially, the Werleins quickly packed their son off to Europe, and beautiful Annie was forgotten.

But when I knew Grandma Annie, she was no beauty. She was large and wore generous print dresses, or just swaths of cloth that wrapped around her sweaty, talcum-powder-caked corpulence, crimped with a big safety pin. Jewelry cascaded from her, clinking as she walked. Some of it was costume, some the real thing: eighteen-carat rose gold deco rings encrusted with swirls of rubies and diamonds, butterfly brooches with sapphires, citrons, and pearls.

Annie walked around Canal Street with a huge shopping bag for her "five-fingered-discount" shopping sprees. She was famous for slipping items from the counters of Maison Blanche and D. H. Holmes. She'd steal even from W. T. Grant, the five-and-dime that paid her thousands of dollars in annual rent. Her accountant had cut a deal with the merchants of Canal Street; they would assign a store detective to shadow her when she crossed the threshold. The store would then send her accountant a monthly bill for the merchandise that had vanished into her bag. This gave not just Annie but also the Canal Street merchants a license to steal: why not pad that bill with things she *didn't* steal? Annie stayed out of jail and littered her sparsely furnished apartment with piles of useless, ill-gotten trinkets. Everyone made out like bandits. Her money kept her out of jail and the Southeast Louisiana State Mental Hospital, colloquially called Mandeville, that Governor Earl Long would one day, in A.J. Liebling's words, have to "legaliz[e] his way out of."[4]

Trying to win Mom back for her son, Annie would send a taxicab full of toilet paper she had gotten a deal on, or thinking of the boys on a rainy day a cab full of comic books. Another day, ten pies arrived from A&G Cafeteria. We'd see the stack of pies with their legendary crusts walking up the drive, only the cab driver's legs and hat visible behind them, and, while Jerry and I ran for forks, Mom would quip, "That woman belongs in Mandeville."

Annie had another purse that some remember as a physician's bag. Dressed in her safety-pinned fabric, she would carry it to Mafia don Carlos Marcello's New Southport Hall on the river road out past the parish line between Orleans and Jefferson. She would approach the craps table, open her doctor's kit—full of money—and take out one silver dollar. She would place it on the Don't Pass line and rejoice when the shooter crapped out and grumble at him if he made his number. "If you didn't watch her," one-time croupier Lenny Ferrara told me, "Annie would steal a quarter off the table." Later when Lenny made a career change, perhaps possible only in Louisiana, from croupier to state trooper, Annie crossed the street rather than come near his police uniform. The uniform blinded her, he believed, so she did not recognize him. Her fear of the police was so great that she didn't report the theft of tens of thousands of dollars of jewelry when her hotel room in El Paso was burgled.

The world in which Annie Fertel grew up was an odd mixture—at once a claustrophobic, Orthodox Jewish mercantile enclave and the epicenter of an artistic whirlwind destined to change world culture. Jazz was being born all around them. South Rampart Street became home to jazz when the whorehouse district Storyville, only three blocks away, closed in 1917. And another part of the mix: just beyond, two blocks away, lay the smaller, unofficial vice district called Black Storyville where Louis Armstrong, born a year after Annie, lived as a boy. It was also called the Battlefield because "those bad characters," wrote Louis in his memoir *Satchmo*, "would shoot and fight so much."[5] Another name: the Swamp, because beyond Rampart was once known as the back-swamp. But perhaps it referred not just to the low ground but also the low morals.

Annie's father, Sam, was widely known on Rampart Street as "Money-bags Fertel," and her mother, Julia, was famous for her tightfistedness. After their nightly dinner in Morrison's Cafeteria on Gravier, Julia had the first cup of coffee and Sam the refill. They never went home without a bottle of ketchup, a saltshaker, or set of tableware in Julia's large purse. Annie got her kleptomania honestly.

But according to some, such loot amounted to chicken feed for the Fertels. Sam, who came to New Orleans in 1895 from Krakow via the Carolinas, had gotten his start fencing stolen goods. He chose New Orleans because he heard that "Spoons" Butler, the Civil War general in charge of the Federal occupation of the city, had made a fortune purloining his Creole hostesses' sterling tableware. Sam felt this was just the place for him and his young bride. They found a location in the 200 block of South Rampart, next to the dirty, dangerous Back a' Town neighborhood, and set up shop. The river was Front a' Town. Rampart Street, named for the ramparts that once held back the swamp and the Indians, was once the edge of town. Back a' Town was edgier still.

Like many pawnbrokers, the Fertels served the underworld. They were known as the biggest fences in the South. Not only did they receive stolen goods; they also commissioned burglars to acquire them. When a mink coat was stolen from their step-granddaughter Wilma's home, the speculation was that it was the Fertels' doing. They were always holding a grudge about something; maybe the missing mink was payback for some imagined offense. Whenever the cops paid them a visit, they'd flush the loot.

No wonder my father would later preach that stealing was a "duty." It was a genetic imperative.

When Annie's mother, Julia, died in December 1941, Harnett Kane, a talented local-colorist who would soon also write of Ruth's *Deep Delta Country*, told the Fertel story—or the version fit for public consumption—at length in the New Orleans *States-Item* in an article I first found, torn and dog-eared, jumbled in with the Super-8 movies in the cabinet in the den. It made me curious.

For Kane it was "A saga in penny-saving" with a woman pawnbroker as heroine. Her "name meant nothing to most Orleanians. She left an estate of $2,379,159.39—one of the biggest of recent history, larger than that of most cotton factors, financiers or bankers of Louisiana. During all her quiet life, Mrs. Julia Deiches Fertel denied herself, accumulated money and bought property after property. She seldom sold. Real estate was the thing; one day she stopped a friend and told him, slapping her hand against the wall— 'Bricks and mortar, bricks and mortar, that is what counts.'" Her estate was the equivalent today of $36 million.

She was, Kane adds, "a stout, a quiet, intense woman who dressed usually in dark and plain attire." He notes how the Fertels had prospered, because "their wants were small, their hopes of property large . . . Day after day, they labored among the brooches, rings, necklaces, revolvers, bits of metal, leather cases, picture frames, belts and miscellaneous items that they had accumulated, and over which they made trades with their world."

But Kane also allows an element of romance, quoting Sam's memory of his wife's talents. A traveling diamond merchant, Sam had walked into the Deiches' store in Dover, England. It was love at first sight: "'She was a magnificent woman—a jewel. Everything I am, and became, I owe to her. I was a tramp before I met her. She is my secret. She was the boss. I was her assistant. We never regretted a single decision she made. She was a salesman; she handled the customers, she argued, she made values, she made bargains.'"

The Fertels never owned a car. Kane noted that "Julia preferred to walk, and she walked long distances. She was economical in the matter of food, as in other things. When she bought a stick of gum, she broke it in half and put only half in her mouth. She saved the rest for another time, or for someone else." Prospering, the Deiches back in England moved from Dover to the fashionable West End of London. But in New Orleans, Sam and

Julia's home above the pawnshop was bare: drop-cord lighting, no indoor plumbing, kerosene heating.

Julia's only self-indulgence was that "she bought dozens of shoes, more than she ever needed. She was determined that she would never go barefoot, no matter what happened to her." According to family legend, she wore only flats—but if she found heels at a bargain she'd grab them and knock off the heel. Another legend, but from journalist Walter Isaacson's family: Julia beat Walter's uncle Julius, a physician, out of a $2 house call fee. He couldn't be bothered to argue with the rich old bat. Why argue with crazy people?

Sam Fertel did not share his wife's frugality. He liked nice clothes. For the high holidays one year, he bought a fine hand-tailored suit at considerable expense at Godchaux's on Canal Street. He knew Julia wouldn't like his spendthrift ways, so he announced that he had made a great bargain on a suit, in pawn. His plan was to leave the suit in the pawnshop until he judged it safe to spirit off to his own closet. Before that time came, however, Julia boasted that while she was minding the store, she had made a great sale: *she'd gotten twenty dollars for that suit!*

Kane records Sam's reflections on first settling on the edge of Back a' Town. "They used to laugh at me when Mrs. Fertel and I bought property so far 'out' along toward University Place and Rampart," Kane quotes Sam. "Everything was centered then toward the river. They said I was crazy. I said nothing." They laughed not only because Rampart was so far—from the commercial center—but also because it was so near: to Back a' Town.

This was the world from which the Fertels drew many of their customers, an often violent world. In 1900, the year of Annie's birth, "Back to Africa" advocate Robert Charles, objecting to police harassment, went on a shooting spree that left seven dead and twenty wounded; he was surrounded on Saratoga Street just off Rampart and riddled with bullets. At one point during the race riot Charles inspired, a mob of 3,000 descended upon the Central Police Station, on Common Street and Basin, less than half a block from the Fertels. Ten years earlier, Police Chief Hennessy was gunned down just off Rampart, six blocks away. His dying words—"The Dagoes did it"—led to the arrest of 250 Italians. Newspaper coverage of the murder trial of 9 Sicilians introduced the word "Mafia" into the American vocabulary. When they were acquitted, a mob of 8,000 met at the Henry Clay statue on Canal Street and then marched to Rampart Street and on to Parish Prison behind Congo Square where they lynched the "assassins."

Across the wide intersection of Rampart and Common lay the small but labyrinthine Chinatown where young Jelly Roll Morton would be sent by older band members "with a sealed note and a small amount of money to get 'hop'—opium."[6] This drug market was not fifty yards from the Fertels, directly across from the Central Police Station.

Across Canal Street, further down Rampart a few blocks, *Place des Negres, Place Congo*, Congo Square—today's Louis Armstrong Park—was the place where slaves gathered in the eighteenth and nineteenth centuries to drum, dance, and chant call-and-response rhythms from their native Africa. Louis's grandmother, Josephine, a former slave, described visiting Congo Square on Sunday afternoons and witnessing the birth of an art form: "All the slaves came in their finest clothes. The women mostly had on calico dresses, and their hair was bound in tight bandannas. Some colored musicians played African music, and we would dance the Bamboula or the Conjaie until we had to go back to our quarters. . . . One would beat the drums, another would scrape a cow's horn with a key, a third would blow into an instrument with slides, a fourth sat on his haunches and rang bells."[7] Congo Square was the center of their social and spiritual world. The first Jim Crow laws banned the drums and dancing in 1875.

In the early 1890s when the Fertels first arrived, the spirit of the drums had resurfaced in Storyville and across Canal in Black Storyville, the few square blocks that for twenty years housed the whorehouses where the ratty, hot bands shaped it into a new idiom called "jass"—a reference to sex. When the "District," as Storyville was called by its denizens, was closed by federal edict in 1917, the movable feast decamped for South Rampart Street. As Michael Ondaatje wrote in *Coming Through Slaughter*, Rampart Street's paving stones were "made marble by jazz."[8] This magic swirled all around the Fertels.

It was on these streets—Rampart between Perdido and Gravier—where Louis Armstrong walked along in 1910 singing for coins with his "spasm band," named for their dancing style. His singing was so good that a friend dragged Jelly Roll Morton across Canal from Storyville to hear him. Louis sets the scene: "[I]n that one block . . . more people were crowded than you ever saw in your life. There were church people, gamblers, hustlers, cheap pimps, thieves, prostitutes and lots of children. There were bars, honky-tonks and saloons, and women walking the streets for tricks to take to their 'pads,' as they called their rooms."[9] Another Fertel Building, dated 1910 on the facade, sat at the corner of Rampart and Perdido. The Fertels lived two

4.3 The Fertel Building at Rampart and Perdido. Photo by Charles L. Franck Studios. The Historic New Orleans Collection, acc. no. 1979.325.782.

blocks away above their pawnshop at Rampart and Common. Only half a block down Rampart further toward Canal, the famous madam Norma Wallace got her first taste of running a bordello. Long New Orleans's most renowned whorehouse, in the 1960s Norma's place, a few blocks away at Conti and North Rampart, would become the subject of many adolescent jokes—*Hey, saw you at Norma's last night*—long before we knew what the joke was or the deep New Orleans history behind it.

Louis Karnofsky, the Fertels' one-time neighbor directly across South Rampart Street, befriended the young Louis, giving him a job selling hard coal from a wagon and collecting junk on another—"old rags, bones, bottles." Louis used coal delivery as an excuse to hang out on the banquettes (sidewalks) of Storyville to hear his hero Joe "King" Oliver at Pete Lala's saloon. The Karnofskys also gave him "the kind of Tin Horn they use at Parties to make noises, while celebrating" to help attract business on the junk wagon and he played it day after day. "One day—I took the wooden top off of the horn, and surprisingly I held my *two* fingers close together where the wooden mouthpiece used to be, and I could play a tune of some kind. Oh the kids really enjoyed that."[10] Another ragman, Larenzo, gave him his first music lessons on such a tin horn.

The Karnofskys had the gift of what Saul Bellow called "cupboard love," that readiness to share the daily victuals, along with their big hearts. They'd often feed Louis before sending him home after a day's work, giving him a lifelong taste for Jewish food that almost rivaled his obsession with red beans and rice. The Karnofskys loaned Louis $2 toward his first trumpet, which he bought on time for $4 from Jake Fink, a Fertel relation by marriage.[11]

Catty-corner from the Fertel Building at Perdido and Rampart sat Fink's Loan Office. Specializing in used musical instruments, Fink's pawnshop was one door from a crossroads that would prove historic when an eleven-year-old Louis was picked up for firing a gun on New Year's Eve, a local custom that survives to this day. Trudged off to the Colored Waifs' Home for Boys, Louis got his first serious instruction in the cornet from Professor Peter Davis.

Some thought the New Year's story was just an excuse Louis made up, that he was in fact aiming at some rival.

Annie's sister Nettie married Jake's son Max, a concert violinist of note and, according to *Variety* in 1932, the best dance-band leader in the South. "Effective in both classical and 'rag time' playing," reported the *New Orleans Item* in 1915, he "often memorizes an entire opera score by playing it only once." His sixteen-piece band regularly played the Saenger, the St. Charles Hotel, and, in the same block as the Fertels, the Little Club on Rampart. He toured the national Orpheum circuit. According to jazz historian Tad Jones, "Max Fink went on to have a big band and became pretty well known. We think that's why Armstrong bought [his first cornet] there"—at Jake Fink's. He adds: "From 1908 to 1918, this is *the* spot for jazz."

For the rest of his life, Louis extolled the warmth and nurture of the Karnofsky family. "I shall always love them," he wrote. "I learned a lot from them as to how to live—real life and determination. . . . I began to feel like I had a future and 'It's a Wonderful World' after all."[12]

And yet, there was Louis's handgun. And there was the Robert Charles race riot, Chief Hennessy's assassination by unknown assailants, and the endemic violence of Black Storyville. Interwoven with the birth of America's greatest art form, a world of violence swirled around the Fertels.

At that same corner was the Odd Fellows and Masonic Hall, where Buddy Bolden, Jelly Roll Morton, Kid Ory, "King" Oliver, and Louis Armstrong himself played. Bolden was known for his power over women, his power on the cornet, and the power of the trance he'd slip into when he played.

4.4 Louis Armstrong nabbed at Perdido and Rampart as imagined by local artist George Schmidt. By permission of George Schmidt.

Once, the trance went too far. In 1907, in the midst of a parade, with his women all around him he halted, screamed, and frothed at the mouth. His family took him to the Louisiana State Insane Asylum upstate in Jackson. He never emerged. Jazz would have to find its way without him.

In the midst of all this, the Fertel Loan Office. On its side wall, this sign:

A FRIEND IN NEED

IS A FRIEND INDEED

IF YOU NEED MONEY

SEE FERTEL'S

LOWEST RATES IN THE CITY

Julia and Sam did not often venture into their customers' universe. The Fertels, says Harnett Kane, were polite but had little to say to others; the neighbors did not know them well. Unlike Tillie Karnofsky, there is no indication that Julia knew her way *to*, let alone *around*, the kitchen. Most days, if they were not stocking up on flatware at the Morrison Cafeteria, Sam and Julia took their children, Nettie, Barney, and baby Annie, across Rampart Street for lunch at the Astoria Hotel. The toniest black hotel in town, the Astoria was owned by the Braden family, prominent Creoles of color. It was holy ground in the history of jazz. All the top black musicians played the Astoria's Tick Tock Tavern and stayed there when traveling through New Orleans. Gamblers in need of a new stake in the game might leave the Astoria's tables for a quick trip across the street to the Fertel Loan Office to

4.5 A Friend in Need—close-up of the Fertel Building. Photo by Charles L. Franck Studios. The Historic New Orleans Collection, acc. no. 1979.325.659. Detail.

pawn a watch—or a cornet, as Louis is said to have done more than once. The Astoria was hopping, its music spilling over late into the night, swirling around the Fertels' cast-iron gallery that overlooked the scene. Surrounded by all that life and all that good Creole cooking, the Fertels lived in this world, but were not of it.

Nor were they of the mainstream, white Christian world. The Fertels' bargain prices were known in the nearby theatrical world, and they were often called in to supply pieces for performances. Once a diamond crown was required—paste, no doubt—and Annie was asked to deliver it to the Saenger Theatre, the grand vaudeville house on Canal and Rampart that opened in 1927. When she arrived, a Passion play was in rehearsal and Annie saw the scene depicting the suffering Christ. My grandmother was so horrified by this exotic display that she ran all the way home, never to return to the Saenger.

When Julia died in 1941, the family discovered that her 1936 will left everything to her husband, Sam, during his lifetime, with her fortune to be distributed at his death to her daughters, Nettie and Annie, and to "my grand son [sic] Rodney Fertel Weinberg." To her son, Barney Fertel, she left "one hundred dollars per month for the maintenance during his life time ONLY to be paid out—of the estate" (her emphasis). Her intent, in effect, was to disinherit him.

By all reports, Barney was the oddest in a family of oddities. According to the family, Barney had both a lazy eye and an eye that wandered. He was an "outlaw," his son Sydney reports, "who loved anything that passed." He married twice, initially to a first cousin. Leaving the family shop, he set up a pawnshop in the 300 block of South Rampart, and he ate every day at the

Walsdorf drugstore at 1036 Canal Street adjacent to Rampart in a building the Fertels owned and the former site of the Pickwick Club. According to fellow pawnbroker Slim Foley, Barney ate like a bit player in a prison movie or a Dickens novel: "He would put his head down and surround his plate with one arm while he scooped with the other hand, and he wouldn't pick his head up 'til he finished." For Harry Latter of Latter & Blum Real Estate, who was maneuvering to buy Barney's stake in the W. T. Grant building on Canal, Barney was "a very low element, runs a loan office and is really the 'scum of the earth.'"[13] My father's half-sister Wilma says he would sit, before the family was divided, in front of the Fertel pawnshop, cross-legged, "looking like an ape." Family legend explained his disinheritance—ill-tempered, Barney was reported once to have struck Julia.

Her will ignored her other grandson, Stanley Fink, the son of her eldest daughter, Nettie, and nine months younger than his first cousin Rodney. One might have thought that Julia would seek to continue her hard-earned legacy by placing it in the hands of someone who shared her frugality and business sense. Stanley was such an heir. Julia lived long enough to see Stanley graduate from Louisiana State University and follow his wife's family into the "rag trade" in Senatobia in the Mississippi-Yazoo Delta. But when he saw his black clientele move away, replaced by mechanical cotton harvesters, Stanley had the good sense to enter law school. Stanley became a successful criminal prosecutor in Memphis. An earnest man, but he did not earn a place in Julia's will.

Rodney, fourteen years old at the time of the will, would not finish high school until a year after Julia's death. (He graduated from Warren Easton in 1942, at age twenty-one.) Still, this hardworking, tightfisted businesswoman—who chewed gum half a stick at a time and walked everywhere in discounted shoes shorn perhaps of their high heels rather than own a car or hire a cab—adored her grandson Rodney Fertel Weinberg. Was it because he was a handsome, athletic young man with a taste for the horses and the crap tables? Did his charm bridge the abyss that separated their tastes and lives? Was Rodney Julia's unlived life?

To my father's dismay, Julia's will ran afoul of the Napoleonic Code. As explained by the *States-Item*, "Like most laymen, she did not know that unique provision of the Louisiana legal system—dating back to the old *Code Napoléon*—that prohibited her from reducing Barney's share of her estate." The $100 monthly maintenance for Barney was Julia's ill-informed effort to satisfy the Code: he was not disinherited, just disrespected. Had she claimed that Barney struck her, Julia would have satisfied the condition laid out by Napoleon as grounds to disinherit. But Julia did not give that incident as one of the "just causes" that the Code recognizes. Pennywise and pound foolish, Julia had been too cheap to pay for legal advice. But the *Code Napoléon* becomes something of a family Bible. That paragraph in the Code, which protects donors from those who would benefit from their largesse, becomes our constant study, and the penchant to disinherit a family trait.

Barney's son Isadore speaks of all this as "the family trouble." For generations, the two sides of the family never spoke. Isadore "Izzy" Fertel easily rivals his dad in oddness, sharing—and then some—his father's interest in women. He swore to his dying day that he went to Newcomb, Tulane's former women's college, not to Tulane. In the 1970s, he was the only male member of an organization known as the Radical Feminists. A recording artist on Tiny Tim's label, Izzy recorded Helen Reddy's "I Am Woman," wrote and recorded a hymn to feminist Susan B. Anthony and another to celebrate the talks of Begin and Reagan. He did a Yiddish version of "Rock around the Clock." Most are available today on YouTube. There you'll find his bald head, Coke-bottle black-framed glasses, broad smile, and an off-key, nasal singing voice, swelling with enthusiasm, which dares the audience to listen. He died in 2008 in a Bronx nursing home.

By contrast, Dad's teenage aspirations were almost mainstream. With cousin Stanley Fink and his friends on Robert Street Uptown, where the Weinbergs settled for a while, Jan Pedersen and Frank Zito, he organized a strike—"picketing with signs and everything" reports the *Orleans Item*—to protest their having no place in the neighborhood to play. Dad had cut his hand playing ball in a vacant lot. Commissioner of Public Property Joseph Skelley brought in several loads of river sand and the football games recommenced. Already a fine athlete, Dad realized he was born to be a coach.

But the aspirations were short-lived. According to court records my father did not receive the $1 million imagined in family legend, but only $300,000 (equivalent today to $5 million). Julia's inheritance nonetheless made him rich enough at age twenty-one that he never had to work. To honor his grandmother, Rodney Fertel Weinberg became Rodney Fertel. There was a lawsuit ahead that would curtail his great expectations, but young Dad quit school and gave up his idea of a career in coaching.

He might have thrived as a coach. Instead he settled for spending his life coaching whomever he could buttonhole about his latest idée fixe or bête noire.

I once asked my father why I had never heard about his father, Cyril Weinberg. Through a friend, I had just met Dad's half-sister Wilma.

"My parents were divorced," he explained curtly. "He wasn't part of my life. I hardly knew him."

Cyril's life with Grandma Annie had been tumultuous. In their 1925 divorce proceedings in Orleans Parish court, Cyril stood accused of "excesses, cruel treatment and outrages" against his young wife. Married at sixteen (according to her testimony—in fact she was twenty), Annie played the child bride victim, claiming "he would make me go to my father's store and beg him for money. . . . Yes, it was always money, money, money. . . . He used to dress me up so he could go to the Roosevelt Hotel and cheat his friends at cards. He plays with marked cards and dice. . . . He beat me and humiliated me and I could not bear it any longer." Not that Annie didn't like a game of cards. Cyril testified that he once found her, in the back room of a bar, playing the Cajun card game bourré with a tableful of blacks. Perhaps it was the Tick Tock. He dragged her away, her thumb-latched coin purse bursting with quarters and dimes, a roll of dollar bills stuffed in her rolled-up stocking.

The entire Fertel family meddled in the couple's affairs. On Robert Street the Weinbergs shared a double shotgun with the Finks, Annie's sister, Nettie, and Max. Annie went back and forth from her marital home in Denver to New Orleans at her mother's beck and call. During one of these sojourns to Denver, Dad was born. When Cyril asked Annie what had happened to the fur coat he bought her for the Denver winters, she replied, "Momma asked for it and I sent it to her." Julia's version was the opposite: "That man went through a hundred and thirty thousand dollars in three years, and I had to go to Denver and buy my child shoes." When, during one of their periods in New Orleans, Cyril was running a pawnshop on Rampart Street and allegedly abused Annie, she rang up the Fertel Loan Office one block away from the Weinberg Loan Office: "Barney, come over quick, he is killing me."

But according to Cyril, Annie was given to tantrums, "liable if you touch her to jump up and down in bed and scream."

Who knows where the truth lies? After all, Cyril testified during the divorce proceedings that he had already been divorced twice and left a

4.6 Dad as baby with football.

widower by the death of his third wife. He couldn't remember his first wife's grounds for divorce and could not recall his second wife's maiden name: "Let me see, Grace, Grace O'Donnell, no Grace McDonald. . . ."

Little Rodney, three years old, is glimpsed only once in the proceedings. Annie is asked to explain why she kept going back to this abusive husband. She replies, "It was account of the love of my little baby." If at first we imagine she is speaking of *her* love for her baby, the next sentence disabuses us: "He really loves his father." Perhaps she displays an element of empathy there, but later testimony is unambiguous. Asked if she "took good care of that baby," Annie replied: "Yes, I take the best care I can of it."

After the divorce was finalized, Annie decided she wanted Cyril back. At his mother's suggestion—*You have a son*—he remarried Annie in 1927 and took her back to Denver, far from the Fertels.

Just before Annie and Cyril's second divorce, determined to be rid of Cyril, Julia proposed to put her grandson Rodney in her will if her son-in-law would get out of Annie's life forever. My aunt Wilma remembers how her father struggled: "He came home one day and you could see how upset he was. He was crying. He loved that boy and he didn't want to give him up."

Wilma's daughter Barbara, heir to her mother's earthy matter-of-factness, clarifies: "He sold your father."

Cyril came back into Rodney's life for a short period in his early adulthood; his half-sister Wilma played matchmaker between them. Rodney had approached her out of the blue one day as she was waiting for the streetcar on Rampart Street.

"Do you know who I am?" he asked. It was 1942. Julia Deiches Fertel was dead and her estate tied up in the courts.

"Of course I do," she offered, "you're my brother." She, Wilma Weinberg Brandt, invited him, still Rodney Weinberg, home for dinner. Home was her mother-in-law's house, where she lived while her young husband was away in the war. Rodney was 4-F, not subject to the draft for reasons that remain uncertain. He ate with them several times, liked the home cooking. One night over dinner he said, "You know, I'm going to be rich some day."

"Yeah, I know," replied Wilma, ever matter-of-fact.

"I'm going to take care of you some day," he offered earnestly.

"Sure you are," Wilma replied, her eyebrow raised.

Eventually she took Rodney to Mobile, where Cyril had a store, because she felt he should know their father. Cyril indulged Rodney's wild streak, all the wilder now as he awaited his great expectations. They shared Cyril's rooms at the swanky General Semmes Hotel, newly opened the year before near Mobile Bay. Rodney would come to Cyril's store in Mobile and ask for $100 to cover his gambling and carousing; Wilma, who worked the store and resented Rodney's scapegrace behavior, was instructed to give it to him. When Cyril was away on business trips, Rodney brought girls up to their rooms. The manager complained to Cyril, whose guilt about deserting Rodney only went so far. He said a word to Rodney. Rodney took all Cyril's shirts and ties and fled back to New Orleans.

In his article written after Julia's death, Harnett Kane seemed struck that, in the $2.5 million declared value of the estate, only one-tenth was *not* in real estate. This is true, no doubt, of the *declared* value. But Kane was not privy to another truth: Sam and Julia hid much of their wealth.

In the 1943 trial challenging Julia's will, the three children—Nettie, Annie, and Barney—mounted the stand one by one to deny that they had met on the Monday following her death to divide Julia's hoard of diamonds. Each testified that their mother did not care for jewelry, wearing only a wedding ring throughout her life. But twenty-two-year-old Rodney drew a contrary picture of the diamond hoard, kept in the second of three safes at the Fertel Loan Office. "My grandmother often let me see them and she would tell me she could make a dress out of diamonds . . . She wouldn't part with those diamonds; those were her life." "Bricks and mortar" might count, but diamonds counted most of all.

In court, Rodney valued the diamonds conservatively at $80,000 ($1.2 million today) and spoke of thousands of dollars kept in the same safe: "*a special roll*, she would call it . . . and she would only let me go to the safe. She wouldn't trust my uncle Barney. She would always tell me, 'Rodney, you are the only one I can trust.'"

He then testified that, on the day after her funeral—Pearl Harbor Day— "Uncle Barney told me, 'Get Aunt Nettie, and bring her down here because we are going to divide up the diamonds.' At this time no will was found, and I was still under their influence and was going to do anything they said." Peering beneath the lowered blinds, he saw his uncle Barney and aunt Nettie inside the loan office. "The diamonds were out on the showcase there and [they] just split it up."

When asked whether his mother, Annie, was there as well, Rodney asked, "Do I have to answer that question?" Pressed by the court, he conceded, "Mamma was in there."

Rodney's momentary attempt to protect his mother seems touching, especially since he later testified that she had acted as "go-between" for Barney and Nettie, just outside the courtroom, in an effort to suborn his testimony. They had offered him $100 apiece—a contemptuous sum since, if Julia's will was upheld, his share would be one-third of the $80,000 hoard (almost half a million today).

The lawyers for Annie, Nettie, and Barney went on the attack:

Q. Did you threaten the life of your uncle Barney?

A. I had never any intention of killing anybody except Japs.

Q. Why aren't you in the army, then?

A. Because they won't take me.

Q. We will come to that.

But first Barney's lawyer put Rodney on the defense about how he spent his time. "You all might not approve," he responded. Pressed, he answered, "Well, I take a chance on different games of chance."

Q. In other words, you gamble for a living.

A. I wouldn't say I gamble for a living, because I have $300 a month income [the equivalent today of $4,500]. I wouldn't have to gamble at all; I do that just to pass the time away.

Q. To pass the time away.

A. Absolutely, pass the time away and keep out of trouble.

Q. You have been in trouble?

A. I have never been in serious trouble in my life.

Q. Weren't you arrested in Houston, Texas, as a draft dodger?

[Rodney's attorney]: Objected to as having nothing to do with the case.

Q. I am going to show he was rejected from the army for a purpose, and he hasn't been taking treatment. What was Dr. Reed treating you for? Isn't it a fact you refused to take treatments from Dr. Reed?

William Arthur Reed was Touro Hospital's nationally known urologist, a specialist in the treatment of syphilis. Then finally the hostile lawyer states:

Q. We say it is a mental deficiency that makes him make these statements.

With that bombshell, the recorded testimony abruptly ends except for the stenographer's unusual notations, "That's all" and "(End of this day's hearing.)" One wonders what fireworks went unrecorded.

In May of 1964, I went with my father to Grandma Annie's funeral. Years before she had suffered an accident in Las Vegas. Crossing the Strip in front of the Dunes Hotel she had been hit by a car. Her embonpoint was such that, according to the police report, the impact made her bounce "278 feet." By that time, Grandma Annie looked so like a vagrant the ambulance didn't want to pick her up.

After the hospital stay in Las Vegas, she mostly took to her wheelchair and her bed. She was ever infirm after that. Diabetic, she died of gangrene in her leg, unwilling to pay for proper care, just as Julia had been too cheap to pay Walter Isaacson's great-uncle for the $2 house call. Build an empire on pinching pennies, and be buried under the quicksand created by the same impulse.

Attendance at her final service was sparse. The closed casket, a Jewish observance, saved me from my first face-to-face experience with death.

After the service, my father explained that he couldn't leave, that Jews "sit shiva" all night with the closed casket, a solitary wake. The next day we buried Grandma Annie near Julia and Sam in the Canal Street Orthodox Cemetery.

It all seemed so odd to me. I had grown up Catholic. Who were these people who I looked like but about whom I knew so little?

I never heard a kind word exchanged between Dad and Grandma Annie. As with Cyril and Annie, the only surviving evidence of their relationship relates to business dealings and lawsuits. In the summary of my parents' divorce proceedings, for example, it was noted that Annie "frequently borrowed funds from her son, and he, in turn, borrowed money from his mother." Their business dealings were conducted, by the court's report, as though they were strangers. On one occasion, Annie sued Rodney for $23,000, and as the papers confirm, "obtained a judgment therefore, and was fully repaid."

The distance between mother and son is most convincingly suggested by the *Times-Picayune* article about the Fertel realty auction in 1955, "one of the biggest real estate sales in New Orleans' history." The sale was held to resolve the succession of Barney Fertel. Uncle Barney died suddenly and his estate included buildings co-owned by other members of the family. Unable to parcel out Julia and Sam's real estate empire amicably, and though enjoined by Julia's will not to sell her property for twenty years, the Fertels forced an auction.

The article notes that "a mother and son provided the action for the two-story building at 232-40 South Rampart, corner Gravier, as they bid against one another. Mrs. [Annie Fertel] Buhberg [she had remarried] and Rodney Fertel did all of the bidding for the property to a total of $82,000. Fertel was highest man."

The building they fought over—232 Rampart—was "Dad's bar," the place where Jerry and I bickered over the pool table and where I got those black-and-white Scottie magnets whose attraction and repulsion so intrigued me.

And now she was dead. After the funeral, I accompanied my father to the bank vault where we opened Annie's large bank drawer. If Annie had been famous for simple dresses that dripped with so many diamonds you thought they were paste, well, here was her hoard, a mishmash of jewelry, some costume, some semiprecious, some valuable, but all mixed up together. And I mean mixed up, jumbled, chains and bracelets and gewgaws all entangled, so that part of my job that day was not to help take inventory—the inventory they had avoided taking in 1941 to beat the IRS—but to disentangle the jumble.

In the early 1980s, coming from a Shakespeare class at the college where I taught in upstate New York, I received a shoebox in faculty mail. All over the outside in my father's unsteady, block-lettered scrawl were instructions:

TAKE THIS IN A ROOM AND
LOCK THE DOOR BEFORE OPENING

I went to my office and locked the door. In the box lay Grandma Annie's hoard, diminished by then but once again a jumble of Victorian and art deco brooches, rings, necklaces, and watches, many encrusted with diamonds, rubies, and sapphires, most stuffed inside thumb-latched coin purses from another day. Some settings were a copper-rich eighteen-carat gold. Some were mere paste. This was, after all, a trove from a pawnshop where the fine stuff was few and far between. But there was, for example, a huge baroque pearl in a platinum setting, with ornate engravings under the pearl which presumably would only be seen by the wearer, a grace note from an era gone by.

My father, I imagine, got tired of hoarding the diamonds he had fought for in 1943, forty years earlier, and then retrieved twenty years later from her bank box. Or maybe he got tired of paying the box rental fee.

Like Rampart Street itself, the lives of the Fertels lay on the margins. Among themselves, like my dancing Scottie magnets, they alternately attracted and repelled each other. Was their oddness a matter of nature or nurture? There seems an overabundance of evidence on both sides of that age-old question.

Throughout my childhood and adolescence I longed for a father who was normal and sane. Fear drove the longing: did some craziness lie waiting in my blood? It was hard to satisfy the itch in my skin. Was there something beneath destined to work its way out? So my mother seemed to fear: I was Rodney, whom I resembled, in the making.

Another itch. My father wasn't the last of my mother's marginal men. Life with Dad wore thin and she managed to extricate herself. But throughout her life she consistently danced a dance of attraction-repulsion with some pretty odd characters. Why would such a brilliant woman surround herself so consistently with men like that?

CHAPTER FIVE

HAPPY JACK

AS I GREW UP, WHEN SHE MENTIONED THEM AT ALL, MOM SPOKE always of perfect parents and a perfect family. Paw-Paw—Arthur Simpson Udstad—*outsold every insurance salesman at National Life and Accident.* He'd sit with potential customers in their cypress-framed houses up and down the river road drinking jelly jars of their thick coffee, roasted dark on the stove and syrupy with cane sugar. Always made the sale. The whole lower coast was his debit. He was so good the firm kept trimming his territory to even the playing field. Mom's mother, Josephine, taught school, the best first-grade teacher Port Sulphur Elementary ever had. Her nickname in the community—Nan' Jo' from "nanaine" (godmother)—was a term of respect. Another nickname among the locals, gulook, referred to her fresh good looks. Light, bright, and sparkling, Jo' cast no shadow. Everyone loved her.

Nan' Jo' died in 1952, before I could really know her. Paw-Paw was a wiry old man with wispy white hair surrounding his bald pate. He taught me to net butterflies. We scrambled together through empty lots in the newly reclaimed backswamp between the city and Lake Pontchartrain to find the beautiful monarchs. To feed them, we stirred a nectar of honey and water. Holding the captured butterfly gently by the abdomen, Paw-Paw showed me the elegant brushworked powder on its wings. We watched the proboscis uncoil into the nectar and then watched the monarchs flutter against the wire screen at the glass-louvered back door on Seville Drive.

5.1 Plaquemines Gothic: Arthur Simpson Udstad and Josephine (Nan' Jo') Jacomine Udstad.

He taught me about eucalyptus trees, how the leaves were silver on one side, green on the other. He had recently planted a eucalyptus tree in the front yard of his house below the levee, a place where I loved to play. The tree was small, but taller than I. Because of Paw-Paw's excitement, I longed to experience the beauty of the leaves as they swayed in the wind.

I remember, too, Paw-Paw's sweaty, back-stiffening work planting St. Augustine grass on the sandy lot surrounding our brand-new tract home. In those more frugal times before sod was bought in pallets, Paw-Paw planted single strands of that sturdy, wiry grass every foot or so, then watered and waited for the thick tendrils to multiply and grow together. Despite his elegant mien, he was a man of the country who'd lean over with a thumb to his nose to clear it.

Mom used her country know-how to take care of Paw-Paw at the end when he was dying of cancer and came to live with us on Seville Drive. Nan' Jo' was long dead. Mom knew both the right thing to do and how to do it. She lifted him and washed him and catered to him with the energy I saw her apply again thirty years later when her brother, estranged from Aunt Helen, was dying in her house.

Mom grew up a tomboy, determined never to be outdone by her big brother, Sig, three years her senior. She skipped two grades in Port Sulphur's

5.2 Paw-Paw with Randy and Jerry before the St. Augustine is planted on Seville Drive.

one-room Rigaud Elementary School, learning, she always explained, by listening in on the grades ahead of her. By the time they moved to Port Sulphur School, she must have breathed down Sig's neck. She always claimed she got her competitive spirit from her dad. *Just tell me I can't do something, and I will do everything in the world to do it.*

Even without running water or electricity, Mom always said, she never knew that her family was poor during the Depression. Their cypress house below the levee uninsulated, they got through the chilly wet winters with a fireplace in every room, comforters and pillows filled with duck down culled from the hunt, and with mattresses stuffed with moss that was taken out once a year, washed, and dried in the sun. "Winter nights, Sig, Ruth, and I," cousin Audrey recalled in her ever-sweet memoir, *Family Affairs*, "would sit in front of a roaring fire and write stories that we would read to each other. Our faces almost got sunburnt facing the fire but our backs were freezing. So every now and then we would turn around and bake the other side." The kids weren't allowed an oil lamp for fear of fire. When they went to bed, they'd wiggle to make a small rut in the tight-packed moss to lie in all night. They never went hungry: all around them, in the deep Mississippi Delta's water and on its land, lay the foodstuffs, ripe for the picking, that graced their bountiful table.

Arthur Udstad came from a long line of engineers. His father and uncles had emigrated in the 1880s from Trondheim, Norway, to St. Charles, Missouri, a well-to-do suburb of St. Louis.

5.3 Ruth with Randy and Jerry in Happy Jack.

"Udstad" means "outer homestead" (out-stead). In 1978, when Mom, Uncle Sig, and I traveled to Norway to meet the Udstad line, we visited the family farm twenty miles outside Trondheim. No longer in the family, the farmhouse contained a corner cabinet dating from 1612 that bore an ancestor's name: Arnt Arntson (he would marry the Udstad widow and take her name—the founding of the Udstad line). We were told that the first Udstad to move into Trondheim from the farm had become the town blacksmith, a position then equivalent in stature to mayor. We saw the wrought-iron fence he made at the town cemetery. Inside, another of his fences surrounded the family plot.

In the next generation, the immigrant Udstads had equal success in their newfound world. Arthur's father, Sigvald, worked for the Union Pacific as a mechanical engineer, earning patents on coupling and braking devices used on train cars. Arthur's uncle moved to Aurora, Illinois, and there invented the interior door hinge for Fisher Body.

Arthur turned the family scientific bent to horticulture. At thirty-four, university degree in hand, he traveled to New Orleans to ship for Mexico where he was to take possession of a banana plantation his father had purchased. Pancho Villa and the Mexican revolution of 1919 put an end to his plan.

Waiting for the ship that would never sail to Veracruz, Arthur journeyed down to the mouth of the Mississippi. He saw the truck farms' black

5.4 Port Sulphur School, 1935, grades 4 and 5: Ruth, 1st row, 3rd from left, has skipped two grades and almost caught up to Sig, 3rd row, 2nd from right.

mud and the lush green that flourished in winter along the levee south of New Orleans, and he decided to stay. He wanted to live in the country where things grew. Soon he found his beautiful Delta bride, Josephine Jacomine, thirteen years his junior, of mixed Alsatian and Dalmatian descent.

In that true alluvial Delta, there was nothing but topsoil, two hundred feet thick before bedrock, the result of eons of silt left by the river in its annual spring inundation. The Delta soil was so rich that, with one crop of Creole lilies (*Crinum scabrum*), the bulbs of which were prized as far away as Japan and Holland, Arthur earned enough to build the cypress clapboard house where Ruth Angeline Udstad grew up. The biggest cash crop Plaquemines Parish ever saw, Creole lilies would soon develop blight and were never grown there commercially again.

This lower Delta is not to be confused with the Mississippi-Yazoo Delta, the floodplain hundreds of miles to the north where cotton thrived and the blues were born. If the blues spun gold from the hard life of picking cotton in the Mississippi Delta, then it was nature itself, brimming with life and mineral wealth, sulfur and oil, that made the lower Delta extraordinary.

But the weather was extraordinary, too, and not only just for its verdant winters. The hurricane of 1863 had washed away Isle Dernière, a barrier

5.5 Mom and Sig visit original Udstad homestead near Trondheim with cousins Sverre and Hjordis.

island and rich man's retreat in the Gulf of Mexico thirty miles due west from Happy Jack. It took 320 men, women, and children with it. The hurricane of 1893 killed 2,500 in Louisiana, 300 in Plaquemines alone. The hurricane of 1915 touched both my father's and mother's families.

In the spring of 1927, it rained for months all through the Mississippi River Valley. Just months after Mom's birth in New Orleans, threatened by the famous flood—"The river has busted through clear down to Plaquemine," sings Randy Newman—the rest of the family, the Hingles and Jacomines, scrambled up to higher ground in New Orleans where they stayed for a while with Arthur, Josephine, and little Sig and Ruth Angeline. In fact the flood never invaded Plaquemines's west bank, the location of Home Place, where the Jacomines had their rice farm, and Happy Jack, a few miles upriver where the Udstads went to live in the early thirties. It wouldn't have drowned the east bank either if the bankers and power brokers of New Orleans had not conspired to blow up the downriver levee to relieve the pressure on city levees and save New Orleans. Promises of reimbursement to the trappers and fishermen of St. Bernard and Plaquemines by those who orchestrated the flood went unfulfilled.

Sometimes the levees were the problem; sometimes they were the solution. Until the 1920s and 1930s when the shell road was built—by raiding the Indian middens for shells and by dredging the marsh—the levee served as thoroughfare for long stretches up to New Orleans. Cousin Audrey again helps us picture the journey: "There was a man who stood at the side of a particularly bad stretch of mud road where many cars got stuck. He had a team of oxen and for a price would pull cars out of the mud. He probably didn't make much money out of this career because hardly anybody had a car. When the man wasn't there, it was necessary to drive on top of the levee where there was a lighthouse. The car was slanted sideways, and I used to get very scared when we did this. I was sure the car would roll down."

Built up by eons of spring floods and bolstered by a century or more of human effort—skills brought from the Cajuns' weir building in Acadie which they first had learned from the Indians to improve their farming— the levees were what made the lower Delta habitable and its rich black soil arable. At one time, levees were also the town commons where neighbors traded gossip and foodstuffs.

So, high ground was key currency in the lower Delta. The prairie (from French *pré* = meadow) is the mostly dry land west of the strip of habitable land below the river levee. At its western edge, the "back levee" held the waters out—most of the time. Beyond the levee is the marsh, and beyond that the floating prairie, *flotant:* soil held together by marsh grasses but not anchored to a bottom. It is also called *pré tremblante*, a prairie that trembled. It rose and fell with the tide. Here even the land was amphibious. Beyond these wetlands to the west lay pirate Jean Lafitte's Barataria Bay and to the south, the Gulf.

All is flat in the marsh except for the *chênières*, where shifting tides have built up isolated silty beaches; there, small oaks (*chênes*) have taken hold and built up a few more feet of soil around them. Here and there, too, shell middens rise where Indians once gathered to feed off clams and oysters. Now and again a mysterious mud lump will rise up in the Mississippi itself and provide a few feet of relief (and a great place to fish for speckle' trout) before it subsides again. But for the most part, it is flat as far as the eye can see, from the river to the marsh to the floating prairie to the Gulf, save the levees.

Paradoxically this levee that made life possible also ensured its eventual reclamation by the Gulf. Without the annual fresh water inundation and the silt it left behind, the land was subjected to the salt-water intrusion that killed off the plant life that held *flotant* together. The marshlands also were jeopardized by the building of canals by sulfur and oil production companies who, for decades, cut through the marsh seeking more direct

5.6 Fishing behind the back
levee in the Cut.

routes to their working fields to pump out their mineral wealth. In lower
Plaquemines, airborne sulfur and salt rusted through car wheel wells at
about the same rate as the marsh eroded away—the size of a football field
every hour.

We were oblivious to the world we were losing. "The Cut"—the nearest
reach of one of those canals—was an exciting place. Behind the company
barracks, Freeport Sulphur Company dug as a fishing and swimming hole
an extra spur in the ten-mile canal used to get men to the sulfur dome at
Lake Grande Ecaille and to get the sulfur back to the river for transport.
Connected to Grand Bayou and beyond it the Gulf, the Cut was the closest
place from Sig and Helen's to fish for redfish and speckle' trout and flounder.

Those fish provided not only good game for us but fine dinner for
sharks. Sighting the fins of small sharks every once in a while insured that
swimming in the Cut was a source of special excitement. A hundred yards
out was a platform we used sometimes for diving, sometimes for basking,
and most of the time for playing king-of-the-hill. When Jerry once pushed
me off and I plunged feetfirst through six feet of water and two feet of ooze,
I got a direct experience of what the Delta swamp is all about. And, for
some time after, the stuff of nightmares.

Sometimes "high ground" wasn't "ground" at all. All the fishing camps
in the bayou beyond the back levee were built on pilings, ten or fifteen feet
high. When I was a boy, the grown-ups sank the pilings for our fishing

5.7 Jerry with flounder.

camp at the mouth of Grand Bayou where it met the Gulf. They built a platform on six-inch steel poles and then got as many full-grown men on it as possible, to jump in unison. The mud gurgled, the poles slipped by jolts into the half-liquid marsh, and the grown-ups cursed and laughed.

We would go fishing by boat in the Gulf or along the edges of the bayou where huge bull redfish fed, or we surf-cast for speckle' trout, wading up to our waists in high-summer water the temperature of a bath, the croakers nibbling at our ankles. I once went trawling for shrimp with Uncle Martin in his skiff in the bay behind the camp, helping him throw out the bycatch—crabs and baitfish—when we hauled up the long net.

At night, if we didn't sit around playing bourré by Coleman lantern, we carried lanterns to go gigging flounders. We would wade along the shallow sandy verge of the Gulf on a cold, moon-filled night, trying to avoid the mud holes that sucked the knee waders off our feet. When you gigged one, you'd get splashed as you struggled to get the wriggling impaled flounder in the gunnysack. We also fished the swirling waters beside gas flares—the marsh was bursting with oil and gas—that attracted the teeming schools of fish and the predators who fed off them: primeval alligator gar, barracuda, porpoise, and shark.

I loved gigging flounders and was entranced by Uncle Martin's country ways and rich French accent. But for the most part I was the odd man out on these excursions, always with my nose in a book—now Edgar Rice

Burroughs's Martian series, now Jules Verne's *Mysterious Island*. If the fish started biting, I might try my hand awhile till I'd cast a bird's nest and have to ask Mom's help to disentangle the reel. There was always a family bet on first, biggest, and most fish; Mom hated to be drawn away from the competition. *Oh, Randy . . . not again. Can't catch a fish unless your line is wet!* Jerry was more her match, his line always wet first and last, long after dusk, till he could hardly see his cork.

For many, those camps weren't for weekend fun but for year-round living. Men fished out there and trapped muskrat, mink, and nutria. They spoke French even though they might be named Petrovich or Folse.

In Diamond below Happy Jack, there was a boat that served as a school bus, picking children up along the bayous. To reach their congregations, priests took altar and Eucharist to the bayous by boat. Early on, peddlers came along the river on boats, called *chalons*, "floating department stores in miniature . . . that bartered for rice, for pelts, for alligator skins." The peddlers, called Arabs whether they were Jewish or Lebanese or French, would call their wares: "I got drawers for the big boys. I got drawers for the big girls." So recorded Harnett Kane in *Deep Delta Country*. Kane adds, "The owner, arriving on an infrequent trip, tooted his whistle and for miles the housewives ran over their lists. This was commerce with a luster; as one woman sighed in recollection, 'It made paying out your money a nice pleasure'"[14]—a phrase which perfectly captures the idiom and cadence of the true Delta.

In 1727, Sister Marie Hachard de Saint-Stanislas, a nun traveling to New Orleans in the first contingent of Ursulines from France, just a decade after Bienville's founding of New Orleans, described in lush terms her weeklong journey by pirogue from the river's mouth up to New Orleans:

> There are no lands cultivated the whole length of the river, only great wild forests inhabited solely by beasts of all colors, serpents, adders, scorpions, crocodiles, vipers, toads, and others which did us no harm even though they came quite near us. . . . The grass is so high in this region that one can sleep only on the banks of the river. . . . We slept two to a pallet with our clothes on and covered our cradles with a large piece of linen in such a way that the Maringouins [mosquitoes] . . . could not find any little passage to come to visit us.

In her next letter she described the cornucopia of this rich land, displaying a degree of appreciation only the French could muster:

> Hunting is done about ten leagues from our city [in Plaquemines] and lasts all winter which here begins in October. Many wild oxen are taken and brought here to New Orleans and nearby areas. We buy this meat for three *sols* a pound, the same as deer, which is better than the beef and mutton you eat in Rouen. . . . Wild ducks are very cheap. Teal, water-hen, geese and other fowl and game are also very common. . . . Really, it is a charming country all winter and in summer the fish are plentiful and good. There are oysters and carps of prodigious size and delicious flavor. As for the other fish, there are none in France like them. They are large monster fish that are fairly good. We also eat watermelons and French melons and sweet potatoes which are large roots that are cooked in the coals like chestnuts. . . .[15]

Mom's maternal ancestors arrived in the New World at about the same time as Sister Marie. A carpenter, Simon Hingle (sometimes Engel or Yngle in the genealogical record), probably settled first in Mobile, then on La Côte Allemande (meaning not German Coast really, but rather Alsatian bank of the Mississippi), a dozen miles below Baton Rouge on the river, then traveled downriver to the deep Delta. By 1789 Jacques-Santiago Hingle is established in Plaquemines. The fecundity that Sister Marie described called them to farm rice, indigo, and oranges. But in their hearts they were all hunters and fishermen.[16]

Angeline Hingle, great-great-granddaughter of Jacques-Santiago, married Nicole "Nick" Jacomine Sr. in the 1890s. Then their daughter Jo' Jacomine married Arthur Udstad from St. Charles, Missouri. It was Jo' Jacomine's Delta world and family, full of vitality and good cheer, unlike his dour and laconic Norwegian family, that Arthur Udstad received in dowry.

The deep Delta's land and the waters brimmed with redfish, trout, shrimp, crab, and oysters, duck, geese, dove and quail, deer, rabbit, and alligator. In the early eighteenth century, Jesuit priests had planted orange trees brought from Saint-Domingue (Haiti). Hybrids from that stock, Louisiana navels, became the best oranges in America, with less acid and higher brix (sugar content). The recipe for Uncle Martin's orange wine went back at least three generations; it was fermented dry and, at 18 percent alcohol

5.8 The Hingles and Jacomines, c. 1940. L to R: Great-Uncle Nick Jacomine and his wife, Lydia, Josephine Hingle (Gr'Mom) and her second husband, William, Grandmother Josephine (Nan' Jo'), Great-Great-Uncle Martin.

and up, packed a wallop. Sig's Orange Wine, sold commercially, was one reason fisherman stopped at the restaurant.

Uncle Martin (really my great-great-uncle) had been wounded in the Great War. Having promised his Savior that if he survived he would never marry, he lived with his mother, whom everyone called Gr'Mom, cooking all the while. He figures in a family story where the revenuers arrived and, not finding any orange wine, aimed their shotguns into the attic and pulled the triggers until wine flowed down the walls.

At Christmastime, we all went to Uncle Martin's place to pick oranges—hard work but fun. We'd haul those oranges from trees high as his house in bushel baskets with wire handles that cut into your palm. En masse, the oranges were so heavy that, with the trunk full, the Grand Prix plowed back to New Orleans with its nose in the air like a speedboat. I would help wash and bag the oranges, then sell them in the neighborhood for fifty cents for a small bag, a buck for a large. Mom was happy to pocket the extra income. Dad was dragging Mom through the courts.

My mother's great-grandmother Gr'Mom was the family's legendary cook. Uncle Martin came in a close second. Gr'Mom's husband Jules had died of lockjaw and she married his nephew William, thirteen years her junior. Every Thanksgiving and Christmas saw a table that started with gumbo and ran through daube (roast beef braised in a red gravy), pork roast stuffed with whole toes of garlic, pique duck (stuffed with chopped garlic and parsley laced with cayenne), fricassée of rabbit, whole fried sweet and Idaho potatoes, broccoli and cauliflower au gratin, and creamed spinach from the expert hand of Uncle Martin. The stuffed turkey was almost an afterthought, a token gesture to local tradition. The pièce de résistance was oyster dressing made, as my cousin Audrey recalled, "in a giant washtub with 17 sacks of oysters that had been fished by the men in the family from the bottom of the bayou and then shucked." It ended with half a dozen pies and cakes. Sometimes thirty-five people sat down to this rich repast, all cooked in a house with neither electricity nor gas, on a wood-burning stove without a thermostat. Ruth Ann looked on with eyes wide.

Food was the center of their world. But their Pickwickian table had another Dickensian quality. Trauma lay behind it.

When she was seven, my grandmother Nan' Jo' lost her mother, Angeline, still in her twenties, to anthrax. In these days of anthrax attacks by mail, we forget that anthrax is a disease of farm animals. Angeline contracted it in 1905 while helping operate on a mule on the family rice farm in Home Place. French was the older generations' first, if not only, language, so they would have known anthrax as *charbon* (coal) because of the black suppurations that form all over the skin.

Jo's brother, Nichole Jr., three years younger, recorded the horrible death in the same handwritten memoir where he described the hurricane of 1915. When Nick was four, Uncle Martin paddled him in an open skiff from Home Place to their mother's deathbed in Buras—fourteen miles downriver. Big sister Jo', aged seven and unmentioned, was no doubt at his side. "I remember vividly," wrote Nick, "when we got there, that she was dying. Her face was swollen to the breaking point and when she saw me she tried to smile, and then she announced that she was to die at a certain hour, which she did at exactly the hour she predicted. I was then about four years old, too young to understand the agony she had gone through."

Maybe Jo' was old enough better to understand their loss. Raised by Gr'Mom, she would spend her life as a first-grade teacher mothering seven-year-olds. She would name her daughter Ruth *Angeline*, Ruth Ann for short, a name that would last through Mom's college years.

After Nan' Jo's death from cancer at age fifty-two, Paw-Paw lived alone in their cypress shotgun house on the shell-paved river road in Happy Jack, at the corner of Udstad Lane. He had trouble keeping up with the St. Augustine grass he had so lovingly planted. Once, his riding mower grabbed the exposed roots of the live oak and started climbing; Paw-Paw tumbled off and broke his arm. Magazines and newspapers began to accumulate. For years he had collected wild irises and other specimens along the highway and replanted them in his yard and in the greenhouse behind the house. Now, neglected, his greenhouse began to fall into disrepair.

Paw-Paw came to stay with us in New Orleans for two weeks. Was it then he taught me about butterflies? While he visited us, Uncle Sig and Aunt Helen cleaned up his house and got rid of what they could. When Paw-Paw returned, he stood in the front parlor looking back toward the dining room with its big mahogany table, the lace runner straight and neat. Paw-Paw looked stunned. His eyes welled up with tears. Sig was anxious he was about to be fussed at again.

"You know," Arthur said finally, "I expect Jo' to come out that kitchen. This is just the way she kept it. I miss her so."

Happy Jack drew us for almost every holiday, and Uncle Sig and Aunt Helen, who ran the first restaurant in the family, re-created Gr'Mom's legendary feast with Mom's help, though I won't venture to say who was in charge. Sig was charged with getting the duck and the rabbit; Mom and Helen had the run of the professional kitchen. The serving table laden with food was often longer than the dining table at which we sat.

Such excess brought with it an insurmountable temptation to gluttony. How could I skip the daube? And of course I had to have spaghettini with the daube's red gravy, rich with beef drippings. The crispy pork roast—always overdone but all the more crispy—cried out for interladlings of oyster dressing, as did the turkey. Each swam in its own rich gravy. It was truly a groaning board. Mom once indulged in a second deep-fried sweet potato; her stomach swelled so much she threatened a visit to the emergency room.

The bounty of Gr'Mom's table resurfaced, first at those holiday feasts, and then again later at Mom's restaurants. Key vestiges appear on the Ruth's Chris menu. In my family, Uncle Martin's creamed spinach was used as a home remedy, meant both to cure and to comfort. Anyone who has eaten that same creamed spinach at Ruth's Chris knows how well it performs at least the latter function.

In the 1950s, Mom's brother, Sig, decided to have a go at a motel, bar, and restaurant. He'd had one last fling in Hollywood after the war, trying to

5.9 Mom re-creates Gr'Mom's Thanksgiving at Ruth's Chris.

make the most of his matinee idol looks, and then came home to work as an oilfield roustabout, learning to fly a seaplane, and putting a life together with Helen, the Croatian beauty from Buras.

Sig was self-taught architect, carpenter, and mason. We all pitched in. I remember carrying mortar, I'm sure more trouble than my help was worth. Even Dad helped, cigarette hanging from his lips, mugging for the camera. And Helen was always scurrying around, making sure everyone was well fed.

Business was good. The oil fields were growing, and there was plenty of traffic on the highway. A workingman liked a drink after a long day in the fields. And after fishing in the Gulf, his trailered boat full of iceboxes jammed with trout, a fellow could use a bite of something more than a ham sandwich on Sunbeam bread. People got so they couldn't do without Oysters Helène or her flounder stuffed with crabmeat.

Every couple of years, Sig added something—a big fireplace, an oyster bar, a patio, or some new nook for cozy dining. The fireplace could burn four-foot logs for long hours. He'd varnish old brick he'd found in crumbling plantations until it shone with a luster. Above the mantle hung the trove of family pictures, blown up and framed. Sig was a scavenger with a taste for history, collecting and displaying antique guns, decoys, and spinning wheels. The restaurant grew back from the highway, toward the river and Arthur and Nan' Jo's house below the levee. The place was festive, hosting big dinners and parties for the oil production companies and rivaling the well-established Delta Club. Those rich Cajun accents roughened by Picayune and Pall Mall cigarettes could be heard over the clatter of plates and the tinkle of ice in highball glasses. Sig told a good *coonasse* joke. The bar did a load of business. Arthur loved to get behind the bar and joke with customers. He loved to buy a round, sometimes forgetting to satisfy Sig's till. He liked his highballs, too, and would forget himself. One day Sig was serving drinks right behind his father. In earshot of Sig's customers, Arthur was saying, *My God, look at that. A bottle without a stopper. A man would have to be a fool to drink out of this.*

Doesn't Dad know he's chasing my customers off? But what could Sig say? He was used to getting the short end of the stick, his GI savings used to send Ruth Ann to college. He was used to his father ignoring him. Ruth Ann always won. *I may as well finish this bottle myself. . . .*

CHAPTER SIX

BIENVILLE SCHOOL

"RUTH, YOU KNOW THOSE FRIED POTATOES AREN'T GOOD FOR THE boys. I can see why they're so fat."

The air—like the cooktop in the yellow Formica kitchen—was electric. Dad was in the house again for the first and last time since the separation.

"Rodney, you used the boys to talk your way in here, but you can't tell me what to do. I'll cook what I want. If you care about the boys so much, why don't you pay for their school?"

The potatoes sputtered in the hot grease. Scrambled eggs with fresh French fries was one of Mom's country favorites—and mine. She added salt and pepper and began to beat the dozen eggs she would pour over the frying potatoes.

"They're getting fat. I know what's good for them. And if they love that school so much, you can send them."

"On the money you give me?"

"You going to invite me to dinner? I miss home cooking."

"Not on your life."

After Dad left in 1958, Mom had stayed in her room crying for a short time. Then she did whatever she needed to do. At first, she made drapes. Our house on Seville Drive became a workplace as Mom crawled around on our parquet living room floor—pinning, hemming, and pleating drapes. She drew on what she had learned from her country upbringing in Happy Jack, basting hems and sewing thick buckram into heavy cloth to make

6.1 At Sam Barthe School, 1955.

pleats, stitching lead disks into the bottom hem to make them fall right. Then it was time to hang the drapes for her clients, all five foot two inches of her, screwdriver in hand, screws clamped between clenched lips, installing the rods. She complained now and again of her calloused knees and aching back and hands. Soon, the sewing morphed into a decorating business that thrived for a while, despite the fact that she didn't have a natural gift for the visual. In her first act of home decorating, she covered our living room parquet floor with a broad expanse of emerald green thick-pile carpet. Perhaps Mom's temporary success at the decorating business was simply an example of her soon-to-be-famous willpower.

That same year, my new school—Bienville School—staged a Mardi Gras parade. Miss Vorbusch's third grade class paraded as conquistadors. Mom sewed my costume of upholstery fabric so thick and shiny that it could have stopped arrows from those pesky Chitimacha Indians. Suitably appointed in conquistador leggings, chestplates, and helmets, we paraded around the block pulling our American Flyers as Mardi Gras floats, pleased with ourselves.

Our class had just gone to the new Union Passenger Terminal to visit the statue of Jean-Baptiste Le Moyne, Sieur de Bienville, the founder of New Orleans, four times governor of Louisiana, and our school's namesake. Bienville was French, not Spanish, but the statue had the same era breast-plate and helmet, nobly held in the crook of one arm as the other arm planted the flag that seized the swampland in the crook of the Mississippi River in the name of the noble Duc d'Orléans. Humbled, admiring Indians knelt at Bienville's statue-feet. Like Bienville, our class carried pennants on poles. I was convinced that, as conquistadors, we were the next best thing to explorers and noblemen. It was pretty grand to my eight-year-old eyes.

Not long after that parade, a high fever laid me low and I, like the Maid of Orléans, was visited by "voices." For the *Catholic Encyclopedia* the "su-pernatural character" of Joan's voices "it would now be rash to question." But for my very terrestrial mother, voices were a bother. At my bedside, the doctor made short shrift of the problem, attributing the voices to the high fever. But I was afraid and so was she.

"Mom, I hear voices. Make them stop."

"No, you don't."

"Mom, I hear voices."

"What do they say?"

"I can't tell. They just keep repeating something."

"Randy, go to sleep. You don't hear anything."

Did I carry the Fertel gene? I wondered. And so did she.

But this was clear: I experienced my parents' separation in 1958 (the divorce settlement would not be completed for almost a decade) as a fall from Sam Barthe School to Bienville School, a local public school half a block from home.

Sam Barthe was housed in an elegant Spanish Colonial mansion in City Park—formerly the McFadden mansion, where its seven bedrooms served as classrooms. One of my earliest memories: as a boy in prekindergarten, I stand at one of its glorious arched windows with two sheets of paper, one on top of the other. The light streams and I am utterly intent on my project, tracing the image underneath. At Sam Barthe, I feel awash in light. And special. Dad loved Sam Barthe School for Boys because Sam was devoted to sports. I love Sam Barthe School in part because it loves me.

The mansion also housed a trophy room, bursting its seams with tro-phies, a giant indoor marble-lined swimming pool, and beautiful grounds with a sunken garden on one side and an Oriental garden on the other.

Sam added a jungle gym where I loved to hang from my knees, upside down. WPA art deco bridges hung over the lagoons where the busses flowed on the way to school and the way home.

Sam—so we called him—had a brush-cut military bearing, with a big gap-toothed grin always ready to break forth from his granite jaw. Sam's martial commitment to athletics pervaded the school. We were the Hornets, well-named, scrappy, and determined. Winning made Sam happy and brought out that grin we loved to see.

He was "Sam," but at Sam Barthe we went by our last names, perhaps because of the founder's military approach. My family name is pronounced with two strong stresses (FER TELL), but my early classmates found various plays on "fertile" too tempting to pass up. When we studied the dawn of civilization I became "The Fertile Crescent," and, though I ran anchor on the relay team, I was dubbed "Fertile the Turtle." Still, at Barthe I was the golden boy, and teasing rolled off my back: head of my class, teacher's pet, and star athlete at a school famous for its athletics. I felt appreciated and liked. I also wore with honor the badge for "most paddlings." Sam paddled us when we acted up, but for all his military bearing, he seemed amused at the trouble that brought me to his office on a fairly regular basis. Boys would be boys, after all. We loved Sam and felt loved by his big toothy grin.

So when the money for private-school tuition went away after the separation, for third grade I trudged half a block to Bienville School where there were no team sports and where all the teachers were women. Not a man in sight, just like at home.

Bienville was an orange brick, postwar utilitarian box on a spacious double-block campus, shaded by hundred-year-old oaks. It must have been an island of high ground (a *chênière*) within the one-time backswamp that lay between New Orleans and Lake Pontchartrain. Any good hard soaking would turn the huge playground back to swamp or at least a temporary pond. We would play touch football, drenched to the skin, splashing our way out for a pass. Or with a stick we'd poke floating red ant pyramids that formed to save the ant colony until the water drained away. The self-sacrifice of those at the bottom of the pyramid impressed us. The blacktop basketball courts compared badly to Sam Barthe's indoor basketball court, the former mansion's ballroom, where our Keds had squeaked across the polished oak floors.

I walked into Bienville an outsider, a status compounded by being a child of divorce. This was 1958; divorce was just beginning to be talked about in whispered tones, a sin that could not be spoken aloud. Suddenly I was an alien with three heads.

I didn't have words for it then, but, looking back, I see that there was also the complicated matter of class. Sam Barthe was tonier by far. An expensive private school, it bussed kids from all over the city but only from the very best areas. At that time, bussing was a sign of privilege. Sam Barthe families were the upper crust in a city highly aware of its hierarchies.

In New Orleans the most fundamental hierarchy is expressed by the height of the home lot. Being a few feet above or below sea level come hurricane season could mean life or death, at least to one's home and valuables. The trees told much of the story. In our neighborhood, the one-time backswamp drained by the Albert Baldwin Wood screw pumps, live oaks were the exception. Newly planted longleaf pines, feathery mimosas, and golden raintrees with their tiny Chinese lantern seedpods were scrawny by comparison. Along the high ground of the Metairie Ridge and of St. Charles Avenue, alleys of live oaks spread in all their age and glory.

Our neighborhood was modest compared to the beautiful tree-lined streets of Old Metairie or the Garden District. Mom and Dad had no pretensions to class. Dad was a Jewish inner-city kid with lots of money, and Mom was a tomboy from the country who would come to hate the white-shoe pretense of Uptown. I was moved by the comfortable cool hush of schoolmate Jerry Wilson's house in Old Metairie with the jalousied sunroom that sported a myna bird that whistled and spoke. Was Jerry Wilson's family part of the true upper crust of New Orleans, the white-shoe lunch clubs and krewes that ran Mardi Gras, the debutante balls, and the city's power structure? I was so far out of this world that I didn't even know to ask.

Bienville was full of people who were my equal in matters of money, especially since Dad was doing everything he could to impoverish Mom. Bienville drew not only from our ranch-house neighborhood but also from Parkchester Apartments. We lived there once, but we had moved up to Seville Drive after Mom had repeatedly begged for a home of our own. From Parkchester, Bienville drew working-class kids who played rougher and tended to perform less well in school. This, too, represented a new and alien world.

At Bienville, I missed the sense that I was special. The tone had changed. While I was still at the head of the class and the teacher's pet, at least up to a point, I also felt I was *that Randy*. In fifth grade, Miz Steer, an ugly old bat who we assumed was an old maid, put me in charge as class monitor whenever she was called to the principal's office. She was assistant principal. She had earned my respect with her intelligence and her twinkling eye, so perhaps I acted out less in her room than I had in previous years. But there was this feeling that she did it grudgingly or by calculation. Perhaps she figured I'd do less damage if I had the responsibility to keep others from cutting up. Somehow I managed to do the job well enough to keep it and yet avoided appearing to my classmates a total suck-up—though they may remember differently. Out on the playground afterwards, it was back to business as usual, climbing the *chênière's* magnificent live oaks or playing marbles in the dirt beneath their rich canopy or teasing the girls at their hopscotch and jump rope.

One day, a storm blew up. Miz Steer asked me to close the heavy metal door that led from the corridor to the playground. A gust of wind slammed the door on my right index finger. I was escorted to the principal's office and my mom was called. I could hear the principal explain to my mother, "Mrs. Fertel, he really needs to see a doctor . . .

"No, we can't take him . . .

"No, he really needs to see a doctor . . .

"Mrs. Fertel . . ." Finally, the picture of exasperation, she came to get me. *That Randy.*

At home I soothed my loneliness and anxieties with Mom's cooking and numbed myself with this new thing called TV. I went from being a skinny, glowing kid in Mrs. Halsey's first grade at Sam Barthe School to a pouting pudge in Mrs. Heinz's fourth grade at Bienville. *Randy Pandy* was now *roly-poly.*

Mom's cooking was simple but always mouth watering. Pan-fried veal and pork chops, panéed meat (breaded veal round), roasts cooked till they were crusty and fell apart, stuffed peppers, shrimp smothered with mirliton, a squash called chayote elsewhere that thrives on New Orleans backyard fences. Of course we ate red beans on many Mondays, a tradition in New Orleans dating back to the time when beans were put on to simmer while the week's wash was done. In New Orleans everyone has their favorite condiment to stir into their red beans. I've known people who liked a big heaping of chowchow, a southern concoction of sweet relish and mustard. Yuck! Until I grew out of the childishness of it, I favored ketchup. Mom and Jerry, who both looked down their noses at me, liked wine vinegar or

6.2 Roly-Poly Randy at Bienville.

pepper vinegar, cayenne peppers soaked in vinegar. Of course we all added Tabasco. It was just a question of how much.

Gumbo Mom made for holiday or special meals, or, creature of whim, if on the way home she found nice-sized shrimp being sold out of an ice chest from a truck along Gentilly Boulevard in front of the track. Maybe someone had just come up from the Gulf or had good luck with his cast net in Lake Pontchartrain. The A&P didn't offer much fresh produce. Like those of most American home cooks of the 1950s and '60s, Mom's vegetables came out of a can—LeSueur early peas, Green Giant Niblets corn—and were cooked to smithereens with generous amounts of butter. She'd ring the tarnished brass bell mounted at the back door to bring us in from playing, or, if I was reading comics in the den, would nudge me to come eat. *Randy, I've been calling for five minutes.*

Mom rarely cooked breakfast—which began my self-taught lessons in the kitchen. But when she did on special days, pancakes were her specialty:

banana pancakes or silver dollar pancakes, or jelly rolls—pancakes folded up around Welch's. More infrequent dessert treats included a huge skillet filled with overripe bananas caramelized in grease and sprinkled with sugar, or rum cake in a Bundt pan, cooled upside down over a glass milk bottle. Once she turned the pan over too soon and the rum cake cascaded down the bottle. Mom had a good laugh and I had the delicious pudding-y detritus scooped up from the Formica counter.

When she was too tired to cook after a day of sewing or, later, working in the lab at Tulane, Mom took us to A&G Cafeteria. We'd wait in the long line—the hungrier you were the slower it inched along—then slide the trays along the stainless steel runners and choose our dinner. Desserts came first—they tempted you before your tray was full. Jerry swore by the apple pie. He hummed when he was happy with his food and the apple pie's crust did it every time. For me, it was a constant debate between the cup custard and the custard pie. The crusts at A&G were legendary but it was such a pleasure to dip my spoon into that pot of eggy cream with its golden-brown skin on top.

For the main dish, Jerry favored the roast beef, a steamboat loin carved behind the steamy glass with roasted new potatoes. For me, the Salisbury steak with mashed potatoes and gravy. I knew Jerry was getting the better dish but my hamburger steak saved Mom money. Sometimes on a splurge, glancing to see if Mom would comment, I added garlic bread. Among the overcooked vegetables, I favored the Brussels sprouts or the niblet corn that I would pour directly on top of my mashed potatoes, the mixture of creaminess and sweetness all I needed to know of heaven. Though Mom's, drenched in butter and hot milk, were better.

Black men in starched white jackets met us at the cash register to carry our trays to the table. I admired their nimble way of sweeping the trays off the stainless steel slides, and their jazzy saunter to the table. Their hustle for the quarter or two my mother would leave on the tray lay in the friendly *Ev'nin', Miz Ruth.* How much could they have been making? Two dollars an hour? With families to feed? In the high spirits of their performance they seemed to be tap dancing through what for them must have been purgatory.

Then Mom's inevitable quip as she surveyed our plates: *Your eyes are bigger than your stomachs.* We didn't dare not finish.

Besides, we had the loss of Sam Barthe to soothe. The move from all-boy Sam Barthe to a coed school was also disconcerting because I had to learn to deal with these new beasts called girls and their strange folkways: adjusting their petticoats behind the metal doors at recess (which I was dying to see, but too ashamed to watch), playing hopscotch and jump rope (which I was dying to do, but too ashamed to join), and, worst of all, having the audacity to be as smart as me (which I was too ashamed to acknowledge). Rebecca Picou captured my heart in Miz Vorbusch's third grade. I never told her. I suffered in silence.

My crushes brought nothing but discomfort. I was powerless even when fat old Miz Vorbusch leaned over to help with my schoolwork, showing wrinkly cleavage. I couldn't take my eyes away, left wondering what this could mean, mesmerized by something so unattractive. In Mrs. Heinz's fourth grade, I never spoke to the tall redheaded girl who favored sundresses that showed off her creamy white legs. In fifth grade, I teased Susan McLean so unrelentingly on the playground that she slapped me. I also pinched her mercilessly at square dancing, every time the *à-la-main*-left brought us together as momentary partners. Square dancing then still thrived in New Orleans, a legacy of the French quadrille. But the Frenchman's savoir-faire was not to be mine. A store by that name sprung up in the Parkchester Shopping Center and I wondered how you got some o' that. What I was more likely to get in its stead was another helping of mashed potatoes.

In a way, religion formed one tenuous bridge between Sam Barthe and Bienville, and for a time was one path I pursued in my effort to find my way in the world. Catholicism had been the resolution of the mixed marriage, uncomfortably for Dad apparently, given the jockey silks he designed that showed the Star of David together with Christ's cross on a field of green satin. Though like his family a thoroughly secular Jew, Dad sometimes reminded Jerry and me, "You know, Jesus was a Jew." Oblivious to the discomfort that must have lain behind those reminders, I took Catholicism fairly seriously for a while. Mom talked a fairly good game, making us go to catechism—*the seven deadly sins are gluttony, . . .*—on Tuesdays and Thursdays and to mass on Sunday. She stopped attending mass herself which made me fear for her eternal soul. Jerry went rarely. I'd walk or bike on my own to St. Francis Cabrini's huge postwar Quonset hut that served the parish until they built the modernist space station *cum* stained glass in the early sixties to replace it. I often wore a tie of my own accord though even grown men came in shirtsleeves. I was serious. I wondered if I had a calling.

This seriousness didn't stop me from being the most obnoxious catechist, peppering the nun or lay teacher with sarcasm: "Mr. Sartorini, do you think maybe Joseph thought that dove did it?" I spent a lot of time in the head nun Sister Mary Joseph's office.

Perhaps it was hard to take catechism seriously because, years before, Jimmy the bus driver at Sam Barthe had been assigned the task of helping prepare the first graders for their first communion. It was hard to shake the image of him explaining the Holy Trinity in the very bowels of Holy Trinity Church on Esplanade near City Park, as he picked wax out of his ear with the school bus key. Nor did Cabrini's Monsignor Frey nurture my seriousness when I asked him which Bible we were supposed to read. Catechism didn't at that time include much Bible reading, just bowdlerized and infantilized narratives. I knew there was something more there. I also knew enough about the Holy Mother Church that they would have a preferred Bible and that the failure to find out which one it was would send you straight to hell. Looking down from his great height, Monsignor Frey intoned, "That's too hard for you. Leave the Bible reading to us."

It didn't help that everyone was as impressed by the monsignor's lineage as they were his holy office. His family owned one of the two local hot dog companies. The Burings—Jews—owned King Cotton, and Catholics owned Frey. Did Monsignor's spiritual authority, I wondered, come from the pope or from his family's wealth? If you ate King Cotton hot dogs were you allying yourself with Christ's killers? By the time I was old enough to hear about how my pubescent yearnings were staining my soul with carnal sins, I was ready to lapse not only from seriousness but from the church altogether. Working at the Jesuit institution Le Moyne College years later in my first teaching job was, I suppose, my penance. If a lapsed Catholic can fall further from the church, working with the Jesuits I did.

Baseball was for a moment the one bright spot on an otherwise dark field. The summer of 1959, I was the ninth player on the second-best ten-year-olds baseball team in New Orleans. I played left field and batted eighth. Jerry and I were on the same team. He caught and was full of hustle. He batted third, right before the clean-up, Bobby Larson—a large, red-faced left-hander with a wicked fastball and curve both.

Maybe Coach Dave Adamson deserves most of the credit, but imagine: double plays around the horn at ten years old: 5 to 4 to 3. Once Bobby Larson hummed three quick strikes past a little tyke before he could dig in and before his coach could call time or wave the kid out of the batter's box. Barely able to hold up his bat, one, two, three, *yer out*, before he knew what hit him.

"He can't do that," yelled the opposing coach.

"Well, get you boys outta the batter's box," explained the ump.

We were out to win and win we did. We came in second in the city championship that year. It was my dropping a simple pop fly in left field in the ninth inning of the championship game that made us lose. That pop-up just looped so slow and languid that I had all the time to imagine the consequences of failing my teammates, and I did.

The next year Coach Dave broke my heart when he left me back with the ten-year-olds while Jerry and the rest moved up to the eleven-year-olds, a city championship and a trip to Atlanta for the nationals where they made the finals. I was batboy, riding my first train and sitting in the dugout, but little consolation.

After that, I became a catcher like my brother. All reaction, no time to think behind the plate. But never again on a great team. And never again blessed with a great coach.

Dad got wind of our success in team sports and came back into our lives. He asked if we wanted to go back to Sam Barthe for sixth grade. *Did I!!* But much had changed. Sam had moved the school to the suburbs in Metairie to a sprawling new campus. Worse, I was no longer a shoo-in for top grades and Sam's gold medal. Had my three years in public school set me back? And when Sam came to fetch his old star athlete from class to see if I made the weight for his 110-pound football team, he shook his head in disgust. Eleven years old, I tipped the scales at 120. Dad disappeared again and it was back to public school the next year.

Bone-tired from making drapes, Mom started a new job downtown at Tulane Medical School. She was hired as a lab technician for Dr. George Burch, the founder of modern cardiology (his bust stands alone in the medical school's lobby) with an international reputation for his research on heart disease. Mom, valedictorian of her high school class, had graduated from LSU at age nineteen with honors in chemistry and physics; she also had pursued a master's degree. At Burch's lab, she ran the Zeiss machine, a spectrometer that measured traces of radioactive isotopes that Burch infused into his cardiac patients. Burch had a special relationship with the Oak Ridge National Laboratory in Tennessee, the first nongovernmental researcher to obtain their radioactive material.

The radioactive material was kept in vials on the counter, placed behind loosely stacked lead bricks with no cover. Mom's job was to take samples of cardiac patients' *piss and shit*—so she called it with a smile—and run them through the Zeiss machine. She said her nails had never been so hard—clicking them on the kitchen table—as when they steeped in urine all day.

Mom was so nimble at what she did for Dr. Burch that he let her bring home the huge Frieden electro-mechanical calculator to crunch the numbers for his studies. Our living room then doubled as a computing room, with the calculator taking up one end of our formal dining table, never used except for poker and bourré games or as underpinnings for a Ping-Pong table. That machine had ten or twelve columns of integers, each running from zero to nine, with a movable decimal place for doing calculations on minute trace elements. Mom's fingers were a blaze of speed, punching in the numbers and then hitting the "go" key. The machine would buzz and whir, and numbers would click into place. The solution was tidy, correct, and inscribed in black and white. There was no possible doubt or question. Just like she liked it.

CHAPTER SEVEN

CONGO SQUARE

BASEBALL SEASON DIDN'T LAST LONG. THERE WAS THE PROBLEM OF what to do with the rest of the year. I started selling seeds door to door, sending off to a seed company from an ad on a comic book's back cover. I sat on my bed with piles of pennies, nickels, silver dimes, and quarters, the next Moneybags Fertel. Paw-Paw had conveyed to me his love of growing things. I planted the unsold packets in the yard: nasturtiums and elysium, radishes and carrots. Never so adept as he, I chose a shady spot for the root vegetables. Beside the carport with better sun, my first hollyhocks grew eight feet tall in the rich once-swamp soil.

When I was twelve, I extended my job mowing our own lawn to others in the neighborhood. Mom paid me $2 or $3, a third of what a yardman got. When I started going door to door, I upped it to $4, which still undercut the competition. I did half a dozen yards regularly that summer and the next, meticulously mowing, edging, raking, and sweeping. It was hard work in the unrelenting sun and humidity of New Orleans, and the afternoon rains that came up from the Gulf made the spikes of St. Augustine grass grow like crazy. Miz Evans across the street, whose Boston terrier, Biff, yapped at me when I passed with my mower, complimented my hard work. When daily rains kept me from cutting lawns and the grass got high, it was a challenge pushing the gas mower through the thick stuff. Of course *Roly-Poly* had that extra weight to heave into it.

That weight might have melted away had I not traveled often by bike to Tasty-Time in the Parkchester Shopping Center for soft-serve ice cream and chocolate shakes and po'boys. It was owned by Mom's college pal Gloria Bowers, also newly divorced. Her housekeeper, May, helped run Tasty-Time, and she knew how I liked my roast beef po'boys—slathered with extra mayonnaise and dripping with gravy. In New Orleans you measure a roast beef po'boy in part by the number of paper napkins it requires. At Tasty-Time I grabbed a handful. Apart from buying these treats, I proudly banked the rest of the money at the National American Bank, conveniently located in the same shopping center.

After the first summer, Mom announced that, since I was using her mower, she would no longer pay me to mow our lawn. She didn't use it as a maternal opportunity to teach me basic economics. Her message was not, *I'm glad you're working hard and saving your money, but.* . . . Nor was it the harder lesson, *This is how the world works, Randy, there's no free lunch.* It was more, *Hey, you've been taking advantage of me! Time you paid the piper.* My enterprising spirit soon petered out and she was back to paying the high-priced gardener. Though she didn't admit it, it was a case of what she called *cutting off your nose to spite your face.* But I felt the real loser. I don't remember what I did with the money, in part, perhaps, because the pride had gone out of it. Call it a Ruth's Reduction Sauce.

Jerry meanwhile was never home. He became an avid hunter and fisherman, casting for bass in the City Park lagoons. A four-pounder sat naked, staring up at us from our freezer for years waiting for the taxidermist. If it wasn't bass it was golf balls he would fish out of the lagoons, then carry bagfuls to sell at the clubhouse. Other times, Jerry went to Uncle Sig's and Aunt Helen's in Happy Jack. There he hunted whatever was seasonal. Or unseasonal. Uncle Sig had grown up at a time when wild game laws and restrictions did not exist, and he disdained newfangled notions about the right time to hunt duck or dove. And why shouldn't they shine rabbit and frogs? There were pots to fill. For generations they had been filled by shining flashlights that froze the prey until you got a bead on them. Jerry went down to Happy Jack almost every weekend. I would sometimes tag along when Mom drove him to the Greyhound bus station at the foot of Tulane at Basin, where Highway 61 begins on its way to the other Delta where blues was born, and on to Chicago. Jerry was going in the opposite direction.

Other times Jerry was off helping his buddy down the block steal and paint my bike so I wouldn't recognize it. It was a gold Schwinn Dad had given me, a twin to Jerry's red one. I learned this a few years later when our cars displaced our bikes. Jerry blithely boasted of the theft.

Dad came back into our lives intermittently, always with excursions to the movies or the zoo. He received mixed receptions. One weekend when Dad was due to pick us up, his knock at the door sent Jerry running for his closet where he shut himself in. Not understanding, I ran into mine. We were eleven and ten. We stayed long after Dad stopped pounding on the front door. Jerry never explained what had spooked him.

Dad began to send postcards of palm trees above sand beaches or the cliff divers at La Quebrada in Acapulco. One day, the call came. *Did we want to join him south of the border for Christmas?* To get the conversation rolling, he deployed the joke that he would never tire of throughout his lifelong travels: *The kids down here are smarter than you: they speak Spanish.*

Jerry was not interested. I was. Telephone connections were scratchy and uncertain. We tried to work out the details. He painted a picture just like his postcards. At least that's what I saw: cliff divers and coconuts, white beaches and blue water. After Miami and Havana, Acapulco was among the first tropical resorts to get wide notice. Dad was staying at La Playa, a hotel on the beach, or did he call it a motel? He gave the impression it was the Ritz of Acapulco.

I would lie in bed contemplating an imagined map on which the countries would turn from black to different colors, like on the world globe that stood on its swivel on Mom's desk, as I grew to know them. I was a stamp collector. Stamps were little windows into the world beyond Seville Drive, but it wasn't the stamps that lured me or even the sun and sand. The lure was the prospect of being elsewhere, *ailleurs*, my longing for the larger world beyond my grasp—a feeling that the French poets would one day identify for me. Sunny Acapulco was a good place to start bringing a rainbow of color to my mental map.

Swirling beneath this glamorous surface was the undercurrent of Dad's seamy world. It was hard not to remember where he lived in New Orleans, the seamen's hotel at the foot of Canal that he owned and where he'd taken me a couple times. It scared me with its unpainted grime and sometimes tattooed, toothless occupants. So I longed for my father and I longed for Acapulco. And I didn't.

The discussion ended as abruptly as it started. The details couldn't be worked out. Did he want to fly me down? Take a bus? Did my mother obstruct the trip? The problem may have been one that a travel agent couldn't have solved. According to the divorce documents, Mom had moved to rescind visitation rights because Dad had taken us out of school during school hours, tried to turn us against her, and used vile language on the phone. In turn, he sued to reduce child support. He loved fighting in court as much as he loved watching cliff divers.

In 1963, my father invited me to Hot Springs. I was thirteen years old. Best of all was that I got to drive the whole way up, four hundred miles. Of course I didn't have a license, but Dad had taught me to drive when I was eleven, going round and round on the deserted roads behind the golf course in City Park. I sat on his lap in his Dodge Dart, unable otherwise to see over the steering wheel. He worked the brake and accelerator.

Now with the seat pulled close, I was just tall enough. Driving up and down those hills on country roads—interstates did not yet crisscross Louisiana and Arkansas—I could really get up a lot of speed, especially when Dad was asleep. Once on a long downhill grade I even got up to ninety, about all that Dodge Dart could do. Sometimes I had trouble staying in my lane. And I got sleepy once in a while. It was lots of fun.

When we first arrived, Dad took me to the fountain in the middle of town, and though it was the middle of the night, we stood around, drank the hot water that came out of the spigots, and filled the plastic jugs Dad kept in the car. He wore his unmatching madras shorts and shirt. Nothing could match his swagger. Dad was all excited. Here was something for free that would make you live forever. *Can't beat that. You'll thank me some day.*

I didn't especially like drinking hot water but I did like the hot glazed donuts that we got at the bakery a few yards away. It was the only time I've had donuts like that, fried in lard, and dispensed by a guy at the back kitchen door in the middle of the night. All that greasy sweetness.

Every morning, we took the baths at the Buckstaff Bath House. It took hours and hours. Walking around draped in a white sheet was cool, but it also made me feel a little weird. After we hung our clothes up, we'd soak first in a big marble tub, worn from years of use. The Negro attendant took the scratchy, hempen glove that is *my* glove, which he put *my* name on, and washed me down, swirling the water around like a handmade whirlpool.

Then alone for twenty minutes, I'd sit in the hot water that was supposed to be special and good for you. They had sitz baths—*very* weird—and a shower with high-power spray coming from all sides—*that* felt *really* great. Then I'd get wrapped in a big sheet and sit in the cool-down room. Or maybe I'd take a steam first in one of those boxes that closed up with a towel around my neck. God, they were hot. Could I stand seven minutes next time? Dad swore by all this and always fell asleep once he got to the cool-down room with its hush and its ceiling fans and its cool-to-the-touch tiles. He snored.

Dad preached to me about how good the water was, how *it would cure everything* because of the minerals in the water and *the radioactivity.* Dad had the kidneys of a twenty-year-old. *That's what his doctor says. It's the water.* The water came out of the mountain too hot to drink—143 degrees. I read at the reception center that this water fell in this forest tens of thousands of years ago, trickles down until it gets hot near the earth's core, then expands and shoots up.

After the baths we'd walk down Central Avenue to the Arlington Hotel, which was really grand. Dad said you should never worry about the money you spent on food. The elderly waiters wore white gloves and uniforms like in *Gone with the Wind.* The dining room was huge and the ceilings tall. There was a lady who played a big Hammond organ, and Dad, flirting, sent me over to ask her to play "Danny Boy." Which made me uncomfortable. Besides he was always preaching, *You can't trust women.*

Why could you trust this one?

The food at the Arlington was the best part. Crisp cornbread sticks that came out of molds that left even crispier edges. I slathered them with butter and dipped them in little glass pitchers of honey. It was like dessert. Then watercress salad, bitter and peppery, surprised me how much I liked it. I was always so hungry after a morning in the bathhouse.

Good for the appetite, son.

I wished we could stay at the Arlington. We stayed across from the bath-houses in a cheap rooming house with no air-conditioning. *Always get the corner room, son, for the cross-ventilation.* But it was still hot. *Air-conditioning's no good for you.*

Dad liked to go to the goat farm south of town to get yogurt and milk. *Goat milk is much better for you, easier to digest.* With a grin, Dad pushed me toward the farmer's daughter, several years older and not especially pretty, a bit horsey in the face. It made me uncomfortable. So did milking the goats, which Dad insisted I do. Dad laughed.

Dad and I visited Mr. Ball, his friend who grew corn and tomatoes in a field behind his house. He had invented Ball's Horse Liniment, bottles of which were strewn about his airless house. He wore a wife beater that pooched over his belt. Dad sent me out to harvest. The corn towered over me. The corncobs snapped as I tore them from the stalks and scrunched when I peeled back the husks. The ripe tomatoes easily sheared away from the rich-smelling vines. Dad loved fresh food, dropping the just-shucked corn in the boiling water, slicing the tomatoes with onions. *You don't need all those fancy sauces, son. This is what's good for you. It's all you need.*

While they played pinochle, I walked to the skating rink nearby. Skating was not a neighborhood pastime, and I spent an hour trying to find my balance. On the way home, the stars wheeled overhead and I felt the longing for something concrete, something I could trust. That didn't seem to describe Dad or Mr. Ball.

I was surprised at how much time I spent by myself, since Dad spent most of *his* time—I sometimes joined him—at the betting parlor in the Southern Club or the pool hall down Central Avenue. I liked the Quartz Cave. It wasn't really a cave but a house where two old crazy guys with too much time on their hands glued quartz crystal on the walls and ceilings and even the windows. I liked the I.Q. Zoo with the raccoon that played basketball and the chicken that beat me at tic-tac-toe—*but they get to go first,* fellow tourists complained. And Dryden Pottery with all those colorful glazes. I liked to climb the mountain behind the bathhouses. There was a lookout tower at the top.

One night, as I was walking back from an evening movie alone, lightning lit up the whole horizon, in every direction. The constant flicker of light halo-ing the mountains was something I had never seen in New Orleans where thunderstorms were a way of life. What was going on? Was it just lightning? Had the cold war heated up since we'd come to Hot Springs? The streets were empty. I wished Dad were here. I couldn't count on his being at the rooming house when I got back, even though it was late. He was probably playing pool. And Mom and Jerry, were they okay? New Orleans was so close to Cuba and the Russian missiles.

When I got to the rooming house, the flashes still flickered all around the horizon. Maybe it was just sheet lightning. . . .

The rain that finally came that night was torrential. A flash flood coursed through Central Avenue—wedged between two hills—while we slept. The next morning we found the Dodge Dart filled with silt several blocks down Central Avenue. A fire hydrant had stopped its progress and pierced the door. I flew home, my first plane ride all by myself. The excitement merged with my relief.

During the times when Dad came back into our lives, sports were his main interest. He paid for golf and tennis lessons and bought the gear we needed to play them. We went often to the driving range in the Marconi Meadows in City Park. He took me to Monday night boxing at the Municipal Auditorium, a thriving, smoky, and raucous tradition. Many of the faces, chewing on the same stogies, were familiar from days with Dad at the Fair Grounds or nights at Jefferson Downs.

For, of course, there was always horse racing, the sport of kings. Because we were underage, Dad had to sneak us through the turnstiles with the help of one of his cronies who worked there. His goal was to teach that *you can never beat the horses.* Now as a teenager, I enjoyed the pageantry, just as I had in the early mornings before the divorce. Jerry came along just long enough to have a winning race season and to gain a lifelong taste for the *Daily Racing Form* and the betting window.

Dad owned horses again and Chico, unlicensed, was training them. Chico had always made me uncomfortable. Now I began to understand why. Some infraction was keeping Dad's horses from being stabled within the bounds of the track. Dad's sermons about this ran along the lines of *you can't trust those racing stewards.* I'd hear, *it's expensive to keep a horse,* so not only should you steal the oats to feed them, but *you had a right and duty to do whatever you could to win.*

You needed to know what drugs could not be detected in the Spit Barn, as it was called, after winning. You needed to know which jockeys were willing to use "machines" like a hand buzzer, hidden in their palms, and which horses—the "machine horses"—responded to them in the stretch, leaping ahead to the finish line. Before the race, you needed to know which horse responded to being jazzed with an illegal electric cattle prod, the horse rearing and kicking the walls of his stall and the trainer taking his life in his hands. More than once Dad sent me to serve as lookout at the corner of the barn. These lessons he offered as important knowledge in the ways of the world. *You'll thank me some day.*

A friend and I trudged up my father's unlit stairway at 208 South Rampart one day to borrow his car. Dad's door had holes in it large enough that I could see him get up from his mattress on the floor. I could also see another pair of naked legs. Dad came to the door and said through it, unopened, *This isn't a good time. Go away.* I was embarrassed, fourteen, in ninth grade. What did my friend see?

About that time Dad took me to see the Broadway touring company production of *Oliver.* Maybe it was the echo of Miz Caldwell's fusty lectures on a condensed *Great Expectations* in ninth grade that prevented my fully warming to *Oliver.* The kid was great, the dog even more so, and Oliver's lilting falsetto compelling—*Where is love? Does it fall from skies above?* The problem was my own distraction. During the intermission, I got into conversation with Dad, and for once, he seemed to listen.

Jerry and I had lately waged some battle on Seville Drive. Our fights were a neighborhood entertainment that began with the announcement, *hey, the Fertel brothers are fighting, let's go watch.* He was ruthless: biting, scratching, brickbats if they were at hand. Whenever a fight broke out, Jerry raced to find his leather-soled shoes, to kick the shit out of me—*where're my shoes?!?* My method was mainly defensive. In one fight, I had landed too solid a counterblow to Jerry's hard head and broke my hand. A few days later, Jerry cornered me, certain I wouldn't use my plaster cast as a weapon. He was right but I surprised him with a lucky left, gave him a black eye and ran like hell. It was the only fight I ever won, but a Pyrrhic victory for which I was paying sorely.

Now, to Dad I poured out my sense of victimhood, crying shamelessly and profusely. *Jerry beats the shit out of me. Mom always takes his side.*

"Why don't you come live with me?" Dad asked.

I imagined it for a moment: up the dark stairway at 208 South Rampart where Dad moved from the seamen's hotel after his mother's death. The door with holes from previous doorknobs. Inside, drop-cord lighting revealed piles of the *Daily Racing Form*, water jugs, and unwashed clothes. I, too, could have a sheetless mattress on the floor, in a room that had seen neither paint nor wallpaper since 1912, and I could pee in a bathroom that had never seen Lysol or Ajax. I could take breakfast with my father at the Track Kitchen with men having their first drink of the day before I took a public bus to junior high school.

Dad didn't try to paint a grand life in his Rampart Street den. He didn't really want this extra wheel. He preached the simple life. I was nothing but complication. Part of me was grateful that my pitiable situation could drag this offer out of him. But worse was the idea of taking him up on it.

We went back into the theater to watch Oliver learn about his true parents.

After making something of a splash at the talent show that same year, I was approached by some of the school's elite. My dramatic monologue spoofing Hamlet's "To be or not to be" speech in different personae made me fodder for Fortinbras' political machine. Imagining himself a kingmaker, the student body president suggested I run to succeed him. How could I resist? I would prove to myself and the world that I deserved to be loved and admired. Unfortunately, Dad got wind of my throwing a hat in the ring. Of the many pieces of bad advice he gave me, the worst was the counsel that I should hand out pencils emblazoned with "Vote for Fertel." He bought me grosses of them. No one at F.W. Gregory Jr. High had ever given out pencils before.

When the election results came in, the teacher in charge ominously asked if we wanted to know the exact count. Forewarned but grandiose to the end, I asked for the tally. My monogrammed pencils had managed in a school of many hundreds to buy seventeen votes.

Monogrammed pencils weren't my only tasteless extravagance in junior high. I became suddenly aware of clothes. At the start of each school year, my mother had always dragged us to Sears to buy a new supply of khakis and tee shirts. Now, I started shopping at the department stores downtown. Madras and Oxford cloth shirts with Bass Weejuns were my crowd's uniform.

I took it further, adopting a tie and leather-soled shoes that echoed in the corridors. I carried a briefcase that my father had given me. It had the initials we shared: RF. It was the only thing I wanted to share with him. Dad dressed not for success but to convey just the opposite: unsuccess. *No mugger's gonna think I have this bankroll dressed **like this***, he'd say, waving his fist-sized roll of twenties, fifties, and hundreds. *Like this* was his madras ensemble—unmatching plaids in shirt and shorts that he bought wholesale by the dozen from Max Dulitz in the 300 block of South Rampart. Or *like this* was his baggy unpressed trousers with lightweight permanent-press shirts that he could rinse out in a basin and dry overnight, exulting that he was beating the cleaners out of a fee. He often wore a thin, loosely knotted fifties tie. His clunky Murray's Space shoes were handmade in New York City at great expense. *They make a cast of your foot; fits perfect; s'all you'll* *ever need.* They were also about as far as you could get from stylish Italian loafers, let alone Weejuns. I didn't know much about style, though I wanted to. What I did know was how unlike my friends' fathers he was. And how I needed to be different from him and more like I imagined my schoolmates to be.

It got back to me that the young art teacher, upon whom we all had a secret crush, commented on my odd dress, saying that I puffed myself up because I must feel so small inside. It hurt. She was a tall, raven-haired beauty. Well-married, she later became a bejeweled fixture at Ruth's Chris on Uptown Sunday nights. We never spoke of our link in the past.

My dad's three favorite subjects were money, food, and women. But money subsumed all. *It's everything,* he would say. He preached to me about how it was my duty to take that newspaper without leaving a nickel on the stand or, if I had to pay, to take two papers, even if the extra went directly into a nearby garbage can. *Steal whatever and whenever you can.*

The truth is I did eventually steal from him and from my mother, but not because I believed his sermons. When I stole from the pockets of his pants, hanging on a hook at the New Orleans Athletic Club, rustling the twenties from his huge roll encircled by rubber bands, it wasn't because I believed that I had a right to relieve him of excess. When I edged quarters out of my mother's three-foot-tall, plastic Beefeaters piggybank, labeled "My First Million," it wasn't because Dad set me to the task. When I lifted a brush from the counter at the D. H. Holmes Department Store, it wasn't because it was too expensive, or because I thought I had a right to it.

My mother came to bail me out of the sordid back office at D. H. Holmes. I was thirteen. I felt embarrassed and dirty. The department store cop offered Mom the two-bit psychological explanation that I was looking for attention. My father was gone. Mom was working long hours. My brother was doing badly in school, running with the wrong crowd and getting all the attention—at least in my eyes. A plea for attention was no doubt an element. But even more, I imagined that some of my friends, who had more and better things than I did, didn't feel the emptiness I felt.

Our walk to the parking lot was one of the toughest promenades of my life. She blamed my father.

"I know your father tells you it's all right to steal. But it's not."

"I know."

I could tell she also blamed his genes but she didn't venture a lecture about that.

But most of life at that age was well beyond the reach of lectures. Junior high school revealed not only girls with budding breasts, but also occasions to ogle and get near them. In New Orleans, King Cake parties—like *galettes du Roi* in France—are part of the carnival tradition. Between Twelfth Night—January 6—and Mardi Gras, a traditional cake is made with a bean—a *fève* or fava bean in France—or later a small ceramic (and eventually plastic) baby doll. Whoever gets the favor is crowned "King" or "Queen" and must bring the next cake or throw the next party.

In early adolescence, King Cake parties were opportunities for low lights and slow dancing and, to my glee and amazement, making out with Mary Wiley, who spurned me the next day—was there something wrong with my kissing?—and lots of uncomfortable longing for Sharon Stanley, Linda Kerr, and Carolyn Warrick. Lying in my bed in Mom's now vacated bedroom, I practiced kissing on my forearm.

New Orleans is a drinking town, and soon many of us found our way to the bars not likely to card us. With access to a car, you could get curb service at the Rockery Inn or at Lenfant's, infamous for its Mob connections and for the steamy car windows in its dark parking lot next to the cemetery. At Nick's on Tulane, mixed drinks came in plastic cups for fifty cents; Cosimo's Bar on Burgundy in the French Quarter was a nicer place and just as likely not to worry about how old you were. Nearby on Rampart, Cosimo Matassa had recorded the great rhythm and blues men—Fats Domino, Little Richard, Ray Charles, Lee Dorsey—who provided the soundscape of our adolescence.

The progress of my tastes was marked by a slow ebb in sweetness. First, sloe gin and 7Up, then, Gallo Sweet Vino. Both made for a horrible drunk and a worse wake-up. Southern Comfort followed, first by the half-pint and then the pint, carried around in a back pocket. Somewhere in there was a short desperate Bacardi 151 period. Finally bourbon—Old Grand Dad and Wild Turkey, until my mother's first restaurant head cook, Vontel, would teach me that my masculinity hung on moving to Scotch.

Every weekend there were fraternity-sponsored parties and dances at F&M Patio and the Union Hall, both on Tchoupitoulas, the street that ran along the river and wharves. The word was Indian, meaning the same as "Metairie": little farms. For us it meant "place to get shit-faced." First we'd work some magic at Hokus-Pokus Package Liquor on South Carrollton where they didn't check IDs and chances were good we could walk out with whatever we needed to make ourselves stupid.

The most desirable destination was Valencia, an Uptown teenagers' club on a tree-lined street where many Uptown kids were members. Well out of my league, Valencia sometimes held open parties where knowing, impeccably dressed kids lorded it over us nonmembers.

The public dances on Tchoupitoulas were crowded affairs and rowdy. The music was local and first-rate. Deacon John was a Creole musician from Treme, the oldest free black neighborhood in America, near the French Quarter and surrounding Congo Square. He knew every rhythm and blues piece that had come out of New Orleans since the 1950s. Slow dancing to "Ruler of My Heart" and "It's Raining" by Irma Thomas, queen of New Orleans soul, was a local rite of passage. Musicians went by the name of their biggest hit: Clarence "Frogman" Henry, Oliver "Who Shot the La La" Morgan, Ernie "Mother-in-Law" K-Doe, who considered himself "Emperor of the Universe." Rumor has it that he once opened for James Brown and upstaged him. I once heard his producer Cosimo Matassa say, "Ernie K-Doe invented confidence," so it was probably Ernie who circulated the rumor. John Fred and his Playboys often traveled down from Baton Rouge with their big hit "Judy in Disguise."

Benny Spellman fronted one of our favorite party bands, his deep bass voice capturing our longing for those *Lipstick Traces* from some *Sinner Girl* whom his *Fortune Teller* might conjure for us. Heaven knows, we all "had a dizzy feeling in [our] head."

Dancing to these greats was mostly an excuse for hard drinking. I became fairly adept at driving while drunk but ended many nights in our backyard losing my dinner. Overindulgence was of course de rigueur on Mardi Gras day. One Fat Tuesday, I gained entrée to Al Hirt's hotel room on Bourbon Street. Jumbo played trumpet from the gallery to an appreciative throng below while I stumbled into the bathroom, lost my lunch in the bathtub, then, shamefaced, hightailed it.

Mom rarely took note of these alcoholic mishaps. By this time she had started her restaurant and was not yet home when I stumbled in. Once a couple of friends indulged in too much vodka during a car wash fundraiser for the high school fraternity I was pledging. I escorted them to my house and let them sober up on my bed. My mother came in and asked what on earth had happened. Terry Tyler told an over-elaborate story about having been bit by a dog, and Mom chuckled as she quit the room. *Boy, your mom is cool, Randy.*

Terry told another story about a cool parent in our circle. Terry was once caught with his next door neighbor Dean painting graffiti on Fortier High's brick wall. Some uncomfortable time was spent in the holding cell until Dean's stepfather, Dean Andrews, came to fetch them. Andrews was the madcap lawyer played to a tee by John Candy in Oliver Stone's *JFK*. One-time attorney for Lee Harvey Oswald and Carlos Marcello, the rotund, Y'at-talking hipster blew through the police station front door in pajamas covered by a trenchcoat. "Hey, d'ey still call you 'da squir'l'?" Terry heard him address the desk sergeant. He knew then everything was going to be all right.

Mom was cool, too, but to those near her, her coolness could be all too literal. It began to dawn on me that Jerry and I both believed that Mom favored the other. Jerry was convinced that I was the favorite son because I was the academic achiever. I was convinced that I made my mother uncomfortable, I knew not why. In looks I favored my father. Did that explain it? Jerry was an Udstad. I was a Fertel.

Because I left the hunting trips to Mom and Jerry, I missed out—to hear them tell it—on the best of times. There was the time they got lost hunting deer on the east bank of the Mississippi Delta. Out of their accounts of traipsing through the east Plaquemines woods that I never myself experienced, I built images of virgin forests and a wild raw nature. The most fun always seemed to come from some failure of judgment or equipment. Once they stayed too long in the duck blind and the wind came up while the tide, unnoticed, had gone out. The three of them—Jerry, Sig, and Mom—had been in separate blinds and now had to drag separate pirogues across the same mudflat toward the boat hundreds of yards away. The wind was icy, the water was icier, their boots filled, the Delta mud gave way beneath them. When they got to the water again Mom flipped her pirogue. With her poor circulation in her arms and legs, she wondered if she would make it. *Never had they had such fun.*

Jerry shared Mom's ability to live in the moment. One acquaintance liked to say that Jerry made a friend for life every time he filled his gas tank. This was truer when there were guys to pump gas, but even now Jerry is likely to befriend the person behind the bulletproof window.

Beginning in junior high, Jerry and his buddies gathered at our house for serious poker and bourré around the dining room table. In bourré, French for "hangman," if you "renege"—don't play according to suit or fail

7.1 Mom on duck hunt with Sig at left.

to use a trump card when the cards call for it—or if you "bourré"—finish a hand with no tricks—you have to match the pot, maybe hundreds of dollars, which grows still larger with the next round of antes and bets. The next hand, if you bourré, you'll not only be "hanged" but flayed, having to redouble the pot.

Many of Jerry's friends were still in high school, though some, having been held back, were crowding twenty. When my mother returned from a night at the restaurant, she would often join in the game. She enjoyed being one of the guys, and they enjoyed her even though she often took their money. The game always grew livelier when she arrived and announced, *Deal me in.* They loved Mom and they loved Jerry, too. Because of Mom, ours was one of those houses friends liked to visit. Because of our housekeeper, Earner, an invitation to dinner was prized.

One day Dad took me to see a track buddy of his who sold Buicks. Dad was giving me a car, and I could order the one I wanted—a yellow Skylark, four on the floor, wire rims, red-lined Tiger Paw tires. I wouldn't have my license for another six months, but what fourteen-year-old could turn down a new car? The Skylark sat in the driveway for those six months.

Unknown to Mom, I had been borrowing Dad's white Electra 225 for at least a year. The fiction between Dad and me was that I would only let a friend with a license drive it. I borrowed it for days at a time, parking it two blocks away from Seville Drive in front of a vacant lot. It was a quick step away from the house, cutting down the alley that bisected the blocks in our neighborhood. Mom never knew, even when I bottomed the Electra at an intersection in Lakeview and broke the car's A-frame—$800 in damage.

In giving me the Skylark, Dad was manipulating my mother into buying Jerry a car, one that would equal mine. By then Jerry would have nothing to do with Dad. Mom offered some choice words, but effortlessly outmaneuvered the competition. Jerry got a handed-down 1964 GTO from Joe, Mom's new husband. Just one year old, it was one of the coolest cars of the decade, easily outclassing my Skylark. Fire engine red with black vinyl top; 3-deuces fueling 6.5 liters of muscle; 4-speed Hurst transmission with chrome-plated shift lever. Jerry was one happy guy. But by then, Jerry and I had gone our separate ways, he with his greaser gang, me with my frat crowd.

It was the eve of the New Year, 1966. I was almost sixteen and told Melissa, my first steady girlfriend, that I was going to see in the New Year without her. In our relationship, Melissa had taken on the task of convincing me I was okay. It wasn't working. I knew I was destined to get desperately drunk that night.

I climbed the narrow winding stairway to the balcony in the Sterns' playhouse where Deacon John and the Ivories were playing. Slipping, I bounced down the steps, a pint of Old Grand Dad in my back pocket, which broke on the last step. The cold bourbon soaked through my slacks, mixed with a little blood. When I looked up, I saw Melissa through the blur. With her help, I got to my feet. We exchanged a few words; then I wove my way outside for air. Just outside was the tennis court where I lost my dinner along with—my true goal—my consciousness.

CHAPTER EIGHT

DAD'S DAY

THERE WAS SOMETHING OF HEMINGWAY IN MY DAD. IT STARTED WITH the good looks: the leonine head with its shock of thick hair, broad forehead, fine nose, strong jaw (if perhaps a bit jowly). I associated my father with all the granite-jawed American leading men I grew up admiring. He also shared Hemingway's love for all the "manly" sports: horse racing, boxing, bullfights, cockfights, jai alai, and the gaming tables.

Gambling was his life. If you dropped your hat, he was liable to bet whether it would land on its brim or its crown. Before going into the operating room for a critical procedure, just weeks before he died, the nurse asked if he was allergic to anything. Though he was suffering from senile dementia, he answered without missing a beat, "Yeah, slow horses."

Dad also had the mixed blessing of never working a day in his life, an eccentricity that enabled all the others. Because he had all the money he needed, he could pursue whatever caught his fancy at the moment. He ran a riding stable in Baton Rouge for a time in his twenties, a bar on South Rampart Street for a short while in his thirties; he owned Thoroughbreds that were trained and cared for by others, and he owned real estate, mostly inherited and largely overseen by Latter & Blum. For the long length of his life, his day was almost entirely his own. While my schoolmates' purposeful dads were commuting to the office, my father drifted through the day in the idle, worldly way of mobsters and Hollywood idols.

8.1 Rodney with swim trophies.

But still, he had that day to fill, a challenge that never seemed to bother or bore him. He didn't give a damn what others thought. If asked what he did for a living, he had a simple answer: real estate. Let them imagine what they would. "Real estate" was what I learned to put on school forms. It always felt half a lie, somehow not as true as whatever my classmates put. What other fathers did at least involved some effort.

Depending on the season, Dad spent his day at the golf course, the track, the betting parlor, or the New Orleans Athletic Club. During the racing season, he rose early to get the *Daily Racing Form* or to oversee tending the horses on the backside of the track, or both. Every morning at 4 a.m., he delivered the *Racing Form* to his handicapper Paul Stern's house. It was in Dad's interest to give Paul enough time to pore over the horses' past performances: what kind of track they preferred, fast or slow, dry or muddy; how they fared in their last outings; what their recent morning training times had been. *I'm not good with figures,* Dad would explain.

Paul the Tout was a wizard and the *Daily Racing Form* was his wand. Pudgy with a dark brow and a diffident, elfish smile, he was always bundled in a cloth overcoat, his hands deep in both pockets. My father swore by Paul's handicapping skills. Paul was the high priest of the tote board, a genius mathematician, a sorcerer of horseflesh.

Paul's fee was based on Dad's winnings and Dad had money to wager. Dad's big bets would wait for the sure thing, often a "chalk bet," which is to say a heavy favorite that Paul felt deserved its favored status. Dad would wager several hundred dollars, or sometimes thousands, to show. By law, the least the track must pay to show, coming in third, is $2.20 for a $2.00 bet. Dad didn't believe in swinging for the grandstands. He was happy to take a 10 percent return on his money every half hour if he could get it, all day long. *You can make a living this way, son. You're better at numbers than me.*

Of course, magician or not, the odds are still against you, always with the house, no matter how you bet. That was the other part of his sermon. *In the long run, you are going to lose.* But that never stopped him.

Dad rose early even when the horses weren't running, a habit he'd acquired in his racing days. In New Orleans, golf is played all year. But in the summer, it is important to start before the sun gets hot. My father mostly played the public links in City Park. He rarely rented a cart. *Walking is good for you; you should walk three miles a day.*

He rarely met a friend for a round but relied on pickup foursomes. Garland Robinette once joined a foursome that included Dad, and they quickly fell into bitter arguments about city politics. Today a radio talk show host who earned international fame for his live broadcasts from a closet in his station after Hurricane Katrina blew out its windows, Garland back then was very visible as a local TV reporter and news anchor. He was well informed. But Dad, who didn't watch TV except for the games, wasn't impressed by Garland's name or by how he marshaled the facts. Despite their endless bickering between shots, at the end of the round Dad announced, much to Garland's surprise, "I like you. Would you like to play again?" Arguing was one of Dad's favorite pastimes.

Other days might start with a long breakfast at the Track Kitchen with the wise guys, men with time on their hands who knew how to sit long over a cup of coffee. Clustered around the tables were hot-walkers, trainers, vets, owners, exercise girls (as they are still called), the usual array of backside hangers-on, people on the make with something to sell, and all of them looking for the inside info to ensure a winning ticket in a "boat," or fixed, race. (If they knew a favorite was going to be "slowed," then their nag had a better chance to place among the winners.)

In downtown New Orleans, Dad might start at Mumphrey's sandwich shop, its simple Formica tables occupied by men with newspapers and plates brimming with grits, toast, and eggs. These were men with much to say. *Can Jim Garrison really prove that Clay Shaw guy killed Kennedy? Who's likely to win the New Orleans Handicap?* Plenty of laughter filled the air along with the smell of coffee, chicory, biscuits, and bacon, and the ever-present tobacco. Most favored Camels, Pall Malls, and Picayunes, the strong local brand that used locally grown black perique tobacco. Or some, like Dad, smoked cigars.

Dad loved an audience. With the right crowd, Dad could make breakfast last until the first race at noon. Sometimes he'd walk over to the New Orleans Athletic Club at the far edge of the French Quarter for a steam and a swim. Sometimes on the way he stopped by Latter & Blum to fuss about the rental property on Palmyra Street. Maybe Shep Latter was in and would see him. *That Shep Latter is smart as a whip.*

A frequent destination was Curley's Neutral Corner on St. Charles and Poydras, part of Curley Gagliano's neighborhood empire: Curley's Corner, Curley's Neutral Corner, Curley's Cozy Corner, and Curley's Other Corner. The Neutral Corner had a bar on one side, a boxing ring on the other, and a large chalk tote board on the center back wall. Some guys hit the bag while others pored over the morning line. Being the only child in this milieu made me feel at the same time special and out of place. I couldn't take my eyes off these men with sometimes natty, sometimes tattered outfits and even more colorful names like Leapin' Lou Messina, Broadway Johnny "The Fox" Cox, Place 'n' Show Joe, Meyer the Cryer, Willie the Weeper, Benny Without a Penny, Sleepout Joe, Hard Times Vince, Steve the Hat, Cream Cheese Louie, Big Time Charlie, Alimony Tony, and Eatin' Pete. I couldn't shake the feeling, *am I really supposed to be here?* Dad's own odd ways did little to allay the feeling. My need for "normal"—9 to 5, wingtips and club ties—kept me from fully taking in the local color.

Mother's Restaurant was just a quick step away and another of Dad's favorites. There, I'd tie into a Ferdi's Special Po'boy—ham, roast beef *and* débris, the leavings at the bottom of the roast beef pan. That might make me feel normal for a little while.

Dad was the only adult in my ken who never owned a phone. His need to reach his bookie should have sufficed to make a phone worth the trouble and expense. But there was little in his latest hovel to make him linger. So, better to get up early and meet his bookie at Mumphrey's or Curley's. Where all else he went, I'll never know.

Like whispering, not having a phone commands attention. I had to work hard to reach him. Of necessity, I learned detective work. He didn't have an office or a secretary. His CPA would know what town he was in, but if it was New Orleans, I was on my own. In season, if I wanted to speak to my father, I was most likely to find him at the track. I knew the spots in the grandstand or the clubhouse to check first. It was a chalk bet that I'd pass by the corned beef counter for one of the thick-sliced sandwiches. Not finding him, I might ask Blackie the golf pro in City Park. Or I might have him paged at the athletic club. I would get transferred to the locker room. I would hear the attendant page him. If the cavernous locker room turned up empty, I was transferred back to the front desk where a general page went out. Perhaps he failed to answer the viva voce page in hopes of hearing his name repeated over the loudspeakers.

Paul the Tout had a certain quiet charm, but not all Dad's friends passed that test. If Paul the Tout was his own man, another Paul, whom to myself I called Paul the Toady, was anything but charming. He was as slow as Paul the Tout was quick. He played Steinbeck's Lenny, goofy and doughy and determined to please, to my Dad's George. Dad liked a good laugh and Paul the Toady was goofy enough to provide plenty occasion for laughter for Dad, if not for me.

Paul the Toady didn't play golf, but once he tagged along, so Dad rented a golf cart, which he had Paul steer. On the first hole, he ran it into a WPA concrete bridge that crossed a water hazard. The fiberglass body came clean off the chassis. They had a good laugh about that, then went back to the clubhouse for a new cart, which I drove.

Living in his seamen's hotel at the foot of Canal Street, Dad talked Paul into planting some comfrey in the yard of his shotgun near the track. That herb was then the darling of the health food world and Dad's latest cure-all, though it's now implicated in liver failure. We went to Paul's to drink comfrey tea, just what a thirteen-year-old burns to do—*cure's everything!*—and grill lamb chops slathered in butter in a toaster oven. I paid for my supper by listening to Dad's sermons about how easy it is to digest lamb and the virtue of spending large sums of money for the best food.

One day, Dad announced that Paul had a girlfriend at another track who wanted a picture of him naked, and I was to take the picture with the

Polaroid camera Dad had given me. I resisted; Dad chided and ridiculed; Paul stood blankly, nakedly, before a blank wall. Thankfully, he didn't strike some pose with his doughy body. Though at thirteen I knew absolutely nothing about girls, except vague longing and acute anxiety, I kept thinking, *My God, there is a person out there who would find this attractive?* I did my best to stay clear of Dad until Paul made his tempestuous exit. I knew it was only a matter of time. Dad could be counted on to take offense at some point and to hold a grudge. Few stayed long in his life.

One exception was Norman West of the famous West twins, another of his friends who gave me the creeps. The twins (Sam was the other) were outstanding track stars in Dad's youth, champions at Fortier High who had gone off to LSU and Rice. Unlike Dad, they had graduated. Both acquired a form of arthritis that emaciated their already-lithe runner's bodies and seemed to turn them to stone. I know because one summer when Dad and I were at the Buckstaff Bath House in Hot Springs, Dad asked me to give Norman horse liniment rubdowns. I was twelve; we were in the cool-down room; there was a masseur in the next room but he cost fifteen bucks. Norman's emaciated back was all rock-hard knots. The Ball's liniment reeked of camphor and alcohol.

Despite my mixed memories, the New Orleans Athletic Club was often my first destination when I started going downtown after junior high classes were dismissed. Housed in a wonderful old Neoclassical Revival building on the edge of the French Quarter, the N.O.A.C. was a lot like the bathhouses in Hot Springs, only more elegant. Because its clientele was less transient, it was even more drenched in tradition. The second oldest athletic club in the country, the N.O.A.C. seemed to promise the rites of passage that I longed for.

Dad showed me the speed bag and punching bag on which hopefuls and champions—John L. Sullivan, Pete Herman, Willie Pastrano, and Roberto Duran—had worked out. We played basketball in the squeaky, polished, oak-floored gym where John Havlicek and Kareem Abdul Jabbar would later shoot hoops and give basketball clinics. With a knowing grin, Dad would show me the tricks that got him to all-state in basketball two years running—like grabbing the hem of my gym shorts as I leapt for a rebound, which forced me, as it had his opponents, to suddenly bend over to cover my privates. We swam naked in the elegant, marble-clad salt-water pool where again I wanted to cover my nakedness. The manly thing was to brave it out no matter how yet-unmanly your thing. Dad's hero Johnny

Weissmuller had once swum there. Dad liked to tell the story about winning a hundred-yard freestyle heat in his jock strap, his suit swept off in the racing dive start. *Winning is all that matters, son. That's how you make all-state.*

Besides the gym and spa area, the N.O.A.C offered a clubby area with restaurant, bar, pool table, and reading room. The city's bluebloods and businessmen often filled tables in the bar for weekly card games. Here they took off their seersucker jackets, rolled up their sleeves, loosened their ties, and ordered Ramos gin fizzes and Sazeracs to go with their cigars. Women weren't allowed past the reading room and the little-used, outermost restaurant near the front door. Members signed in at the front desk; I had to page my father to be admitted into the cool inner recesses where tiled floors, high ceilings, and ceiling fans produced a civilized, hushed din despite the nearby bustle on Canal and Rampart streets.

The New Orleans Athletic Club was exclusive in other ways, too. Blacks were not made members till the late eighties—and not without a fight that was plastered in the media. At the time I never doubted what Dad insinuated, that he had been excluded for many years for being Jewish. But, according to a 1972 centennial issue of the members' magazine, Judge David Gertler was elected the club's first Jewish board president in 1962. That was just when I started visiting Dad there. (Gertler would one day figure as Dad's legal and political nemesis.) Anti-Semitism may have lurked at the N.O.A.C., but it was not official policy as it was at the Boston and Pickwick clubs, home to the most famous Uptown Carnival krewes.

Even so, my father entered each time with a chip on his shoulder, convinced that his club was filled with Jew-baiters. And he wasn't going to let them ignore him. When we sat together in the restaurant or reading room, he would often ask me to go to the front desk and page him.

Daaaaad. . .

Go page me. Important people have their names in the air.

If Dad longed to feel important, his native city once truly had been. Before the Civil War, New Orleans was, per capita, the wealthiest city in America. In the 1920s, it was the wealthiest city in the South and as late as World War II, dominated the South as its largest and fastest-growing city.

At the center of all this wealth and power lay the white-shoe clubs. If the Carnival balls were exclusive, the New Orleans luncheon clubs were the inner circle within the inner circle. When President Teddy Roosevelt visited the city during the yellow fever epidemic in 1905, he was made an honorary member of the Louisiana Club so that he could attend a luncheon in his honor. Nonmembers were not allowed in, even to visit.

Club members ran the city. The Pickwick Club was so named because the members imagined themselves as good-natured as Dickens's eponymous hero. But while they may have seen themselves as enlightened despots, by modern standards they were anything but enlightened. The undemocratic, aristocratic traditions of colonial France and Spain shaped New Orleans's social structure. When newly prosperous Americans built their manses in the Garden District, they modeled themselves on a society stratified by parentage rather than merit, a society of exclusion not inclusion. The blueblood members of the Rex Krewe and Comus Krewe, of the Boston Club and Pickwick Club, led the southern resistance to Reconstruction in the 1870s and resistance again to integration in the 1950s and 1960s.

So, when a Fortune 500 company moved to New Orleans, its CEO would wait long at the altar hoping for a proposal to join any of these exclusive clubs. Tired of the wait, the CEO would move to Atlanta, Houston, or Dallas, cities which soon left New Orleans in their wake. Fewer and fewer new companies came New Orleans's way.

Jews fared little better at their hands. Jews had been founding members of the Boston Club, and in 1872 Louis Solomon, the first Rex, was Jewish (though, some argue, a fully assimilated Jew). Yet, by the twentieth century, Jews were excluded. Dashing young Baron de Rothschild had been received in all the royal courts of Europe, and when he came to New Orleans, Mardi Gras historian Robert Tallant points out, "society ladies prostrated themselves *en masse*. But then came Mardi Gras" and "he was allowed to attend no carnival courts of New Orleans." In the 1920s, Jews began a countertradition of taking skiing trips during Mardi Gras season to spare their friends and business associates the embarrassment of not inviting them to the grand balls.

So my great-grandfather "Moneybags Fertel" was in good company when the Pickwick Club snubbed him. The club was the public face on the secret society "The Mistic [*sic*] Krewe of Comus," the first of the New Orleans Mardi Gras krewes. Comus essentially made Mardi Gras into the event we know today. If Dad was sensitive to anti-Semitism, it was both a New Orleans and a family tradition.

In the first of three family legends, Sam Fertel assumed the Pickwick Club would honor the membership that he negotiated in the club's new lease on the building he owned on Canal just off South Rampart. He showed up and was told, "Yes, you're a member, but of course you can't enter. You're Jewish."

In the second version, Sam didn't own the building, but he loved to play pinochle. When the Pickwick Club denied his application, he promised, "I will own this building one day." He bought it and refused to renew the lease.

The third is the most elaborate version. Sam had been so successful that he guaranteed payment of city bills when New Orleans was on the verge of bankruptcy. As a reward, he and Julia were invited to the Pickwick Club, but when they showed up, they were refused admittance. Sam learned that a New York company held the Pickwick Club's mortgage. He bought the mortgage and foreclosed.

The club's official history explains that the move was due to financial difficulties. Whatever the cause, it is a matter of historical record and, as far as I am concerned, a matter of deep family pride that in 1927 the Pickwick Club left the building just off Rampart on Canal Street owned by Sam Fertel.

For Dad, belonging to the N.O.A.C. was not just so he'd have a place to shower and work out. It was Dad's way of revisiting his grandfather's vengeance on the Pickwick Club.

The day filled with whatever delicious tidbits of vengeance he could manage, then there was the matter of dinner. Dad would eat nightly at the same restaurant for days, weeks, and months on end, until the restaurateurs inevitably offended him and he'd vow never to return. When he first came back into my life—I was twelve—it was the House of Lee whose lobster Cantonese with a sprinkling of fresh scallions on top I adored. I got to tour their large kitchen. I was impressed by the fast action in the prep station—all those Chinese cleavers flying—and by the line where the wokking was faster than my eye could follow.

Dad swore by Chinese food: *Who ever saw a fat Chinaman?* he'd ask. That I could have jerked a thumb over my shoulder to prove my point didn't much matter. Harry Lee weighed about 250 pounds when he would seat us at the House of Lee. After he got his law degree and became the famous Chinese cowboy sheriff of Jefferson Parish, his weight famously soared above 350 pounds. His diets became the subject of front-page stories in the *Times-Picayune*. But for my father, it was the idea that counted. Once we got into an argument when I reminded him that rice was a starch. *How could rice be a starch*, he insisted, *who ever saw a fat*

Chinaman? Circular arguments have that advantage—like a fortress, they are impregnable.

The Lee family got their start in a laundry near Rampart Street, then built their restaurant in the burgeoning suburb of Metairie. Through the restaurant Dad became fast friends with Harry Lee's younger brother Frank, a dapper man-about-town with a wicked tennis game. Dad, Frank, and I travelled to Mexico City. Frank and I hung out together while Dad wandered off. Frank was smart and worldly, adept at classical guitar and photography. He treated me like the adult I longed to be. Dad, of course, found some grievance with Frank and their friendship came to an end. Frank and I stayed friends while I was in high school and he let me use his darkroom for printing as I tried to learn that art.

Dad spent a lot of time in bars and poolrooms because that's where the bookies and his cronies were. I can't remember Dad ever ordering a bottle of beer or wine even to help wash down dinner. Certainly not Coke. *Sugar's bad for you, son.* Water was his drink, Mountain Valley if he could get it. That trip to Mexico was the only time I ever saw my father take a drink. He bought a bottle of Chivas at the airport because "tax-free" meant an opportunity to beat the taxman. It sat around in our triple room at the St. Francis on Paseo de la Reforma for most of the week staring at him like a Hitchcock MacGuffin. Finally he decided he had to drink it or lose his vigorish. He lay around for the day drinking scotch and smoking H. Upmanns from Cuba (which I misread and long thought of as Hupmanns)—smoking Cubans was another opportunity to thumb his nose at The Man. I'm sure he regretted till his dying day that he couldn't kill the bottle before we left.

Dad's day began and ended at "home." After the divorce, his first "home" was a huge room in a seamen's hotel he owned at the foot of Canal Street, hard by the Mississippi River. The building, across the street from the U.S. Custom House, was shooting distance from the site of the infamous Battle of Liberty Place in 1874, when New Orleans bluebloods led by the Pickwickians and their volunteer militia, the Crescent White League (an urban version of the Ku Klux Klan), struck the blow that led to the end of Reconstruction and the birth of Jim Crow. And today Dad's seamen's hotel is the site of Canal Place, which houses Gucci, Saks, Williams-Sonoma, and Brooks Brothers, among others. An embattled monument to Liberty Square is sequestered behind it, out of sight.

During my dad's heyday, this waterfront was the scene of seamen's groggeries and flophouses. And these characters were tough. Getting past the bars downstairs and the lurid reception window—*hey, Cap', who you like in the feature race?*—set me back on my heels. I didn't venture there often.

When I finally made it to Dad's room, the ceiling was draped with a colorful parachute, perhaps to hide water damage from the mid-nineteenth-century roof. One time, he was having work done on the bathroom and proudly showed off the showerhead. *Always pay good money to get a good showerhead.* Yet, beyond the shower stall, the building seemed to be tumbling down.

I would learn later that the hotel brought about his arrest for "maintaining a nuisance." Before pursuing Kennedy's assassins, New Orleans District Attorney Jim Garrison had made his reputation by waging war against B-drinking and prostitution in the French Quarter (even though he was a well-known habitué of Norma's). In one minor skirmish in that war, Garrison charged Bessie Ann Lippert, Jack Wainwright, and Rodney Fertel at 211 Canal: "Bessie Ann's, a place in and upon which assignation, prostitution and obscenity is practiced and carried on, conducted, continued, permitted to exist, and exists." In short, Dad's tenants were running a whorehouse and, as landlord, he was implicated. I was shocked when this turned up in my researches. And I wasn't. Dad had always been comfortable in this twilight world, and never gave a second thought to how he made a buck.

Dad's next "home" was on Palmyra Street, two blocks off Canal in a black neighborhood. The roof leaked and his ever-growing piles of stuff made navigation a challenge, especially when the lights stopped working as they inevitably did. I can't remember a working kitchen nor a fully functioning bathroom. One reason he was devoted to the N.O.A.C. and the bathhouses in Hot Springs: for all his commitment to showerheads, his own bathrooms rarely functioned.

On Palmyra, Dad made a short-lived gesture of fixing the house up. He always hired laborers from the railbirds he met over discussions of the daily double. These laborers would always prove untrustworthy, and he would quickly show them the door, happy to find more evidence of the world's untrustworthiness. He never took care of the yard; it grew in such disarray that the city pestered him to trim it back, for which he'd curse them. Then, as he began to feud with his neighbors, he installed iron bars, huge chains, and padlocks across the front door, and barbed wire topping the fences. Elaborate hand-lettered signs appeared on his door and threatened trespassers within an inch of their lives. His signs always made me wince.

Dad's modus vivendi was in full force by this time. He would leave one address when it had become uninhabitable and, spewing venom at his neighbors who had inevitably done him wrong, move to another marginally habitable property in his portfolio. He had a large inventory, all inherited. When I was fifteen, he gave me the grand tour: unpainted, ramshackle shotgun doubles sprinkled around the inner city. Julia and Sam had stockpiled them for a pittance. He wanted me to collect rents for him to save the fees Latter & Blum levied. But it was more than this suburban white kid in madras and Weejuns had the stomach for: to wheedle a month's rent from women holding babies in their arms and standing on galleries about to collapse. Collect rent? I wanted to give them my allowance.

Sometimes the racetrack itself served as Dad's home. From time to time, he stayed on the tackroom cot. He was proud of his ability to "rough it." *Roughing it is good for you. You don't want to get soft.*

And think of all the money to be saved.

Years later I learned where all this led. Vicky Bailey, manager of the track and fiancée to its owner, Louis Roussel, told me that while she found the Gorilla Man endearing, in response to the many complaints from track patrons about Dad's not bathing, she had to rule him off the track. Perhaps his membership to the N.O.A.C. had lapsed.

First the Fair Grounds ruled his horses off the track, then the Gorilla Man himself.

CHAPTER NINE

TRAVELS WITH PAPA DAD

DAD WAS PROUD OF HAVING BEEN AROUND THE WORLD FIVE TIMES. He spent months at a stretch in Havana and Acapulco and traveled frequently back and forth between them and New Orleans. He lived in Cuba in the 1950s during the Batista regime, the time of Hemingway and the La Floridita Bar famous for its daiquiris and mojitos.

From my dad's traveling and sporting world, I learned a few things. How to find my way around a bathhouse. Where to sit at a baseball game (first base side where most of the plays are) or a bullring (on the *sombra*, or shady side). To appreciate the beauty of a veronica pass and a well-killed bull, what a trifecta was, how to bet on the fast-moving game of jai alai. I would come to know from experience that the front row seats for Thai kickboxing in Bangkok were a must if you were to witness, at close quarters, the men's prayers before the bout, their teeth being kicked out, and the warm hugs afterwards when the bloodied opponents renewed their friendship. One could do without such knowledge. And yet somehow it has served me well.

Dad first took me to Europe when I was fifteen. It was 1965; Mom had just opened her restaurant. Dad was not yet the Gorilla Man. I had just gotten my driver's license—back then, you could drive at fifteen in Louisiana. We were flying on my birthday so Dad enlisted his state trooper friend Lenny Ferrara to license me a day early. But even a license didn't make me quite legal to drive in Europe. Dad wanted a driver, however, and

9.1 The future Gorilla Man meets his match.

I was dying to drive in Europe—all those M roads and autobahns with no speed limits! We tacitly agreed that we wouldn't ask Hertz if I was street legal. Through Ireland, Scotland, England, France, Germany, Switzerland, and France I did most of the driving. Not through Spain. My driving was over by then.

Dad was a well-seasoned, though difficult, travel companion. He had a penchant for carrying oddball props. A golf club was one of his favorites. *You don't want to lose your swing,* he would say as he stroked imaginary balls in airport concourses waiting for flights. (Imagine now getting a golf club through the TSA's metal detector.) Then there was the garlic. As we drove through the Norman countryside that first day after landing at Ostend, he made me pull over to a farm stand. *Garlic, fresh garlic,* he rejoiced and repeated the inevitable lecture as he peeled the cloves and popped toe after toe into his mouth. I opened the window, to fill my lungs with the sweet air of the countryside and my ears with the sound of the road.

Surprisingly, traveling was a way for Dad to close, rather than open, doors. He traveled in order to develop new prejudices. The Irish were this and the English were that and *the French, oh my God, the French....*

To Dad, the Scots weren't thrifty, they were cheats. While I was buying a forest green cashmere sweater at the Pringle Factory, Dad was getting a tip from the sweater salesman on the Derby, the biggest race of the British Isles. Not his usual chalk bet, but a long shot. Dad played it on the nose just for fun. When it won, he was told long distance that his prize was £80 for his £20 "show" bet. He had expected £800. He *swore* that he had wagered *on the nose*. I couldn't convince Dad it was a misunderstanding, caught between the bookie's Highland and his own New Orleans brogue. He would have none of it. *The Scots are cheats.*

By the time we hit Basel, Switzerland, he added a new twist.

"The Swedes," he announced, "are very rigid."

"Dad, they're Swiss."

"The Swedes are very rigid."

"No, Dad, they aren't Swedes. The Swedes live in Sweden. In Switzerland it's the Swiss."

"They don't care what I call them."

"Dad, what if someone called you an Armenian rather than an American?"

"I don't care what people call me. Wait, I'll show you, I'll ask a waiter. . . ."

A few weeks later, one rainy evening at the Barcelona Ritz, we shared a cab with Mafalda Davis, a New Yorker also looking for dinner. Before the night was out, I was invited to Salvador Dalí's house on the Costa Brava where Miss Davis had a project to discuss with Dalí. She was an Egyptian by birth and a jet setter by virtue of having been King Farouk's wife's unofficial lady in waiting. During our stopover in New York, I had spent many hours at the Museum of Modern Art, taken by Dalí's melting clocks and Christs floating above Catalan seascapes. I was ecstatic. Dad declined.

Two days later after a train trip north with Miss Davis, I found myself in an open-air restaurant in Cadaqués facing a rocky cove, a few fishing boats and sailboats riding at anchor, a sky as blue as those in Dalí's canvases, and my first paella. After lunch, a younger woman who had recently divorced one of the Guinness heirs joined Miss Davis and me. The three of us traveled by hired car over the mountain to the next cove, Port Lligat, and to Dalí's home, seven fisherman's huts stitched together by corridors. A pink stuffed bear with a purple owl on its shoulder greeted us in the foyer. A German TV crew was that day in the midst of filming a documentary. Dalí's behavior before the camera was insistently meant to shock. Estranged at that time from his beloved wife and muse, Gala, Dalí paraded a leggy blonde model on his arm.

It was as if during the stop at MOMA I'd dreamed Dalí, that surreal dreamer, and now awoke in Spain to find him before me.

Dalí impressed me, but his pet ocelot entranced me even more. Though declawed and his teeth filed, the feral jungle cat was nothing but writhing, lean muscle, rubbery like one of Dalí's watches. It gnawed my earlobes with its filed-down teeth—what chills!

A few days later, Dalí—complete with cape, outrageous moustache, ocelot, and entourage—showed up at the Ritz in Barcelona. For my dad, it was love at first sight. Wild eye met wild eye. Dad had found a soul mate.

Dalí invited us to a bullfight held in his honor. We journeyed to Vinaroz on the Costa del Sol, caravanning down the coast, stopping for lunch. The bullfight in a small provincial *corrida* was uneventful, but the drama of a day spent as honored guests in Dalí's entourage put a gleam in Dad's eye.

The next day, Dad announced that he had a present for Dalí. We were in the Ritz's grand sitting room, filled with overstuffed velvet sofas and wing-chairs with antimacassars. I cringed. *What's Dad thinking now?* With all the flourish and fanfare that one drama king can muster before the drama king of the century, Dad produced a trophy of our visit to Switzerland: *my prize compass.*

The compass was well-tooled and elegant in its own way. Well-made things impressed Dad. But it was just a compass. Dalí turned it over, bemused but waiting for the punch line that would turn this toy into the tribute promised by Dad's ecstatic look. Misled by Miss Davis, Dalí had taken Dad for a patron of the arts. You could see that illusion melting away in Dalí's eyes. As for me, I sat there wishing I could melt into that velvet couch.

Meeting Salvador Dalí was a thrilling experience. But the real thrill I was seeking then and for years to come was to find a father. I was traveling with my dad, but I was looking for a father. Even for that passing moment, I sensed Dalí didn't fill the bill any better than my dad did. It's said that kids are always waiting for their parents to grow up, and it was clear to my fifteen-year-old eyes that as far as Dad and Dalí were concerned, I could wait till hell or Dalí's melting clocks froze over. Not that I consciously understood any of this. But to be around Dalí was to be around someone always playing to an audience and I must have known instinctively that real grown-ups didn't behave that way. Besides, like my Dad, he was crazy. And crazy, even Dalí's cultivated kind of crazy, was something I just didn't want to be.

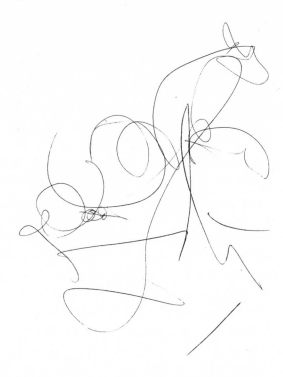

9.2 Dalí's signature as horse that
Dad in 1965 convinced the Hot
Springs *Sentinel-Record* was worth
"$60,000–$100,000."

The truth is, Dad didn't come to Dalí's house on the Costa Brava because
he sprained an ankle when I rammed our rented car into a plane tree in
Montpelier, France. I was turning a corner when suddenly the leather sole
of my new Swiss sandal caused my foot to slide off the brake and onto the
pendulum accelerator. (If only the Swedish leather hadn't been so rigid!)
As I tried to get back on the brake, the sandal slipped again and I hit the
accelerator again. One minute, stopped in heavy traffic at a red light, the
next minute bucking headlong into a tree and into a trailer truck that I
creased on Dad's side. Dad hit the windshield and suffered a cut between
his eyebrows. Lots of blood. His ankle twisted. Dad wailed along with the
ambulance claxon. The car, the Peugeot 504 we had picked up in Ostend,
totaled.

For the next week, nuns cared for Dad in a small provincial hospital. I
was shepherded around by a police officer who found me a little hotel on a
tree-lined boulevard. More plane trees with their mottled trunks. When the
accident happened, we realized on the spot that, for the sake of the Hertz
people and the police, a lie of convenience was in order. I *couldn't have been
driving.*

Having hurt Dad, I felt awful, but the situation had its advantages. Riding in a French ambulance with *The Pink Panther*'s odd claxon brought a knowing grin. In between frequent visits to my dad, I was hanging out with a police officer right out of Georges Simenon who spoke barely any English but who showed me how to play *pétanque* in the dusty playing grounds beneath the shade trees. And how to taste wine. His method was to gargle, then swish the wine noisily through the teeth. The house wine from thick-glassed liter carafes was pretty rough stuff and could stand up to such treatment. He was kind to me and patient. Was it his kindness that kept them from nailing the obvious culprit in the accident? There had been a witness at the scene pointing his finger, and there was the broken glass on the passenger side where my father had hit the window. Somehow, all that got ignored. The French might, *ohmygod*, be French, but they were letting us off the hook. Inspector Clouseau was missing his man (or boy) not out of clumsiness but, rather, generosity. It was unspoken but I breathed a sigh of relief.

A week later when Dad was ready to move on, it fell to me to arrange for passage to Barcelona. Dad asked that I look into a car and driver; he didn't want to venture riding the train on crutches, nor have me at the wheel of another Hertz. Unfortunately, my police friend misconstrued the zeros in conveying the driver's price in French francs. Was it 300F or 500F? I forget, but the fee was astonishingly low for an eight-to-ten-hour ride across the Pyrenees and Dad jumped at it, an unexpected opportunity to take advantage of a cast-against-type, naïve Frenchman. When we got to Barcelona, we learned there was meant to be another zero, not $60 or $100, but $600 or $1,000. Stern looks from Dad. *Who's naïve now?* The policeman had nabbed us after all.

Still angry about the accident, shortly after our adventures with Dalí, Dad decided it was time for home. As would so often happen after our travels, Dad stopped talking to me.

It had been a summer of accidents. After our encounter with the Swedes in Basel, we drove down through the French Alps into the Rhone Valley. One day Dad was driving. As he started to pass slower traffic, there at our side trying to pass us was another car. Dad had not checked his side mirror. The other car swerved left and lost control, traveling off the shoulder and into a field where it bounced heavily over the rutted rows. Dad, much rattled, drove on. He managed as the miles sped away to figure out all the ways that it had been their fault and how *they* had victimized *him*.

Fifty miles down the road, we were slowly moving along in a traffic jam and a car some ways back started honking madly. In the next town when the traffic came to a halt, suddenly a man's face was in the window, and he was agitated, pointing and waving a finger. Dad played the dumb American. Even without knowing French, I knew just what agitated the Frenchman. I'd seen his face before, framed in another car window. Exasperated, the man went away red-faced and shaking his head. *Cons d'americains*, I now imagine him saying. *Well*, I thought, *at least one had walked away from that rutted field*. What injuries his companions suffered haunts me still.

A few months later, playing JV basketball, I arrived early for a game and was approached by a man whom I vaguely recognized as one of Dad's acquaintances, the father of a classmate.

"I know what you did," he said.

"Did? What did I do?"

"I know. What you did. Your father told us down at Latter & Blum."

"What I did?"

"You tried to kill him in that car in France."

". . . ."

All forgotten, if unforgiven, the next year Dad invited me along on his first trip around the world. He needed company.

As we neared the airport Dad yelled, "Pull into that gas station!" Did we have a flat? Had he forgotten his passport? Was he having a heart attack?

No. Dad was working another of his props.

"You can't go to the beach," he announced, "without a beach ball." Dad got out of the car and inflated a colorful beach ball at the air pump. But only after he had asked me to do it, and I said no.

This trip, like all the others, would eventually come to an abrupt end because of the seeds of some conflict sown at an early moment. Perhaps it was when I declined to fill and then again to loft the beach ball back and forth at the concourse gate, a teenager more than a little self-conscious of the astonished eyes all around us. Dad could always dredge up some grudge to support some new imagined injury.

When we landed in Hawaii, Dad learned that Japanese yen were a steal outside the Land of the Rising Sun. The opportunity to avenge Pearl Harbor—a handy grudge to invoke—and make a buck at the same time was too good to pass up. He could make better on the yen exchange than he did on his chalk bets, and, he thought, the yen were in no danger of breaking a leg. While I worked the waves on Waikiki, Dad found the best exchange rate and purchased from his thick roll $10,000 worth of yen. We had to purchase a separate gym bag to carry, like a bagman for the Mob, the stacks of yen.

In Tokyo, our next stop, we learned that if we didn't have a receipt for buying yen on Japanese soil, we couldn't turn them back into greenbacks. Not just the legs, but his yen's back was broken. Dad cursed the "Japs" all the way to Hong Kong where he took a beating worse than the killing he had planned.

Meanwhile, I was enjoying my first taste of the Orient. I was shepherded around the Tokyo Ginza by the very young ambassador to Japan from El Salvador whom we happened to meet; he belonged to one of five families that America would, years later, do so much to prop up at the expense of the left who sought land reform for the peasantry. Oblivious to the retro political world of which he was a part, I was happy for the ambassador to show me the hip Ginza bar scene and very pleased the next morning when he shared his cure for a hangover: having a beautiful Japanese woman walk on my back after bathing me in the public bathhouse. Travel sure was opening up worlds and filling in my map with vivid colors.

Some colors faded into jungle camo on that trip. In Hong Kong I shared a beer with a soldier on R & R from Vietnam. I didn't yet know the term "thousand-yard stare" but he gave me a preview. He was only three years older than me, but it felt like he'd lived several lifetimes. Like me he was a reader; unlike me he had already discovered the need to write. The bar of the Hong Kong Hilton was an incongruous setting for the recitation of a poem he'd written while on patrol. "Loneliness is / A sense of / Onlyness / When in a room / With someone you know." Simple as it was, it seemed to capture the experience of being the kind of grunt who would write poems as he tried to get through a long night in the bush, surrounded not only by the enemy but also by fellow soldiers who would have looked at him funny had he mentioned the word "poem."

Flying from Hong Kong to Bangkok a few nights later, our plane passed over Vietnam. Who knew then how deeply the land would touch our lives and how much we would do to ravage it? It was 1966. The previous March, LBJ had begun the bombing called Rolling Thunder that softened the beaches for the Marines' landing a week later in Da Nang. At a protest rally in New York City, veterans from both world wars and Korea burned their discharge and separation papers. America was about to tear itself apart while killing two to three million Vietnamese in the name of freedom.

The pilot called our attention to the lights below. I thought of my new friend; my dad slept.

Dad's diminished-though-still-large bankroll of greenbacks became an issue again as we were leaving New Delhi, our next stop after Bangkok. The difference between the banks' exchange rate and the black market was a temptation he couldn't resist. As we left New Delhi, a government official, looking at the paperwork stapled in Dad's passport, asked how much money Dad would be taking out of the country. Dad mentioned some innocuous amount that jibed with the couple thousand dollars he had declared upon entering the country. *Why let anyone know your business,* he'd explain. *I don't declare my losses to the taxman; why should I declare my winnings?* The official then asked him to empty his pockets. Dad timidly produced his roll, a bolus large enough to choke a Burmese python. The official asked if these hundreds of hundreds added up to the amount he'd declared. Dad stood there dumbfounded by his fear and his anger. The official lowered his dark eyes on me.

That summer, India was experiencing one of its worst droughts. The summer monsoons had not arrived. Scrawny sacred cows filled the streets, picking their way among the emaciated populace. Thousands slept nightly on the sidewalks. As the official looked me over, all I could think of was how thin the gruel must be in Indian prisons. I burst into tears.

My "faucets" saved us. The official said, "I just wanted to see how little sahib would react." A cooler response might have confirmed his suspicions. Apparently, black marketeers were less free with their tears. We were allowed to take our flight to Athens and then home. The plan to revisit Europe on the way home was forgotten as Dad's grudge set in.

A period of silence followed, as always, but two years later Dad again needed company to hit the road and invited my friend Ricky to join us. Ricky Permutt and I had been best friends since seventh grade. It was 1968, our summer before going off to separate universities. I hoped that having company would abate my fights with Dad.

Before the trip, Dad sent me down to American Express to buy "tip packs." Tip packs, he had discovered, solved the problem of waiting in line each time we crossed a border. *Besides, those exchange offices in airports and at border crossings are nothing but a pack of thieves.* But tip packs created other problems. First, the exchange rate was at least as unfavorable as that at the *cambio* windows. Second, since each tip pack was worth the equivalent of $10, there were pence, centimes, and pfennigs to deal with. These coins added weight, and traveling light was one of Dad's cardinal rules. He instructed us to remove the offending coins from each plastic pack, which meant we had even fewer pounds, francs, and marks for our dollar. Ignorant of their worth, we gave the coins to Ricky's sister who was also traveling in Europe that summer. She later reported that the coins added up to hundreds of dollars.

We started in New York. Dad spent the day as always on his own, cutting Ricky and me loose to make our time in the Big Apple the trip of a lifetime that marked the beginning of *our* sixties decade. On the bus from the airport, we met two young women in paisley bell-bottoms who worked for CBS Records; they decided we were two rubes sorely in need of guidance. They took us to West Village clubs, to a recording studio where we met the legendary producer Tom Wilson—who produced Bob Dylan, Simon and Garfunkel, the Velvet Underground, and the Mothers of Invention—and to the midtown offices of CBS Records. Dressed in our Gants and Weejuns, we smoked pot with the owner of the legendary Café à Go Go where, later that night, we heard the southern boogie band Canned Heat. The ceiling was low and the volume high. The heavy bass line made my chest vibrate sympathetically. The next night, in an outdoor café on Bleecker Street, the young women introduced us to the great Al Kooper, the keyboardist who played Hammond organ on Dylan's "Like a Rolling Stone."

The trip abroad started on a terrible note. We left New York on June 6, 1968, the day after Robert Kennedy was shot at the Ambassador Hotel in Los Angeles. When we boarded the plane, his death was still uncertain. By the time we landed at Shannon Airport, Ireland was deep in mourning for the loss of their second beloved American son. But, like New Orleans D.A. Jim Garrison, Dad had fully investigated the assassination. He had a theory.

At our first breakfast—a mural of John Fitzgerald Kennedy being welcomed by the people of Limerick filled one wall—Dad announced the results of his investigation. "Robert Kennedy was killed all because of modern transportation. If Sirhan Sirhan hadn't been able to get to Los Angeles, he couldn't have killed Kennedy."

"Say wha?" I replied aghast. "What does that explanation explain?" My generation's early adolescence had been traumatized by the first Kennedy assassination, and for the last few years, the Vietnam War had taken American boys just a little older than us across the globe to lose their arms, legs, and lives. Martin Luther King had recently been gunned down upriver from us during the Memphis garbage strike. Dad's theory didn't speak to my raw emotions; his cold reasoning rubbed my emotions more raw.

This put a chill in the air and set the debates in motion. It wasn't that Dad disliked arguing. He enjoyed the back and forth. What he didn't like was the hint that he might not be winning. Worse, he hated my tendency to take things so personally. Ricky, too, wondered why I hammered back so hard. But the loss of RFK, the peace candidate who was displaying an idealism that appealed to youth, meant something personal. Understanding ideas and through them the world, not just belaboring one's own idées fixes, meant something personal. My dad seemed crazy to me—*that* I took all too personally. If I could just argue him out of his crazy ideas, would I myself have a hope of sanity?

The what-killed-RFK-theory led to a discussion about the virtues of travel. Now Dad's preachment was, *Travel is the best teacher.*

We rebutted that with a thought experiment worthy of Einstein. "If travel is the best teacher, then if you flew nonstop around the world, you'd be smarter than the guy you left behind. When you landed you'd be able to do the higher math and he wouldn't." To our surprise, Dad found this logic impeccable. We mocked him with our ironies.

By the time we got to Antwerp, I decided to join my girlfriend Elissa Zengel in Freiberg, Germany, for a few days of fresh air. Antwerp had birthed the Gorilla Man campaign. Dad had discovered the gorillas there on our first trip and was captivated. When I returned from Freiberg, I found Ricky and he announced the bad news: "We're going home."

Over a Belgian beer, I learned what had happened. A band that we adored at the time had a hit song, "Fresh Garbage." One morning at breakfast, Ricky was doodling the letters "Fresh Garbage" in the popular balloon style of Peter Max, adding a "Fertel For Mayor" squiggle on the same page. Dad had by then announced his Gorilla Man candidacy. Ricky showed his page of playful doodles to Dad, an offering for his upcoming mayoral campaign. Dad hit the roof. There was no convincing him that "Fresh Garbage" and "Fertel For Mayor" were not linked. He was certain Ricky had disrespected him.

I spoke to Dad and tried to extricate us from this conflict. "Dad, why would Ricky be so nasty? It makes no sense." But Dad's mind was set, his idea fixed. We went home.

• • •

9.3 "Fertel" peaks out at the bottom of the list of mayoral candidates as assassin hunter D.A. Jim Garrison gloats over his win. © Christopher Harris 1969.

That fall Ricky and I were transformed into college kids and hippies (of a sort) and Dad into the Gorilla Man. In 1969, New Orleans was famous for potholes, poor schools, a failing economy, ongoing civil rights struggles, and official corruption of a high order. But my father's platform bypassed all these minor issues and went to the heart of what ailed the city: our zoo lacked a gorilla.

If, as some say, one test of a good city is how it treats its eccentrics, Dad helped New Orleans set its benchmark. The Gorilla Man campaign was appreciated by some in the electorate for what they saw as Rodney Fertel's sense of fun. But if there were a test for eccentrics—nuts, in my book—Dad set the curve.

My father campaigned in a safari outfit, complete with pith helmet. Invited to ride in a parade during the election, Dad tracked down a man whose gorilla suit he had admired on the streets during Mardi Gras. They rode together in a convertible and every few blocks Dad would send the gorilla to the sidewalk to make a show, sniffing at some unfortunate Faye Wray and beating his chest.

Dad printed his campaign slogan on business cards: *Don't settle for a monkey. Elect Fertel and get a gorilla.* He promised if elected to "conduct a personal safari to the Belgian Congo at my own expense and bring back to New Orleans two live gorillas for the Audubon Park Zoo."

A hundred years earlier during Reconstruction, members of the White Citizens' Council led the Carnival Krewe Comus in silver hoods and rode on floats to belittle the principal figures of Reconstruction as "The Missing Links in Darwin's Origin of the Species." A grinning gorilla on the climactic float represented Louisiana's black Lieutenant Governor P. B. S. Pinchback. Nonetheless, to my knowledge Dad's Gorilla Man campaign did not read to black or white New Orleanians as racist. In fact, Dad had plastic gorillas manufactured by the gross in Hong Kong and, at the corner of Rampart and Canal, handed out black ones to black passersby and white ones to whites—"to show," in his telling, "that he wasn't racist." Just inside at the Woolworth's lunch counter a few years before Dad's run for mayor, sit-in protests had challenged Jim Crow. And yet, no one to my knowledge made these connections. It helped that there were no blacks in power at that point. Moon Landrieu's victory in that election enabled him to change all that, integrating the city's power structure. Dutch Morial, who succeeded Landrieu, was New Orleans's first black mayor. Today, his widow, Sybil Morial, remembers no hint of racism in Dad's campaign. Civil rights attorney Lolis Edward Elie dismisses the notion: "I didn't pay any attention to that."

Not racism but rather New Orleans's political three-ring circus helps explain Dad's hijinks. Dad's campaign manager and sidekick, Allen "The Black Cat" LaCombe, was a perennial candidate himself and one of the minor ringmasters. The New Yorker's A. J. Liebling immortalized LaCombe in The Earl of Louisiana. Covering Earl Long's theatrical run for governor, Liebling records this bit of madcap campaigning:

> A customer came over from the bar and said [to the Black Cat], "I'm going to vote for you, Governor; you're better than them other sons-abitches, anyway."
>
> "What precinct you vote in?" the candidate asked and, after the man told him, said, "Well I'm going to look at the returns Sunday, and if I don't have one vote in that precinct I'll know you're a lying sonofabitch."[17]

LaCombe was called the Black Cat, he was happy to tell you, because of his legendary bad luck. He bet on everything, even wrestling matches he knew were fixed, and lost on everything. During a stint as the sports page

9.4 Allen "The Black Cat" LaCombe, 1986. © The Times-Picayune. All rights reserved. Reprinted with permission.

handicapper he recommended seven winners one day in his column in the *States-Item*—quite a feat—then bet against each of them. In his own words, he'd "got touted off my own selections."[18] The new nickname stuck.

Like my dad, the Black Cat probably never had a day job. The closest he came was being the Fair Grounds press agent, a sinecure if ever there was one. More than once Dad took me up the ladder and across the catwalk to the press box high in the grandstand where the Black Cat in his bowler held court. Through his eyes, Raymond's Beach—that part of downtown that the bookie joints shared with the old city hall and *Times-Picayune* building—had all the glow of Damon Runyon's Forty-second Street. The Black Cat coined the wild monikers that were the social currency at Curley's Neutral Corner, like Alimony Tony (always late with his support) and Curley Gagliano himself (he was bald).

I wish I had known the Black Cat better. My discomfort with my father's zaniness made me less open to the Black Cat's. In zaniness they were soul mates, but the Black Cat's was free of the bitterness that sometimes turned Dad's fun into vengeance. "Nobody's had more fun than me," LaCombe was known to say, "and when I die, I'll know I never missed a thing. God looks after you and I figure He's on my side."

By contrast, Dad's sense of fun wasn't the whole story behind his Gorilla Man campaign. Another man running for mayor in 1969 was David Gertler. As the judge for my parents' divorce proceedings, Gertler had given the final word on custody and child support matters. In 1968, though I had attained my majority, which by law should have let Dad off the hook, the judge ordered him to pay my college tuition.

My father had inherited large parcels of Canal Street from his mother by then, so he was in a position to fund my education. In fact, he had accompanied me to visit colleges that spring. But Dad was playing both sides against the middle. While preaching the importance of higher education—*stay in school as long as you can, son; best years of your life*—he was fighting in court to avoid paying for it. He was still angry with my mother. And he loved a good grudge, one that generated lots of righteous anger, preferably combined with lots of court appearances. If that meant legal fees, well, he could afford them better than she. Besides, it gave him something to do. One good grudge led to another. But this time when he took Mom to court, Judge Gertler ruled against him. "You can afford it, Rodney," Judge Gertler announced from the bench.

In open court my father shook his fist and announced, "I'll get you! I'll get you!" Judge Gertler had him escorted from the courtroom.

Gertler finished fifth in the mayor's race the next year, and he believed that Dad's candidacy hurt his own. He took it personally. Gertler had joined the race proud to be the first Jew to run for mayor. To his dismay another Jew mounted the hustings with something less than the gravitas Gertler wished to project. Judge Gertler's memoir *Man in a Hurry* describes Dad as "a fringe candidate" who "joined the race . . . as part of his demented pledge. Holding press conferences in a khaki safari outfit, Fertel made a mockery of the political process. It was an expensive form of revenge but he was rich and hateful with nothing better to do. Throughout the race he never missed an opportunity to rail against me."

The Gorilla Man collected 310 votes. The Black Cat quipped in his Y'at accent, "I didn't know dey had dat many gorillas in New Oryuns." But Dad won the mock election at the University of New Orleans. Kids know a good joke on their elders when they see one. It was the sixties and maybe this was more of that street theater they'd seen on the six o'clock news. Maybe the Gorilla Man was related to Abbie Hoffman, that other latter-day surrealist.

Losing freed Dad to pursue his favorite occupation other than litigation: travel. Returning from Singapore, Dad brought back two baby lowland gorillas for the Audubon Zoo, calling them Red Beans and Rice. He announced that he was the only candidate in history who had kept all his

9.5 Gorillas in Antwerp, 1965.

campaign promises, even though he'd lost. Coming from, sure enough, the Belgian Congo (we probably don't want to know how), they were named Grandeza ("the great one" in Portuguese) and Boneca ("beautiful"). Dad informally launched a renaming contest, the informal result of which were the names he desired: Red Beans and Rice. The zoo in its wisdom went for plain vanilla: Scotty and Molly.

"It looks easy when you see 'em in the zoo," he said, explaining his safari, "but I challenge anybody to go out and get gorillas. Anybody can buy an elephant or a tiger—just pick up the phone and go buy them. But try to get a gorilla."

Dad had his deep, vengeful agenda, but his obsession with gorillas was no joke. During our first trip to Europe together, he had discovered gorillas at the Antwerp Zoo and was thunderstruck by their massive presence and, to his mind, apparent intelligence. He talked long and often about how much you could learn, just watching gorillas. "Gorillas have their own language," he once said in an interview. "If we could understand what they're saying, we might solve all the problems of the earth." That he wasn't kidding did little to console me about such notions.

Dad's gift earned him entrée to the Uptown ladies who met on Audubon Place to discuss overhauling the zoo, at that time among the nation's worst, so bad the feds were threatening to close it. The oldest gated community in the nation, Audubon Place is the kind of enclave that sent for Blackwater security forces when Katrina struck. My mind reels at the thought of my father in pith helmet having his name checked off at the massive Green and Green stone gate, at the notion of former queens of Comus listening to his soapbox discourses in the hush of their elegant homes. Did they really give him a hearing? Certainly I didn't. And yet in part because of him, the zoo was redone: the gorillas' bars melted into moats, their cages into habitats.

Suddenly he was a gorilla expert counseling Ron Forman, the zoo's new head, on everything they needed. From his travels he would send special letters destined for his darlings. He asked Forman to read them *to my gorillas* and there would follow a bunch of gibberish that was his version of gorilla-speak: *chee-chee ooh-ahh ooh-ahh.* He decided they were bored so he bought them a used TV. He announced Johnny Carson was their favorite. "Heeeere's Johnny" brought howls and chest-beating, its absence, melancholy. So Dad bought a VCR and asked the zookeepers to play *The Tonight Show* often. When he learned they weren't mating because, captured as infants, they had never seen gorillas couple, Dad bought porno tapes hoping the apes would, well, ape us. "I'm all for letting nature take its course," he announced, "but sometimes you can help it along a little." They never did mate and finally were sent to other zoos to fulfill their destiny. Dad then mounted a campaign in the press *to track down the gorilla-nappers.*

"People can learn a lot from them," he argued. "They don't worry, they don't need automobiles, houses, jet planes. They're the most contented people in the world. They wear the same clothes all the time. They pay no income tax, no state tax, and they have humans working for them. I feel safer around the gorillas than a lot of people I know." He thought the Saints could learn some moves from them to use in the Superdome and objected that "a northern dog, a Saint Bernard named Gumbo" was their mascot. He bought a filly that he named Fertel's Gorilla and wore a gorilla mask down to the paddock to watch her get saddled. The track stewards were none too pleased, not for the first or last time. He later named a horse Randyand-Jerry Fertel, much to my chagrin.

The 1969 Gorilla Man campaign was Dad's most memorable, but not his last. In 1973, he campaigned for mayor again, on the promise that he would bring the Blarney Stone from Ireland and place it temporarily in the

9.6 Dad with baby gorilla.

Superdome. He planned to split with the Irish the fee to kiss it. I guess the proposal alone was proof enough that he had himself once kissed it, but I could have offered an affidavit. In 1974, he ran for Congress against favorite daughter Lindy Boggs, whose husband, Hale Boggs, had held the seat for more than a quarter-century before disappearing in an Alaskan plane crash and who was to represent the district herself for nine terms. Dad insisted with southern grace that he wasn't running "*against* Lindy but rather *for* the seat in Congress." In 1977, his platform's theme for another mayoral run was water. "And another thing," he proclaimed from his sound truck riding through the streets of the city, "water. We're surrounded by water." Then, incredulous, "Why do we have to pay for water?" He promised if elected to swim in the Mississippi River at Canal Street "for at least five minutes to show that it was safe." Who needs science or scientists for such matters?

For Iris Kelso, a long-time New Orleans political journalist who covered the mayoral campaign, "Rodney was tons of fun. I often thought he was putting us all on and having a ball doing so. After I wrote my column about him, he was a pal for life. I used to get postcards from him from all over the world. Rodney was the kind of rich person I would like to be. He was

9.7 The Gorilla Man and his muses.

self-sufficient enough not to care whether anyone thought he was making a fool of himself or not."

Reporter Rosemary James, who made her name debunking D. A. Jim Garrison's effort to pin the JFK assassination on Clay Shaw, undermined her reputation a bit with her coverage of the Gorilla Man. Charmed, she wrote about him so often that she was known at the *States-Item* as the Gorilla Man's publicist. Dad often came to the newsroom in safari gear, but once, when everyone was feverishly writing on deadline, in full regalia. She had wanted to ask his gorilla some questions.

"Well, he's smart enough to do the interview," he'd replied, and was there to prove it.

"Sit here, Rodney," Rosemary told him, pointing to a chair near her desk. And he did so as meekly as a man in a gorilla suit can manage.

Rosemary wasn't alone in loving my dad. Dad's mercurial virtues—his good humor, spontaneity, and devil-may-care outlook on life—were real. There is the innocent rapture I see in a picture of Dad with Red Beans and Rice. Soon after his safari to fetch them, I joined him for a day at the Tulane

Primate Center, their home while their cage at Audubon Zoo was being readied. The photo shows them well before they've been renamed, less than two feet tall, still innocent of the zoo's bureaucracy and cold steel bars. My Nikon F, which Dad handed down to me in high school when he tired of it, captures a moment that's a bit goofy—Dad sports a ball cap and a silly grin. He sits on the floor, the baby gorillas before him, holding hands—as if playing ring-around-the-rosy, or in imitation of Colin Clout and the Graces. Who could begrudge him such joy?

A man of ideas, most of them fixed, Dad liked to preach. *Use this soap,* he told everyone. *Neutrogena. It's so pure you can wash your hair with it. Then you can brush your teeth with the same bar.* Dad was a snake-oil salesman with the unique quality that he wasn't in it for the money. Perhaps that's one of the sources of his charm. He was happy to tell you what was good for you—and, believe me, he knew. But he wasn't going to make a dollar if you bought his latest idea. Even so, money and its importance dominated his sermons.

His virtues were real, maybe, but for me the shadow of craziness obscured them. Dad's playfulness was not just to my self-righteous adolescent eye inappropriate and uncouth. It was poisoned by motives like anger, scorn, and revenge. In his book, someone had to win and someone had to lose. Your loss was his gain, and he was happy to take it. Your gain was his loss, and he would never forget it nor forgive you.

Dad had something of the mythic Trickster in him, always ready to stir things up, puncture the self-important. Like Trickster, Dad was an inveterate thief, sometimes just for fun. But to my eye his trickster-thievery was not amoral but immoral. His version of the Signifying Monkey was more like—of course—a six-hundred-pound gorilla who was prepared to do you harm. Dad's con games weren't just for fun. He was *entitled* to their proceeds. If his cons hurt you, that was your problem. Besides, they were meant to hurt. No doubt, there was some grudge lurking in the background, proof that you deserved what he gave you. Spite stole from Dad his sprightliness and his interest in any community in which he was not the center and beneficiary.

I had examples of "normal" and "sane" all around me in suburban New Orleans that served to highlight Dad's oddness. I longed to attain normal, but I didn't know how and feared that I wasn't destined to get there. It would take me a long time to realize that normal might not be the goal I *should* seek. In the meantime Dad's abnormality was to me unpardonable.

9.8 A local cartoonist salutes Fertel for Mayor eighteen years later. By permission of Bunny Matthews.

I called him weird once. Only once. I saw how it shocked and hurt him. I thought it so obvious I was a bit surprised. To some degree his weirdness was cultivated and he was proud of it, so why should he object? I wish I had said, *that's weird*, like it was just his behavior that I was judging, like one is supposed to do with kids. But I *did* think him weird. I didn't see why he had to behave, to be, that way. With the arrogance of youth, I thought he had chosen his way, as I imagined I was choosing my way. It made me sad to see his willingness, his need, to be different in everything. I didn't long to conform. Or maybe, looking back on it, I did want to conform just a little too much—and at some subconscious level knew it. So his eccentricity also made me angry.

The Gorilla Man continued to haunt me. Dad's legacy was everywhere, dogging me even into the classroom. After the very first class I taught at Harvard as a graduate TA, a student approached me. "I'm from Cleveland," she explained, "and I'm related to some Fertels in New Orleans.... Are you related to the Gorilla Man?" William Blake, the visionary poet I had just been teaching, who saw angels in trees, suddenly felt admirably sane.

When I graduated, PhD in hand, I was excited to learn that there was a job opening in my hometown. At the interview, the Tulane University English Department popped its first question.

"Are you really related to the Gorilla Man?"

"Yeah," I admitted. But in a last-ditch effort to woo them, I added, "But my mother is Ruth's Chris." Maybe if I had managed to reproduce the sizzle....

CHAPTER TEN

CHRIS STEAK HOUSE

I DIDN'T HAVE TO SEARCH FAR FOR ONE VERSION OF "NORMAL." Mom married Joe in 1964, although according to the divorce records, they had been an item at least since 1958.

They met when Joe—Officer Salvador J. DeMatteo—stopped Ruth for speeding her pink convertible Cadillac DeVille down Gentilly Boulevard on her way to tend the horses at the Fair Grounds. Cops almost always let my mother off with a warning. For years it was her dazzling fresh good looks. Later it was her sizzling steaks: *O.K., Miz Ruth, please watch the heavy foot. But tell me, before you go, are your steaks as good as they say?*

Once again in my litigious family, court records provide a window into the action. In May 1958, Mom legally separated from Dad. Rodney then accused Ruth of adultery, "publicly seen hugging and kissing Salvador Joseph DeMatteo. . . ." Ruth's counterclaim was that "Rodney did commit adultery with one Scarlett Fleming in the Jung Hotel." *Scarlett Fleming*: so the court record states.

During the court proceedings, Rodney claimed that Joe threatened to do him bodily harm: "Joe DeMatteo pulled a gun out of his car where the petitioner could see it and advanced on Mr. Fertel with the gun in his pants pocket until he was almost face to face with petitioner, and told the petitioner, 'If I catch you in this house or in this yard again, I'll blow your g-d— [*sic*] brains out.'" A later document transferred the threat to Mom: "She called [Joe] to repel with force the peaceful visit Rodney Fertel made

10.1 Mom in her early twenties.

to his own residence for the purpose of photographing the boat of his wife's boyfriend and narrowly escaped death which was instigated by Ruth Fertel. . . . She said that if he came around the house she would kill him."

Dad did not tell me about his adultery charge against my mother until I was well into my teens. For years, he periodically preached to me about the harm women would do me if I didn't watch out. But his insinuations about *that cop Joe* came through loud and clear.

One memory seems to support his charge. I was seven or eight, my parents still married. One afternoon, Mom took me to the horse barn on the backside of the track. Joe, a motorcycle cop, met us there. Mom asked me to wait outside while she and Joe went inside to care for the horse. Joe invited me, while they were gone, to play on his police-issue Harley-Davidson, black and white with sirens and a shiny fairing. In the joy of imaginatively taking this police Harley through its paces, I managed to topple it and pin myself beneath it. My screams brought Mom and Joe running. I was unharmed. Joe was concerned about the motorcycle. The look Mom threw me showed her complete exasperation. As she returned to the barn I heard over her shoulder: *That Randy.*

10.2 Joe and Trouble.

Forty-five years later, sitting in the bowels of the city archive, I found the divorce documents that corroborate Dad's anger and gave meaning to this early memory: "the evidence having been before this court that they committed adultry [*sic*] in the Tack Room of the Racetrack."

Well-schooled by the fight over Julia's will, Dad reminded his lawyers about the Napoleonic Code. In the same divorce papers, I learned that Dad used the Napoleonic Code to rescind his "donation" to Ruth of the seamen's hotel on Canal Street, for "ingratitude."

"Ingratitude," the court documents explained, "can take place if the donée has been guilty toward the donor of cruel treatment, crimes, or grievous injury"—a paragraph in the Napoleonic Code obscure to most Louisiana families, but not the Fertels.

In the late 1950s, Joe became part of the household, sharing everything except my mother's bed overnight. Joe was dark and wiry, a man's man, a grunt who had survived the Italian campaign in World War II, a motorcycle cop, small plane pilot, and gas station owner. Like him, Mom began to smoke filterless cigarettes, Pall Malls. In Joe's presence, I heard curse words from my mother's mouth for the first time. Surely not her first, they bothered me and I imagined Joe was their cause.

Mom, Jerry, and I would spend afternoons and evenings at Joe's gas stations, first a little Texaco at Paris and Foy, then the Parkchester Shell at a better location, the intersection of Paris and Mirabeau, and nearer to Seville Drive. Though a gas station owner, Joe was no grease monkey. He counted money and gave orders from the office at the back of the station. His shirts were always starched and carefully tucked in. His initials shone in his gold belt buckle. His shoes were spit and polish, a vestige of his stint in the army. He liked his wavy hair to lie just so and showed me how to train mine using pomade and my splayed fingers so that the oily waves would, like his, break upon my forehead like a set of waves on Waikiki. I didn't throw away my Vitalis.

Joe also liked to take us out to Little Woods, a deserted area east of the city, to shoot bottles with his pistol. As an ex-cop, he believed in self-protection. A revolver stayed in my mother's bedside table drawer for the rest of her life. She was an enthusiastic competitor at these target practice episodes, and Jerry liked to tag along and squeeze off a few rounds, even when, at eight or nine, he was barely able to hold up the blue-metal gun.

Joe was competitive. When first Jerry, then I, started lifting weights, Joe laughed at our Pillsbury Doughboy arms and displayed his sculptured biceps. This display took place at the kitchen table. Joe took the table's head, Mom the side nearest the stovetop. Joe had been raised in a traditional Sicilian family near the racetrack. He liked to be served. He liked his food items separate on the plate, ate sliced bread with every meal, and kept in a sealed jar a hunk of Parmesan that he religiously grated on his pasta. He liked his Sicilian momma's red gravy, tomato sauce so thick it bubbled up in slow-motion volcanic bursts. He made sure Mom and our housekeeper, Earner, learned to reproduce the daylong procedure, sweating the onions and garlic in olive oil, adding tomato paste to make a kind of red roux, churning whole canned tomatoes through the vegetable mill, and adding sugar at the end to cut the tomatoes' acid. It rivaled Turci's. Mom and Earner learned to fry thick slices of eggplant and slide them into the gravy to soften and meld their flavors into the rich red sauce. They learned the proper way to make meatballs and the Sicilian specialty of frying boiled eggs to give them a crunchy texture before they joined the other heavenly spheres in the gravy.

During their long courtship, we fished on Joe's 14½–foot lap-sided speedboat with a single 35hp Evinrude. We would wake before dawn and Joe would trailer it across the Mississippi River Bridge, under the Intracoastal

Waterway through the Belle Chasse tunnel that sweated and leaked so much that we held our breath till we saw daylight coming at the other end, then past the Gulf chemical plant where we closed the windows and held our breath again against the chemical stench. After Belle Chasse, there were few landmarks to keep our young eyes occupied during the long drive down to the river's mouth. Judge Perez's huge house back off the highway with its moose head on the porch was a sure bet. Then Myrtle Grove and West Pointe à la Hache where pirate Jean Lafitte once supplied the slaves for Magnolia Plantation where Mark Twain once stayed. Now we were fully awake because Happy Jack was just a few miles on. Ten miles beyond Uncle Sig's, we would launch in Empire at Battistella's Marina. Out Grand Bayou, a few scraggly cypress trees soon gave way to expanses of marsh with nothing more substantial than low wax myrtle bushes. We'd cross Bay Adams, then Bastian Bay where you'd smell the menhaden or pogey boats whose purse nets haul in that stinky fish by the billions. Beyond the bays, the rest was marsh grass. Orange-toothed nutrias and masked raccoons fed along the muddy bank, the only break from the monotony while Mom and Joe expertly monitored the impossibly subtle landmarks (watermarks rather) that were their guides. *Turn right at the second cane pole. Bear left at the second sign for underwater pipelines—"Do Not Drag Anchor."* We'd fish the lower reaches of Grand Bayou where Mom once caught a thirty-six-inch bull redfish, fighting it on her light tackle for forty-five minutes, or "the Rocks," an outlet to the Gulf that had been reinforced with granite boulders that came from somewhere far, far away—nothing here but alluvial muck. If we stopped to cast from the bank rather than the boat, if you ventured at all back into the marsh, you could find your foot suddenly deep in the smelly muck of the *flottant* or *pré tremblante*. Despite the boat's diminutive size and no backup power, on calmer days we'd venture miles into the Gulf of Mexico to fish the oilrigs.

The Mississippi Delta was a thing of great if subtle beauty. The expanse of marsh and slow-moving bayous—distributaries from the Mississippi River—went as far as the eye could see. The only visual relief (to my untrained passenger's eye) came from fish camps on stilts along the bayous' banks. Sometimes we would use their docks to fish. If we returned at night, New Orleans, eighty or ninety miles to the north, was at most a faint glow. I never saw a creamier Milky Way. As the engine roared in your ears, you'd look down at the folding arc of water cast by the boat and the wake behind and see just as many stars in the water: plankton and other sea life lit up

10.3 Mom with trophy redfish.

by the agitation of your passing. You could reach out and let stars rush through your outstretched fingers. You'd feel both how vast was the universe and how close the vastness.

A few times Mom hired a deep-sea boat and guide to venture into the blue waters of the Gulf. Once she hooked and landed the six-foot sailfish that hung, stuffed, on the den's paneling on Seville Drive.

More than once on these excursions, it was just Mom at the tiller taking us out beyond the relative safety of the more sheltered bayous and bays. We knew we were safe in Mom's hands. One afternoon Mom, Jerry, and I were out on the clear, blue Gulf water, beyond the muddy silted mix thrown by the Mississippi. We tied up to a rig, fishing on the bottom for sheepshead, drum, redfish, and whatever came our way—mostly triggerfish that we'd throw back. Suddenly a large fish with the shape and dorsal fin of a shark passed beneath the boat, ten feet down in the crystalline water. Even though our lines were on the bottom, I yelled, "Shark, shark, reel your lines up!" I guess I was afraid the shark would swim up the line and eat me. Mom took one look and said, "Shark?! That's a lemonfish!! Great eating!!!!" Passing me a look, she reeled in enough to get the bait at the right depth. But the lemonfish was long gone, scared off by my fracas.

Once on the hour-long ride from Empire out Grand Bayou to the Gulf, a boat just ahead suddenly made a hard right and veered into and up and over the low marsh bank, out of sight. Anxious glances were exchanged. *Should we do something, anything*, I wondered? Joe coldly explained that the boat's steering cable had severed. Having left well in his past his former New Orleans Police Department motto—"Serve and Protect"—Joe kept his heading toward the great emptiness of the Gulf, his wavy hair buffeted by the wind.

Joe was never my stepfather. Not when I rooted around for a father figure to help me carve my Cub Scout pinewood derby. Not when I sought a sponsor for my Catholic confirmation. He was just Joe, my mother's boyfriend, until he became, for a short time, her second husband.

Joe's rapport had always been with Jerry. They shared a love of fishing and hunting; they could talk car engines. When it became clear that I preferred my *Martian Tales* to discussions of fishing reels, shotguns, and spark plugs, Joe stopped making an effort—if he ever had made one. We went our separate ways and kept a safe distance.

The only moment I remember feeling a warm regard for Joe, we were driving in the dawn light to the Empire boatlift. We were in our burgundy Grand Prix. I had snot on the tip of my index finger and, about to rub it on his upholstery, I caught myself. *No, Joe is too nice a man to put a booger on his back seat.*

I can't remember ever having such a thought again. Other than his Sicilian threats to *scapit' ta fundi* because I *had a head hard like a cacuzza*, and the wide, police-issue belt with which he made good on them, it's not that Joe did anything to turn off that warm regard. It's just that he did little to turn it on. I longed for a nice man in my life, and for a moment I made him up.

Mom and Joe both learned to fly single-engine aircraft. Joe had moved up from his Texaco to his Shell station by then and bought a Cessna 172— one engine, four seats. I was in the back seat when Mom performed stalls for the instructor. To stall, she nosed the plane up till the engine, no longer taking the strain, stopped. The nose dipped, and the plane picked up speed on the way down, spontaneously starting the engine again. Besides the thrill of flying for a few seconds with just the sound of the rushing wind, and wondering if the engine would catch or if we would plummet to earth, there was an added frisson, that, if I hadn't buckled my seat belt, as the nose dipped at the height of the arc, I was weightless for a moment. It made me giggle. For a second, it was me and John Glenn.

But Mom came home one day with tales of a different frisson: she had cracked up the plane. She and her instructor were coming in for a landing down in Happy Jack on their way to visit Sig and Helen, when a gust of wind blew them astray into an upright object that clipped their wing. Mom spoke with excitement of the pilot's skill, toggling off the engine and fuel tanks before the plane came to a stop nose down.

Joe seemed to me more concerned about his formerly pristine plane than about my mother. "Why didn't you put a match to it and make it the insurance company's problem?"

Joe was particular about his possessions. He once got angry about something one of us did to his boat, a boat worth brandishing a gun to protect, and left us at the camp where Grand Bayou flows into the Gulf of Mexico, an hour from drinking water and grocery stores. Luckily a friend from Happy Jack lumbered by in his skiff and hauled us slowly back to the dock.

Another time, in the process of building the fishing camp, we were returning to the boat ramp. Joe's boat was riding deep in the water, filled to the gunwales with acetylene torch tanks, excess metal pipe for pilings, and tarpaper rolls for siding and roofing. When they tried to haul it up, the load was so great that water poured in at the stern, making the boat heavier and harder to winch onto the trailer. As the boat sat, half-foundered, half-trailered, cigarettes were smoked and angry words filled the air. One option was to unload the boat, then reload it when we finally got it ashore. Joe's solution combined his meticulousness, his laziness, and his reliance on insurance companies; he wanted to unhitch the boat, take it into the channel, and sink it.

My cousin Jo Ann once asked Mom *why she married that man?*

"I felt I had to," Mom replied, leaving Jo Ann with new questions. *Even Aunt Ruth follows the herd?*

Mom drifted into her second marriage just as she had her first. She didn't give it much thought. She felt she had to.

But the divorce settlement with Dad made not only remarriage a possibility. If feelings and relationships were not her cup of tea, numbers she could analyze. She now owned the house on Seville Drive free and clear. She was earning only $4,800 a year as a Tulane lab technician. She could mortgage the house to buy a business and surely clear more than that. She was "ready to lay it all on the line," she said, so that she "could send my sons to college."

Though forever after a part of the Ruth's Chris corporate narrative, that part of her analysis rang hollow. It was clear that Jerry didn't care about college; he preferred the betting windows to the classroom, and, fatefully, McDonough High was the school nearest the racetrack. Failing out of Mc-Donough, he was sent by Mom to live with Helen and Sig to finish at her alma mater, Port Sulphur High. Now it was not horses but fish and duck that lured him from his classes. He didn't finish the year and never did graduate. Jerry later received his GED in the army.

But in my college decal–laden bedstead I was dreaming of college. So one feature of Mom's employment at Tulane had always been of special interest to me. After five years as a Tulane employee, her dependents would get free tuition. By my own calculations, she would pass the five-year mark just as I graduated high school. Mom wasn't just betting the house, she was betting a free Tulane education.

But determined to put everything on the line, Mom pored over the classifieds. She came across a three-line ad under Businesses for Sale:

> ESTABLISHED STEAK HOUSE
> FOR SALE AT REDUCED PRICE.
> OWNER RETIRING. APPLY 1100 N. BROAD.

It was a restaurant she had long known, serving prime beef she had long enjoyed. Chris Steak House had been in business for thirty-eight years, opening on February 5, 1927. *You've got to be kidding*, she told the owner, Chris Matulich. "That's the exact day I was born." A devoted crapshooter, Mom saw another auspicious omen in the address: *1100 had to be a winner!* Chris, too, was from Plaquemines Parish.

The price was $18,000. Determined and self-assured—*steak house? I can do that*—she approached her banker. Perhaps she wasn't entirely business savvy yet. James Fallon Quaid looked the deal over and said, "What are you going to do for working capital, Ruth? How you going to buy the inventory? Maybe you ought to borrow $22,000." She would always attribute her success to that insightful, generous gesture. Her brother Sig and her Tulane boss, cardiologist George Burch, both asked, "Are you crazy, Ruth?" Which no doubt helped her competitive juices flow. She took possession May 24, 1965.

10.4 The original steak house.

Chris was supposed to show Mom the ropes for six weeks, but on the first day he came in, emptied the till, and walked out. She never saw him again except when he came to pick up the rent. With Chris gone, Mom had to teach herself to butcher the meat, give orders to purveyors, take orders from customers, pour drinks, and deliver the steaks.

Meanwhile men continued to disappoint her. Joe brought to this new situation both his Sicilian paternalism and his years of experience—in gas stations. He thought she should take his advice. She thought differently.

It was Joe's laziness that finally set Mom off. In their final confrontation, she came home from the lunch shift and found him napping. This was the man who dared to tell her how to run her restaurant, who thought he was half-owner though he had staked nothing? On his way out the door, Mom sailed a pot of half-cooked rice at his head. Earner and I watched. My excitement, surprise, and trepidation at Mom's sudden new adventure was joined by a sigh of relief.

That pot freed Mom to marry her true destiny: the Empress of Steak.

Her original menu was three steaks—filet, strip, and porterhouse for two, three, or four—with them, all à la carte, she served a few sides and four salads: regular, head lettuce wedge, white asparagus, and Wop—the name for an Italian salad that passed muster in New Orleans well into the eighties. Nothing came with the steak but French bread. Steaks were $5.50 and sides were a buck or so, drinks a couple more. The dressings were equally simple but rich and tasty: oil and vinegar, Thousand Island rich in hard-boiled eggs, or Roquefort that was crumbled from large blue-cheese wheels. The menu would grow very slowly over the years, always with the first eye to quality. The initial addition became the stuff of legend: Uncle Martin's creamed spinach. No homage on the menu to the recipe's source tipped you to the family legacy it represented.

Other than Uncle Martin's ambrosia and her fresh potatoes, Mom's vegetables weren't much better than those that A&P had offered in the fifties. Broccoli or cauliflower, with butter or au gratin, came from frozen blocks of florets. Peas came frozen, too. The white asparagus that graced the Wop salad or that were served on their own, smothered in blue cheese dressing, came from cans that she bought by the truckload when in season. White asparagus couldn't be gotten at a fair price off-season. Later they were just too expensive and Mom switched to canned colossal green asparagus that were mushy and mostly tasteless. Some people loved them. For many years iceberg was the sole lettuce. This slowly changed in the eighties, when more lettuces became prevalent, and broccoli, cauliflower, and asparagus came in fresh by the crate. By then, many a vegetarian swore by Ruth's Chris's fresh veggies. They came in huge mounds and of course a huge dollop of butter. But there were some who swore by the frozen product, too. One customer in Baton Rouge begged the franchisee never to take the peas off the menu.

"They're just frozen peas with a pat of butter," explained TJ Moran.

"Yeah, I know. But, cher, I just can't believe I can afford a $5 bowl of peas."

As at Galatoire's, customers learned to order just what they wanted, building a meal out of our simple menu's basic ingredients. Those mad for a salt fix would ask for their blue-cheese laden, iceberg lettuce wedge draped with a dozen anchovy filets, otherwise destined to drape across the asparagus on the Wop salad. Or maybe they liked blue cheese on their filet. Certain combinations took on the customer's name: there was the Schwegmann's salad ordered every time by John Schwegmann, founder of the city's favorite discount grocery store and later the state public service commissioner who fought for the people's right to competitive prices on their milk. His famous "Schwegmann's bags" promoted his latest political issue. At Chris's, no matter how many guests he had, he ordered one

Schwegmann's salad split for the table. Every waitress knew how to make it and if the pantry was backed up, she would jump on the salad station and knock one out. You didn't want to make John Schwegmann wait. It was less about special ingredients than his ability to get special treatment and make a head of lettuce stretch around the table. John Schwegmann knew how to get as well as give a bargain. He insisted a porterhouse for two could serve eight even though it came to the table carved into six pieces, two on the tenderloin side, four on the strip side. Perhaps he counted on one guest enjoying the bone, like Jerry and me, and the last being a vegetarian. However customers wanted it, that's how they got it (unless they were John Schwegmann's hungry guests).

The two main dining rooms, separated by a varnished plywood partition, held only seventeen tables. Around the main dining room hung nostalgic renderings of gargantuan Hereford steers that seemed likely to burst the picture frames. The partition was stained by years of nicotine and airborne butter thrown off by the sizzling steaks as they were hurried to the table. In a nook toward the rear of the main room, one large table could seat eight or ten. Above it Mom put up caricatures of her best, most notable customers. As at the Palm in New York, being on Ruth's wall was a token of having arrived.

The main dining room also contained three infamous tables enclosed by wood partitions and entered through green curtains. These "booths" were much in demand. When the horses were running, bookies often sat long hours playing cards. But their true mission lay in the sheets of recorded bets at their elbows. The action wasn't fast enough at the track to keep their adrenaline buzz going. Because phones were illegal within a mile of the track, the bookies had runners who biked results from the tote board to them. These private booths also served businessmen in getting in one another's pockets and lovers in getting inside one another's apparel. After her waitresses accidentally walked in on one too many moments of indiscretion, Mom installed switches that controlled a service light. As on an airplane, you called for service by switching on the light. If the light was out, waitresses knew to knock discreetly before entering. These booths later helped Chris's get voted the "sexiest restaurant in New Orleans" in a magazine poll even though the Playboy Club then flourished in the French Quarter.

The "front" had the mahogany-sided and marble-topped bar that probably dated from the day Chris opened in 1927. Here people who had reserved a table waited in line for an open table, entertained by their drinks and the TV that was almost always on, just as it was on Seville Drive or in many of Ruth's customers' homes. Tables up front were less desirable unless you wanted to catch the news or a ball game. The restaurant also had a third dining room upstairs, used for overflow or for private parties, through the kitchen's swinging door and up a short flight of stairs. There, banquets were held and acts of civic or moral indiscretion could be consummated under the discreet eyes of the waitresses.

At $5.50 a steak à la carte, Mom was pushing the limit of most wallets in 1965. She believed people would pay a premium for the best. But just a few months after she started, Mom sat with a customer after lunch, bemoaning the slack business. Selling thirty-five steaks a day was not going to improve her lot. The customer said, *I didn't know you wanted more business, Ruth. All my buddies in the oil patch across the river are from Texas and they know a good steak. I'll bring 'em over.* Customers began to line up to the point that Mom opened a second restaurant across the river in the oil patch's backyard. Quickly renovating a failed restaurant, The Italian Village, in a strip mall on the West Bank, Mom worked with the makers of Montague stoves to make the broilers as hot as possible—eighteen hundred degrees they claimed. She called it Chris II.

Slowly the word got out that Chris Steak House was the place to indulge in the finest beef money could buy. It became the place to celebrate and where deals, aboveboard or below, were cut, inked, and toasted. As Mets baseball great turned New Orleans journalist Ron Swoboda once said, "It was a place where carnivores behaved carnivorously."

Mom liked to say she had adopted the golden rule, to treat customers the way she liked to be treated. She worked hard. "I'd leave the kitchen door cracked open so people could see how hard I was working," she'd say years later when asked to explain her rise, "and seeing me work so hard, they wanted me to succeed."

Another element of Mom's success was warm, friendly service. Service in fine restaurants in New Orleans had been an exclusively male domain for nearly a century. Tuxedoed waiters at Galatoire's and Antoine's were career professionals who earned good livings by catering to their guests: they knew what brand Miz Uptown Blueblood liked in her whiskey sour and how Mr. Metairie Parvenu liked his pompano, and expected a good tip and a better one at Christmas. Women servers would not break into that world for decades. Mom's "girls" provided the same level of service and professionalism, but added a good measure of warmth and sass. They probably made what the French Quarter waiters made. Mom knew she could count on single mothers, who got along with people and needed the job to raise their kids—as she had done. Her waitresses prided themselves on personal service—knowing the customer's regular order from drink to dessert. Many had call-parties, customers who insisted on being served by Doris or Shirley.

Three waitresses prided themselves on being there with Mom from the beginning. Myrtle Bijoux was part Polynesian, a beauty in her day whose dark hair had a gray streak swept up and held by a broad comb. Myrtle had been Chris's sole waitress for many years and lived next door in a shotgun cottage Chris also owned. She opened and closed the restaurant as needed. Her daughter Delilah worked as a Playboy bunny and often dropped by in the afternoons, visits that got my full fifteen-year-old attention. Doris Brouillette was my mother's first hire, a country girl from near Mobile; Mom stole her away from A&G Restaurant on Canal and Broad after years of serving our family on all-you-can-eat nights. Betty White's raven black hair, porcelain skin, and fine features belied her cracker background that her way with the English language instantly betrayed.

Every time I came into the restaurant, Myrtle, Doris, and Betty found a smile for me and a "darlin'" or "suga.'" They offered to feed me whatever I wanted. Mom made it clear that this could go too far, but Doris liked to tempt me with vanilla ice cream dosed with Crème de Noyaux. Later, when I came to work at their sides, they gently taught me the ropes and covered for my gaffs and blunders.

At most restaurants each waiter and back waiter worked a particular station; in contrast, the famed Ruth's Chris "gang service" emerged from the necessity of working together to get the steak plates out sizzling. Waitresses had assigned tables, but they helped one another serve them. Besides, the original Chris Steak House was too small for stations. Mom developed the rule that if a customer asked for something from a passing waitress, she was never allowed to say, "This is not my table." Customers came back in part because they knew they would want for nothing.

Early on, Chris Steak House became famous for huge slabs of prime beef sizzling in butter on a hot plate, generous sides served family-style including potatoes done nine ways, and huge drinks. Free pouring, rather than measuring with a jigger, was the absolute rule. She used Beefeater and other call brands in the well. In New Orleans, Chris Steak House *invented*

10.5 Salad days: sassy Ruth with her Lincoln Mark III in front of original Chris Steak House.

the stiff drink or at least set a very high benchmark, quite a distinction in what must surely be the hardest of hard-drinking cities. Mom used a famously large rock glass and for a while advertised that *all our drinks are doubles,* until her lawyer envisioned lawsuits. When an evening got rowdy, Mom would take the girls aside and warn, *Easy on the drinks, girls, easy on the drinks.* But she knew that dispensing pleasure in generous amounts would keep the front door swinging open.

Mom's move to Chris Steak House in May of 1965 made for many changes at home. Suddenly Mom was working a split shift—coming back to freshen up before the dinner crowd, after a day of ordering product, butchering steaks, helping to take and serve lunch orders, and spending the afternoon on bookwork. If I wanted to talk to Mom, I sought her out at the restaurant, preferably not during the lunch or dinner rush. Sometimes, during her break between shifts, I joined her in her room while she remade her face at her vanity. I would lie on her bed and carry on a monologue about books I was reading and friends that was counterpointed by her interjections.

—*Uh-huh.*

—*Uh-huh.*

A few years later, after my mother and my high school girlfriend dropped me off at the airport for the journey to my freshman year at college, Elissa said, "I sure am going to miss him." Not to be outdone, Mom replied, "I'll miss our conversations while I get ready for work."

I started working in the restaurant that first year. I was fifteen. I wanted to make money and I wanted to help my mom. A studious underachiever, I also wanted less time for my studies.

I had just started Ben Franklin, the first magnet school in New Orleans, ranked nationally in its number of National Merit Finalists and Presidential Scholars. Although always a reader, I mostly read what was *not* on the class syllabus. There was a lot of brainpower at Franklin, but most of it was in the seats rather than at the blackboard. The number of weak teachers managed to convince me I had good reason not to apply myself. The classic underachiever's goal of not being shown up by the stiff competition this magnet school suddenly presented was an added benefit. In tenth grade biology I had a eureka moment when the process of photosynthesis suddenly made sense to me: *oh, I get it!* Ms. Haas's response—schooled to my misbehavior—was to send me to the principal's office for misconduct. Another morning, she took away my copy of *Atlas Shrugged* when I was 50 pages short of terminal page 1,200. My offence was that I was poring over it in homeroom. An avid Rand objectivist, when I went to buy my second copy, I pictured her grande heroine Dagny Taggart ripping Ms. Haas's throat out.

I squeaked by with the retention grade average of B; when the school board lowered the retention average to C+, my grades slid down to meet it. Part of the problem was that my favorite authors—Stendhal, Dostoevsky, even Lenny Bruce—seemed better father figures than the few male teachers we had at Franklin. Mr. Thayer—Mr. Physics we called him—was a typical kindly but bumbling geek. Mr. Duplantis in English was too tightly wound. Mr. Phelps would read introductions from textbooks as his lectures in English; worse, he would get entirely too close to my shoulder when he looked over my work from behind. He lived in the French Quarter. Dr. Romeo, with his odd literary name, was the most sympathetic. His PhD certainly intrigued me. A paraplegic, he had pursued advanced studies in Romance languages, Latin, and Greek. For him the ancient languages and literature were still alive. He was on a good-humored basis with "whining Achilles" and "mealy-mouthed Aeneas" whom he held up to us as models to avoid. *Don't ever treat your Dido that way, men.* When we translated well we were *gentlemen and scholars.* He had a weakness for athletes and, he explained, had decades before offered gut courses at Fortier for those who needed passing grades to keep playing ball. He had taught Dad Italian. He spoke highly of my father's skills as an all-state pulling guard but, when he saw Dad was getting to me, also counseled me that I wasn't making up Dad's strangeness. I had experienced it firsthand, but Dr. Romeo gave me my first objective sense of the marginal world Dad came from.

In the matriarchal world of Chris Steak House, I mainly set and bussed tables. I took pleasure in learning to carry plates mounded with salads and sides, fanning and stacking three or four in my left palm and up my arm, another in my right. I learned the trick to not spilling full cups of coffee: *don't look, just carry*, the waitresses explained. And it worked. Sometimes I helped deliver sizzling platters of steak to a large party. Handling those hot platters in multiples greater than two was an art I never ventured to learn. The waitresses lined the platters up their forearms, balanced on napkins meant to insulate against the heat. Then they'd race to the table. *Hot plates, hot plates! Who's got the medium rare filet?* If the busboy hadn't cleared the salad plates, or the customers hadn't moved their heads to let the plates pass—the heat of those platters was sure to find its way through the napkins. Napkins were scorched and the waitresses displayed battle scars up and down their forearms and told stories to go with them.

In the beginning, Mom butchered the meat herself. It all came in as short loins weighing as much as thirty pounds each, dry-aged for twenty-one days, wrapped in cheesecloth and tucked into oak-staved barrels. When you peeled back the cheesecloth, a huge slab covered with green mold—the aging—was revealed. Your first job was to carve away the aging, maybe a quarter of an inch thick. Initially, she used a hacksaw to cut through the short loin's T-bone to get the two or three porterhouse steaks in each short loin. These were used as "doubles," "triples," and "steaks for four." The rest of each loin—strip on one side, tenderloin for filet on the other—she boned out, then trimmed off fat and silver skin, and cut to size, sixteen ounces for strips, fourteen for filets. Within a week she saw there was no future in that hacksaw, which had served Chris Matulich well for thirty-eight years, and bought a band saw.

I filled in as butcher. Hack sawing short loins was brutal work. I was fifteen and five foot eight, weighing 165 pounds. Mom was thirty-eight, five foot two and 110 pounds. How did she do it? The band saw made butchering easier but more dangerous. With no safety guard, the whirring band was ready to slice off a thumb. For the next few years, my mother's hands and arms were full of nicks and burns. She filled in for the broiler cook on Mondays and as needed on short orders.

I loved the hard work, especially when we were busy. I loved the camaraderie with the waitstaff and kitchen staff. I was proud to be helping my mom. But Mom gave me the same rough handling at the restaurant as when I cut her grass. She declared that I would be paid minimum wage but couldn't share in the waitresses' tip pool, like the other bussers who did it for a living. No doubt Mom's policy stemmed from sympathy for her workers, an important gesture in keeping them in her employ. She knew what it was like to be a struggling single mother. But it made me feel like I was taking advantage rather than helping.

The one exception to her no-tip rule was that if a customer handed me money and said, "This is for you," I could keep it. Once, a tourist, who needed the menu explained at some length, consumed a porterhouse for two with all the fixings. In his cholesterol haze, he asked how I was compensated and when I explained, handed me a $5 bill, almost the price of a steak. I received it beaming. Mom's policy, on the other hand, left my high-beams begging for juice. I stopped coming in to help.

Nonetheless, I was happy to come to her aid when called. I became the emergency bread delivery guy. Hot French bread was a crucial fixture in the Chris Steak House meal. After being heated in the oven, slices were scored through the crusty loaf, then lopped off depending on the size of the table. So when they ran out of bread, Mom would call me at the house, and I would rush to the Reisling Bakery near the French Quarter and deliver dozens of long French loaves, then go back home to my novel.

The only other male in this matriarchal world, lanky Vontel had worked for years as a pot cook. He made heavenly crew meals—stews, beans, greens, chitterlings, and gravies as only New Orleans Creole cooks know how to stir up. Mom had stolen Vontel along with Doris from A&G Cafeteria, and he effortlessly made the transition to broiler chef. Customers in the know came into the kitchen to pay him homage, a $5 bill ensuring that their next filet was the finest center-cut high-rise in the reach-in cooler.

However, there was the problem of the thumbnail. At A&G Vontel had let his thumbnail grow until it curled back on itself and looped around again.

"No, Miz Ruth, I'm *not* cutting my nail. I been growing that left thumbnail for two years. I got the kind of nails only *mens* have."

"Vontel, cut the nail."

"Miz Ruth!" Even at six foot ten Vontel's voice went falsetto when his emotions rose. "You just don't understand. Mens got to be mens."

"Cut the nail."

"But you got to understand, Miz Ruth, I'm a man."

The "Miz Ruth" locution is what we call "real New Orleans" and a more respectful, not overly familiar, salutation than you might imagine. No one called her Miz Fertel. The battle over that nail was a test of wills and a skirmish in the battle of the sexes that Betty Friedan failed to cover. Vontel's real point was his unshakeable belief, like Joe's, that, since he was a man, he was right. For her part, Mom would not bother to list all the good reasons for that nail's removal—could Vontel hold the tongs properly to turn the steaks? Hold the knife? Was that nail sanitary? Most of all, Mom was still proving herself and couldn't let Vontel seem to have the jump on her. She was new at this and her staff was watching. The nail went. Perhaps it was here that Mom decided never to call her broiler chefs anything but "steak turners." Vontel had enough bravura as it was.

To watch Vontel on a busy night was to watch a master. He presided over the long narrow kitchen, the space filled mostly by the butcher-block line in front of him and the broiler and range behind. Vontel was long everywhere—arms, legs, neck, face—and sported a thin mustache and soul patch. He wore a bandana on his neck or forehead or both—the broiler was famously 1800 degrees in an unair-conditioned New Orleans kitchen.

When they were busy, Mom worked as expediter, making sure the steaks and sides came out together, ladling the butter on the sizzling steaks and garnishing them with parsley. Vontel was good but on a busy night if the tickets came in all at once he could find himself overwhelmed by the ten orders—forty steaks all on the grill at once, each a different degree of doneness. If the line really got behind, Mom would step behind the long butcher-block table, with its hollows where the knives had bitten for decades, to assist on broiler, feeding Vontel the raw steaks, salted and peppered, or, on the shorts side, ladling out Lyonnaise potatoes and creamed spinach, and dropping the battered rings of onion into hot grease.

On less busy nights, Vontel would treat us to his honeyed falsetto a cappella. He had sung backup on some fifties R & B sides. But though his falsetto voice sometimes spoke otherwise, Vontel modeled for me how a man should keep his cool. He'd explain that my acne was due not to adolescence but to my not *gettin' enough lovin'*. And, *if you could be a black man for just one Sa'day night*, he'd intone, *you'd never want to be a white man again.*

Vontel was his own man, accent on *man*, and he could see that I needed instruction in that regard. I didn't do any cooking in those days, but in my

10.6 *Mom at her desk.*

apprenticeship to Vontel, I learned how to sharpen a knife on a steel, drawing it toward me and sliding the blade against the rough shaft, alternating sides at just the right angle. Under Vontel's tutelage, I would learn how to drink Chivas, eat pork skins and pickled pigs' lips (once), eat gumbo at Dooky Chase, and party with the kitchen crew in after-hours black bars. Many a late Saturday night spent dancing with Fran the alluring short-order cook, I was tempted to find out what Vontel meant.

Mom located her desk at a table near the bar and front door where she could keep an eye on everything, including the till. She'd clear her desk to use for diners only on the busiest of nights. People also got to keep an eye on *her*, to see how hard this slip of a thing from the Delta worked, half glasses poised on her nose, the paperwork neatly arrayed before her, the daily sales receipts and private customer accounts. Customers loved to display their low Chris Steak House account number: it was a badge of honor to have been Ruth's customer for so long. Her personal phone book lay open at the ready. A giant-size jar of Cremora awaited the next fresh pot of coffee.

Long hours of keypunching for Dr. Burch made Mom sure-handed on the desktop calculator. A foam rubber cushion tilted the calculator toward her hand. A question would come up: Mom would lean forward in her swivel chair, crunch the numbers, and offer the answer. Before hand calculators became common, waitresses would bring her page-long bills for large parties, and in a glance Mom would add up the numbers in her head, starting at the left column and moving right. *It's faster*, she'd explain. She never lost the knack.

In later years, many long-time customers would invoke the image of Mom with a full ashtray at her elbow and a game of gin spread in her left hand. Her other important "desk" was the table in the corner used for receiving her challengers with endless sheets of Hollywood Gin. Hollywood Gin is played with three simultaneous games in three columns, your second score added to the first and second columns and so on. Mom liked a challenge and a gamble: at a dollar a point (called a penny) or five dollars a point (called a nickel), a sheet of Hollywood could add up to hundreds of dollars, and a night of Hollywood to thousands. Men came to make their bones by challenging her. Her winnings she often put into the tip pool the waitresses shared, a regal gesture that managed to rub the loser's nose in his loss when the chorus of waitresses chirped their thanks.

Mom once beat the nephew of Carlos Marcello at gin. Carlos Marcello was the head of the Louisiana Mafia and, in the minds of some, the man behind the Kennedy assassination. In my mother's telling, Carlos brought his nephew into the restaurant and wanted Mom to play him one sheet of gin for $15,000. Mom said, "I don't play for those kinda stakes."

But Carlos pressed, so she played, "and I had him skunked in ten minutes." Carlos then insisted that she give his nephew a chance to get his money back. She did and another ten minutes later, she had won $30,000.

"So Mom," I asked, pulling the story out of her, "what happened?"

"Well, Carlos was slow to pay."

"So what did you do?"

"I called Carlos and he sent my money over."

That was Mom. She had Carlos Marcello in her Rolodex.

That was Mom. She dunned the Don. I don't think those winnings found their way into the tip pool.

Mom's games were fueled by her intense competitiveness and an endless flow of coffee and cigarettes. She liked her coffee freshly made. Whenever a waitress brewed a pot, she knew to bring Miz Ruth a cup without asking, and the waitresses were under orders to pour out any pot that stood too long. When Mom bought the restaurant, Chris served Try Me coffee, a local family-owned brand from the Ninth Ward. She remained loyal to Try Me. No national brand at any price could tempt her away. She special-ordered 4-ounce (rather than the standard 2.5-ounce) packets for the automatic drip machines. Try Me was delicious but the special Ruth's Blend did not hold long over the hot plate. She refused vacuum pots that would hold the coffee longer. You'd see waitresses smelling a half-full pot, then pour it out. Also at hand were her Cremora and a bottle of saccharin tablets. If the doctor made her swear off cream—the woman who had coated America's arteries with butter and lard—nothing could make her give up saccharin. When it was taken off the market for causing cancer in lab rats, Mom bootlegged saccharin tablets from Mexico. She carried it everywhere, bitter aftertaste and all.

Her smoke ring was another fixture on Mom's desk. It was a heavy metal disk, perhaps an inch and a half across, with a ridged hole at the center barely smaller than a cigarette. She'd run each cigarette through this device, which crimped the paper and produced, she said, a cooler- and safer-burning cigarette. But so treated, they were no less offensive. Louis Roussel, part owner of the Thoroughbred Risen Star that won two legs of horse racing's Triple Crown, gave up his regular gin game because he couldn't stand the pall of smoke or the overbrimming ashtrays. *It's me or the cigarettes, Ruth.* She chose the cigarettes.

When Mom made a go of the business, far surpassing his success, Chris Matulich resented it. During that first year, she suffered a rash of flat tires; the repair shop next door dug out slugs from a .22. She heard the stories. This was not the first time Chris sold the restaurant. His gruff way with customers—*Do I have a menu? If you need to know the price you can't afford my steaks*—became even surlier during the transitions. He would downgrade his meat from prime to choice, pocketing the extra margin and ensuring that customers would be less likely to return once the new owner opened. Chris would end up getting his business back for a song. Mom *put the kibosh*, as she liked to say, *on that game.* Chris never forgave Mom her success. He raised her rent in quantum leaps each time her lease came up for renewal.

In September of 1965, less than four months after the transfer, Hurricane Betsy almost put an end to Mom's success even before it took hold. Power outages forced the restaurant to close. However, she still had gas for her broiler, so she cooked up all the perishables to send to Sig's in the "country," where winds had been clocked at 136 miles per hour. I carried hundreds of pounds of steak in the trunk of my yellow Skylark. A roadblock stopped me at Belle Chasse High School where everyone had sheltered through the howling night. There I heard parish president Chalin Perez, Judge Leander's son, announce with a catch in his throat, "If your home is below Empire, it is flooded up to the roof line." There are twenty miles of highway and homes below Empire.

I delivered the steaks to Uncle Sig's restaurant in Happy Jack, a low-slung brick structure that had weathered Betsy's winds. Aunt Helen's father recounted his Betsy story—everyone had one. A stocky man with a heavy Croatian accent, Mr. Garma looked battered and shaky. In his thick, guttural voice, he told us of manning one of the parish pumps that couldn't keep up with the rising water. When the windows blew out, the glass cut through his heavy rubber raincoat, slashing his back and arms. He had survived by winching himself with block and tackle to the building's peak, lashing himself to the rafters. His house in Buras, well below Empire, was gone. Happy Jack was fifteen miles above Empire, much the worse for wear but not under water.

As electricity returned neighborhood by neighborhood in New Orleans, word of Ruth's great steaks and big heart got out among the phone and electrical line workers who had flocked from all over the South to deal with the disaster. Their expense accounts were generous. The food was fantastic. Business boomed. Hurricane Betsy for New Orleans was a bitter lemon. Mom made lemonade, not for the first or the last time.

From a sleepy little racetrack specialty restaurant, the place to celebrate your winning the daily double, Chris Steak House soon became famous for the people you saw there. First came the Texas oilmen, followed by politicians with a nose for good expense account food and for knowing whither and whence the money flows. In New Orleans, because of its peculiarly "aristocratic" heritage sustained by the Mardi Gras tradition, public servants are largely funded by blue-blood green, and for the most part do their bidding. If the oilmen and the blue bloods from Uptown had discovered Chris's, the mayor and his cronies, the city council, and all those who batten at the public trough followed. A lot of that business was carried on at—or under—Mom's tables. The buzz was: *Chris's is where it's happening.*

The city council often retired to the large dining room upstairs after Thursday night meetings, their checks quietly picked up by some private concern with an eye on public funds. The grand jury, including Jim Garrison's infamous Kennedy assassination grand jury, often took lunch at Chris's, heard the "evidence," and then finished out the day over Mom's generous drinks. The district attorney in New Orleans is powerful in part because of his generous budget to feed and water his flock. What do you say to the guy who is buying you your third Beefeater martini and piling your plate with more Lyonnaise potatoes and creamed spinach? *Sure, hang the guy . . . hey, would you pass the Chateauneuf du Pape?*

The comfortable tone she set had an effect in the dining room. Everyone felt at home. Not only were most of the political deals cut at Ruth's Chris, but a political tradition emerged to gather on the eve of an election for last-minute deal making and for election handicapping. The Monday following the Saturday polling, the tradition was that the winners would come in to eat steak and the losers to eat red beans and rice, for many years cooked by Mom's hand and sold at the price of a steak.

Perhaps this is characteristic of Louisiana politics but at least one precedent comes from close to Mom's home: Leander Perez was known for complete control of the Plaquemines electorate, able to deliver consistently over 90 percent of the electorate to the candidates he favored. When called before a Senate committee in 1965, he explained the "venerable practice of selling votes." Senator Hugh Scott of Pennsylvania termed the practice "the current Louisiana Purchase." One of the few *legal* techniques he indulged in was meant to inspire competition amongst his ward bosses. The ward that turned out the highest percentage of voters was thrown a barbeque. The ward boss who produced the lowest percentage was invited but was served only beans.[19] Maybe Mom's traditional consolation prize came from downriver. Certainly some of the happy steak-eating winners ended their political careers when they were sent upriver.

The racial integration of Ruth's Chris happened in a moment of such political power broking. Despite Mom's roots in Plaquemines Parish, I have often heard it said that Ruth's Chris was the first fine dining restaurant in New Orleans where blacks felt comfortable. Lolis Edward Elie, a member of the most important civil rights firm in the city, Collins, Douglas and Elie, broke the race barrier when he was brought to lunch by a conservative white politician who needed Elie's clout in the black community. The candidate was unlikely to secure support from a radical civil rights attorney, but Elie, a bon vivant, understood the good meal he was being bribed with. The Public Accommodations Act had been made the law of the land a year before Mom took possession of Chris's, but, as throughout the South, the law took effect storefront by storefront. Suddenly Chris's dining room was in a tizzy. A white oil man from the West Bank (adjacent to bigoted Plaquemines Parish) approached my mother and in that drawl bigots seem required to assume even if they were not born to it, told my mother, "If that boy [two syllables] eats here [two syllables], I'll never eat at Chris's again [one and a half syllables: 'uh-g'n]." I imagine him towering over her five foot two inch frame. "There's the door," she replied. I imagine her presence filling the room. But it always did.

When in the late 1970s the power shifted in city politics, Ruth's Chris, long the premier power lunch in town, stayed that way. Mayor Sidney Barthelemy's right hand, Hank Braden, whose grandparents had fed my great-grandparents daily at the Astoria Hotel on Rampart Street, now ate every day with the Fertels' great-granddaughter-in-law.

There were other tests besides Hurricane Betsy and bigots in the early days. In November of 1971 while I was studying in Paris I got a phone call: *your mother's been shot.* I rushed home on a very long plane ride.

Leaving the restaurant late one night with the day's proceeds in her purse, she was confronted by a man with a gun. He tried to wrench the purse from her shoulder. She didn't let go. He fired his .22 pistol and it pierced her shoulder. Still she would not let go. He ran.

Chris's neighborhood had never been the best. Many a regular customer proudly dragged some pal to his favorite restaurant only to hear, *you're taking me in there?* Many with a bullet hole in their shoulder would have deserted the location. Instead, Mom hired an off-duty cop who walked folks from and to their cars.

I stayed with her until the next semester started. New Orleans was increasingly dangerous. This incident followed several burglaries on Seville Drive and more middle-of-the-night confrontations at the rear glass-louvered door: *I've got a gun.* And she did. She decided to move to safer quarters. The Park Esplanade Apartments on Bayou St. John worked for a while but even there she felt unsafe walking from her car to the door.

As the empire grew, the empress had yet to find the place to house her throne. Then came the fire.

"What am I gonna do, Jim?" my mother asked her banker, almost in tears.

A fire had severely damaged the restaurant. The tables were cleared one night and the ashtrays, as always, were dumped into tablecloths that were then taken to the linen room and put away in the laundry bag. One of the ashtrays contained a smoldering cigarette that reignited and caused a fire throughout the back of the restaurant. The kitchen would need to be gutted. For the time being, smoke damage made the dining room uninhabitable. It was 1976. She had just signed a new ten-year lease.

"Do you still own that building down the street?" her banker, Jim Queyrouze, asked.

Yes, she did. Four blocks down on Broad and Orleans was an office building that Mom had been using for catering. She called it the Prime House. She had catered cousin Audrey's daughter's wedding there, the best the family ever saw. When she purchased it I was still in high school. When she showed me the piece in the *Times-Picayune*—"Building Purchased for $172,000"—I had wondered if my mother was crazy and if I would get to go to college. But Mom was on a roll that not even a fire could stop. The contractor Jim recommended, Ed Taylor, a tall brash Irishman with a hulking frame and always with a drink in his hand, worked seven twenty-four-hour days to transform the catering hall into a restaurant.

Once installed, she seized the opportunity to solve a longstanding problem. She bought the two shotgun doubles behind the new restaurant at Broad and Orleans, linked the shotguns with a sunroom, trussed the roofs to create cathedral ceilings, and created a spacious home finished in varnished, new-milled cypress. Broad and Orleans wasn't the safest corner in New Orleans. They needed an off-duty cop there, too. But, as lagniappe— something extra, the thirteenth donut in a baker's dozen—that cop was there when Mom walked across the parking lot to her front door. She felt safe, and she would spend the rest of her life there.

CHAPTER ELEVEN

ESHU ON THE BAYOU

BACK IN 1960, LONG BEFORE ANY IMPERIAL THOUGHTS, WHEN MOM first started working as a lab technician at Tulane University School of Medicine, she put the word out for a housekeeper. A young woman called for an interview, and a time was set for Sunday morning. The appointed hour came and went. Tired of waiting, Mom went fishing. I was home reading.

Hours later, there came a knock at the door. When I opened it, I learned that the young African American woman was Earner Sylvain, who had "come for the job."

"Okay."

That was the interview. I was ten years old. Years later, when Earner told me the story of how I had hired her, she added with a cackle that she didn't meet my mother for three weeks. Mom would leave money on the kitchen counter for the shopping.

On the strength of that interview, Earner Sylvain landed a job that lasted forty-two years, the only job she ever had. In addition to becoming the best of my mother-surrogates (alongside Mom's waitresses), Earner was also an important—though little-known and never recognized—factor in Mom's growing empire.

Like my mother, Earner came from the country—Edgard, Louisiana, in St. John the Baptist Parish, about the same distance upriver as Happy Jack is down. Edgard is just above Boutte, where Louis Armstrong's parents were born. Her name is pronounced "Earn-ah," but she was indeed the "earner" in her family. She lived with four generations of Sylvains under the roof that my mother later helped her purchase on Arts Street near Elysian Fields and not far from Desire. Earner started very early to produce children, each with a different man. But *mens*, she would say, *who needs 'em?*

And *Sylvain*: she is well named, a hardworking nymph of the primal cypress forests. Though I don't think nymphs cackle and guffaw quite like Earner, or prefer wigs to doing their hair, or sometimes forget to put in their false teeth.

Earner was my mother's girl Friday. She cleaned house, cooked dinner, and ran errands. For eight years, until I went to college, it was Earner who made tuna sandwiches, with egg (how I liked it) and with sweet relish (how she liked it) on doughy, white Sunbeam bread, which, back then, we all liked. I would urge the addition of bacon, a luxury she sometimes indulged. Earner would tease me about the empty plates I'd leave under the bed, too engrossed by my French and Russian novels to bus them to the kitchen.

When Mom got tired of cooking the steaks on Monday, Vontel's day off, Earner took her place. When someone on the line was out, Earner stepped in. When Mom got tired of paying for the restaurants' linen service, she bought a double-roller mangle. Earner washed and ironed the tablecloths and napkins in the dark hallway on Seville Drive. When that operation couldn't keep up with her growing empire—four restaurants in New Orleans alone—Mom built a complete laundry in her new house behind the restaurant and hired workers to run it. Earner graduated from ironing to toting the linens around town in the white Nissan station wagon Miz Ruth bought for her.

With the restaurant now adjacent to the house she kept, Earner was always running next door. The restaurant's walk-in coolers and storerooms became her larder and pantry where she would "make groceries," as we say in New Orleans, translating the French *faire les courses*. Butter, milk and eggs, potatoes and broccoli—all within easy reach. The restaurant's salad station was a cornucopia with a panoply of house-made dressings: fresh-made chunky blue cheese, garlicky remoulade, paprika-laden French, Italian, and Thousand Island with relish and lots of minced egg (the recipe, which makes five gallons, called for ten dozen). If I was dining with them, I was the designated salad maker, a role I delighted in. I would go next door with a big bowl and come back usually with a chef salad larded with artichoke hearts, chopped hard-boiled egg, Creole tomatoes, asparagus spears,

11.1 Earner vamps.

shrimp boiled in Zatarain's Crab and Shrimp Boil, "fatigued," as the French say, with Italian dressing, and topped with crumbled blue cheese.

Mom's tastes at home ran to chicken stew over rice or veal roast with mashed potatoes and LeSueur peas with onions. Of course, red or white or baby lima beans on Mondays with plenty of local pickled pork and ham hocks which Mom ate with smoke' sausage or pork chops fried in a black skillet. Some nights, it was mirliton, which Earner stewed down with shrimp and plenty of butter. Other times Mom would have Earner stew up the "beef tips" that were left over from butchering the tenderloins. The result: fork-tender, melt-in-your-mouth. No friend of mine ever turned down an invitation to dine *Chez Earner.*

Ever competitive, Mom allowed that *Earner can cook,* but in her telling, *she couldn't boil water when she came to work for me.* But, having tasted her mother, Pearl's, crawfish bisque, I doubt Earner came to us a tabula rasa.

If Mom had an *envie,* as she'd say, a desire, to cook one of her favorites herself, it was an event: crawfish *cardinale*—crawfish with lots of hot red peppers served over pasta—or BBQ shrimp, a New Orleans dish that had nothing to do with a barbeque pit and everything to do with butter and pepper. Mom would produce this dish whenever she got wind of the lake shrimp running big, six to the pound. She would send Earner out to some pickup truck she had seen parked on the street with ice chests filled with loot culled from the brackish waters surrounding New Orleans. When

Miz Ruth served as chef, Earner did duty as *sous*-chef and scullery maid, rounding up ingredients, chopping, serving, and cleaning up. This always involved some fussing because Earner couldn't always read Mom's mind and Mom considered that a failing.

Mom couldn't cook in small amounts, so I'd get a call to come help her get through five pounds of shrimp. The leftovers would sit in the refrigerator, marinating in the sauce, still on their platter, and covered with Reynolds aluminum. She'd enjoy them for breakfast cold, peeling them at the sink and throwing the shells into the disposal.

Though she was rail thin, Earner's own eating habits mostly added up to bagfuls of Hershey bars and Snickers. Sometimes we'd find her leaning long at the counter, pushing around her red beans and rice on her plate, or picking at her (matchless) fried chicken, a bag of chocolates nearby. Only Chinese takeout might induce Earner to join us at table if we had enough pork-fried rice. Not that she ate much. Or she sometimes brought home yakamein, a thin, salty noodle soup with roast pork available in corner groceries. Her diet basically boiled down to sugar, salt, and pork in its various south Louisiana permutations.

Earner was gregarious, and housekeeping was a lonely occupation, especially when her mistress worked fifteen-hour days. So, more lagniappe, Earner could now cook many of Mom's meals across the parking lot at Ruth's Chris. Mom fussed at Earner when her good household pots and knives disappeared into the black hole of the restaurant kitchen, but the cooks and waitresses were a lot of fun. They laughed and they cut up, especially when Earner was there, stirring the chicken stew—or *stirring the pot*.

Earner's hobbies—bingo, betting the ponies, playing the slots after Governor Edwin Edwards made casino gambling legal—partook of a world overseen by Eshu, the trickster god of her ancestral West African homeland. According to the Yoruba, Eshu invented divination and has a hand in all matters of chance and coincidence. (Was it not fate that brought Earner to our door to receive the "okay" of a ten-year-old?) But, like Eshu, Earner's true calling and principal hobbyhorse was to set other hobbyhorses rocking. Sometimes when she got started, dropping bits of information sure to inflame, we in the know would share a look and make a broad stirring motion like the weird sisters in the Scottish play. If she caught our mimicry she'd cackle in delight. She was a master stirrer and she knew it.

Like Eshu, Earner had an unerring eye for human weakness and pretence. Surviving the Middle Passage, Eshu became Compair or Frère Lapin, and later Br'er Rabbit, in Senegalese slave tales first recorded in French by folklorist Alcee Fortier at Laura Plantation in Vacherie, just a few miles upriver from Edgard where Earner was born. Compair Lapin likes to stir the pot. Better to stir the pot than provide the stew meat. In this, Earner was master of her mistress. Earner worshipped Miz Ruth. But she had Mom's number. These two Mississippi River nymphs relied on one another. But that didn't mean a competition of wits wasn't part of the game.

Earner was mistress of idle banter, greeting everyone with her shrill, *Where you at, cher?* and *How's your mom 'n 'em? I seen your auntie at bingo last week, chère. Yeah, you right!* Earner knew everyone, people from the country and the families for whom they worked, people in the fine dress shops where she shopped for Mom, and people with whom she played bingo or the slots. She knew the railbirds at the Fair Grounds. One of Earner's seasonal errands was to place boxed daily double bets for her boss. The track was just a half-mile from the house. If she stayed for a few finishes, she still had time to smother the snap beans with ham and new potatoes. Besides, Miz Ruth liked to know who won the trifecta in the last race.

Earner carried a marked-up Fair Grounds program and *Daily Racing Form* as she went through her day, comparing notes with her fellow gamblers and touts. But it was not in Earner's nature to analyze. She went on instinct emboldened by gris-gris, the hoodoo amulets of her youth, now found just a block away at the F&F Botanical and Candle Shop on Broad and St. Ann, along with devotional candles and magic oils. Earner liked to cover all bases. If she was having a bad racing meet, she might say a novena at the St. Jude Shrine in Our Lady of Guadalupe Church—also known as the Church of the Dead—at Rampart and Conti. Just across the street from St. Louis Cemetery No. 1, the shrine sits in the burial chapel built during the nineteenth-century yellow fever plagues. Earner and Mom shared the belief that a novena—nine straight candles, nine straight prayers, or in the worst case nine straight masses—to the patron saint for lost causes turned your luck around. Earner performed Mom's novenas by proxy, though I suspect she killed two birds by sneaking in a prayer for her own hopeless cases. They sometimes attended wakes together—my mother hated funerals, the moment of interment gave her chills—and Earner would socialize with the families' retainers while Mom paid her respects.

Earner was less likely to light a candle to another local favorite, Saint Expedite, patron saint of rapid solutions. Earner was not by nature prompt. She would arrive at my mother's house around 10 or 11 a.m., in part because she slept fitfully on her couch with the TV blaring. When she arrived, she'd find my mother, up since 5 or 6 a.m., still in her threadbare, cigarette-burned housecoat and ratty pink terrycloth scuffs drinking her fifth cup of Try Me coffee and finishing the crossword puzzle while she watched the news and game shows. As Mom started to put on her face and get ready for her day, Earner began bustling. Her job was to do whatever Miz Ruth needed done. Earner worked till 8 or 9 p.m. when the dishes were done.

One of her jobs was to ready Mom's suitcase for the many restaurant openings, starting with Baton Rouge and Houston in the mid-1970s, that took her away from home for three weeks at a time. Not trusting hotel room service or the coffee drunk outside New Orleans, Mom travelled with her own percolator and Try Me coffee. Earner's main task was folding Mom's slacks and pantsuits and blouses, all still on hangers, into her large leather Hartmann suitcase. When she arrived, Mom would grab the hangers and sweep them into the hotel closet. *That's done*, she'd declare brushing her hands together expansively. *Now, where's dinner tonight?*

Earner's errands were less efficiently pursued and often errant. To get Miz Ruth what she wanted, Earner needed a certain freedom of movement. She would disappear for hours and rarely bothered to explain her long absences. Sometimes, exasperated, Mom might ask, "What took you so long?" Then we would hear Earner's standard litany. *I had to pay the light bill. Traffic was a rat's nest. Then*, she'd rattle on, *I had to go to four stores to get the veal roast the way you like it, baby veal, see how white that is? The Schwegmann for your good veal, cher, is on Vets*—in the suburbs five miles away, not the store just three blocks up Broad. John Schwegmann knew his customers as well as Mom's waitresses knew John. And, unsaid, after all, there were all those people to ask what horse they liked in the third race, or to stir the pot about their neighbor's misdeeds. Mom enjoyed fussing but knowing that gave Earner carte blanche. Eventually, realizing more fussing was pointless, or worse, counterproductive, Mom would roll her eyes and Earner would disappear into the kitchen.

But these labors for my mother were mere time fillers for Earner, taking her away from her true vocation, the sowing of discord. When Earner shopped or ran an errand for the corporate office, she was sure to keep the rumor of the day at a rolling boil. At the restaurant, she played back of the house against the front, staff against management, black against white. When the managers tired of Earner's troublemaking, they might ban her

11.2 Earner hangs with Aaron Neville at R & B singer Lee "the Tan Canary" Dorsey's funeral.

from their kitchen for a week or two. But eventually Mom would make a call and Earner would be back, returning from exile with pot stirring redoubled to make up for lost time. Earner's troublemaking was an unstoppable force. Her defense was simple and definitive: *I don't work for you. I work for Miz Ruth.*

Rare was the Ruth's Chris executive or manager whom Earner admired. The vice president of operations, Earner said, would always be *the man who drove a ratty old Chevrolet when he came to work for your mother.* The vice president of franchising, *can't keep his hand out of your mother's pocket. But, cher, she gots a weakness for dat Ralph!*

Earner's efforts to protect the family were pure of heart; she belonged at Miz Ruth's right hand; other retainers didn't deserve to carry her train.

Mom and Earner once came to visit me in my apartment near Audubon Park in Uptown New Orleans. Earner looked at the high ceilings and old pine floors and said, "*Cher,* this is so Uptown. This is you, *cher.*"

Mom thought a second and said, "Yeah, Randy's my Uptown son . . . and Jerry's my out-of-town son."

Uptown son for Mom wasn't necessarily a compliment. The businessmen who most often came to cut deals at lunch and brought their families back at night came largely from Uptown New Orleans. Uptown meant good business. But it also represented everything she wasn't: pretentious, exclusive, privileged, entitled, concerned with parentage and inherited wealth rather than merit and hard work. She put up with her lawyer (and my trustee), Uptowner Philip Schoen Brooks, but not without having often to roll her eyes. If you knew how she felt about Uptown New Orleans, her distaste was palpable. In calling me her Uptown son, Mom wasn't just referring to my comparative sophistication. It was another version of *That Randy.*

Likewise, "out-of-town son" wasn't in Mom's lexicon exactly what it seems. It suggests a picaresque image of Jerry cruising Kerouac-like across the American landscape. Since Vietnam, Jerry has lived much of his life on the road and often slept in his car, usually in parking lots, according to his son Rien. I guess Jerry harkened to Dad's lesson about roughing it and like Dad he hates to pay for a hotel. Both his Crown Victoria, driven for most of the seventies, and his Buick Roadmaster, driven for most of the eighties, had hundreds of thousands of miles on them (and more than one engine) by the time he bought his SUV. His vanity plate read **I BET U.** Like Dad's cars, Jerry's interior and trunk were a jumble of golf bags and water bottles and whatever he picked up along the way.

Jerry's travels are legendary if not apparently broadening. When he took his kids, Rien and Tommy, for the summer, he asked them where they wanted to go. Of course they wanted to see Disney World, seventeen hours away. Jerry drove straight through the night, stopping in parking lots as needed. Then they wanted to see Mount Rushmore. And so on, zigzagging across the country. When the boys would call their mother, Rosemary, from a pay phone, she would plead with Jerry to be sure to keep shoes on them and *to, please, sleep in motels, not parking lots.*

The most telling Jerry legend is the time he walked up on the Unangst brothers on Bayou St. John packing their car for the drive to Las Vegas.

"Whatcha doin'?"

"Packing for Las Vegas."

"Great. I'll come."

"Well, get your things, we're almost packed."

"I'm ready right now."

And they drove to Nevada. Without even a Schwegmann's bag to carry a toothbrush, Jerry stayed three months. Once there, he bought what he needed—not much. Then one day he just left, without a word of farewell or thanks, again with only the clothes on his back. Sometime later Dicky Unangst ran into Jerry. "Jerry, how 'bout that $300 you owe me?"

"Sure, come and get it."

Jerry opened the trunk of his car. There, among three sets of golf clubs and assorted junk, was a paper bag full of $100 bills.

Had he hit the daily double? I don't know.

Mom's "out-of-town" son also often conveyed Dad cross-country, along the route of Dad's favorite triangle: Las Vegas, Hot Springs, and New Orleans. Dad never liked to drive and later was not fit to drive. Whenever Dad tracked him down, Jerry dropped everything to transport Dad from spa to casino and from casino to the Fair Grounds.

Another time Jerry joined Mom at the last minute for a trip to China. This was in the mid-1980s, fairly early to be traveling to post-Mao China. His suitcase was a brown Schwegmann's paper grocery bag with a single change of clothes. Mom said that Jerry entered every kitchen in China and carried on sign-language conversations. Without a word of Chinese, Jerry made "friends for life" all through China while checking the cleanliness of the kitchens.

Among Earner's special missions was the challenge of calming the waters whenever the Uptown and out-of-town sons came together—or trying to get me and Mom, or Jerry and Mom, back together. While Earner had better sense than to get between me and Jerry in a fistfight, she became determined to make us friends. She usually managed at least a temporary truce by putting a good plate of food before us.

Her best peacemaker was a bowl of crawfish bisque, learned from her late mother, Pearl. Crawfish bisque is the true test of a south Louisiana cook, days in the preparation. Every spring, Earner would get a forty-pound sack of crawfish and, enlisting the extended family that lived beneath her roof on Arts Street, begin the tedious labor of making the crawfish bisque that her part of the river was known for, a dark gravy filled with crawfish heads stuffed with minced seasonings and crawfish, and bound with bread crumbs. These all swam in the rich elixir that, as we poked out the crawfish-rich stuffing and stirred it in, became richer still. It was the Sylvains' annual gift to the Fertels, the fee Earner paid her liege. Pearl's bisque was sure to set Jerry humming, sign of his satisfaction, as he ate.

When Pearl died, my eight-year-old son, Owen, expressed what we all feared, "Does this mean no more crawfish bisque?" Earner took a couple years off, perhaps out of respect. Then one spring, there it was, as good as ever.

The only time Jerry and I have had a moment's peace was when we were spooning up Earner's bisque. A crucial factor was this: made by the gallon, there was always enough, so we didn't have to worry who got the bigger bowlful.

CRAWFISH BISQUE

1 sack crawfish (about 40 pounds)
Scald crawfish in almost boiling water for about 15 minutes. Drain and cool. Peel crawfish and save the fat in a separate bowl. Grind the crawfish. Clean about 200 heads to stuff.

For the gravy:
2 large onions
4 ribs celery
¼ bell pepper
4 cloves garlic
10 sprigs of parsley
1 cup cooking oil
2 cups flour (about)
4 teaspoons tomato paste (heaping)
½ of crawfish fat
9 cups hot water
2½ cups ground crawfish tails
5 teaspoons salt
2 teaspoons red pepper
6 green onions

For the heads' stuffing:
2 large onions
3 ribs celery
¼ bell pepper
4 cloves garlic
10 sprigs parsley
Rest of ground crawfish tails

¼ cup cooking oil
Rest of crawfish fat
2 eggs, beaten
2 cups dry bread crumbs (or more)
4 teaspoons salt
2 teaspoons red pepper
Flour
6 green onions

To make gravy: grind onions, celery, bell pepper, garlic, and parsley. Make roux with oil and flour. Stir constantly until browned. Add ground seasonings. Cook on low fire about 30 minutes. Add tomato paste and crawfish fat. Cook about 30 minutes. Add hot water and let cook on low fire. Add ground crawfish tails, salt, and pepper. Cook on high fire about 20 minutes.

To make stuffing for heads: preheat oven to 400° F.

Grind onions, celery, bell pepper, garlic, and parsley. Fry crawfish tails and ground seasonings in hot cooking oil; cool. Add crawfish fat and eggs. Mix in bread crumbs, salt, and pepper. Stuff heads. Dip the stuffed part of head in flour and place on cookie sheet. Bake for 20 minutes.

Add baked crawfish heads to gravy. Cook on low fire about one hour. More hot water may be added if too thick. Stir carefully. Serve in soup bowls over rice.

Garnish with green onions.

CHAPTER TWELVE

SEARCHING FOR ODYSSEUS

IN 1967, THE SPRING OF MY JUNIOR YEAR IN HIGH SCHOOL, MY guidance counselor, Ms. Guichard, asked where I planned to apply to college. Franklin, a magnet school, was full of National Merit Finalists destined for top universities throughout the country.

"I always wanted to go to Harvard," I announced.

Not bothering to dissemble, she laughed right in my face. "In that case, Randy, maybe you might have applied yourself a bit."

We settled on a few colleges where, with my mediocre grades, SATs, and recommendations, I might have a chance. I had decided to study political science or international service, something that might enable me to live abroad—an aspiration I owed to my travels with Dad.

The following January, Dad took me to Washington, D.C., to visit American University and George Washington. Even though he was fighting to avoid paying my college tuition, he preached to me all the way about staying in school as long as I could. He didn't want to hear about international service—*don't ever desert New Orleans, son*—but seemed pleased about political science as a good pre-law choice, and after all, his own political career was about to emerge in the "Gorilla Man" race.

My interviews did not go well. When Ms. Guichard called American University to see how I had fared, the admissions officer said that *the young man seemed immature.* As I listened, Ms. Guichard promised that, if American let me in, I would do fine.

They took her advice and accepted me. When I got there, I wasn't completely inept socially. I knew how to take a girl to a restaurant and order a bottle of wine, and I made a few friends. I was past my hard-drinking days and recreational drugs were not a big problem. Still, I was lost and lonely. I got talked into rushing a fraternity where I spent only one semester; I had so little in common with my "brothers" that I felt all the lonelier. Most of the students gave the impression that they were putting in time before returning to their fathers' businesses. Not only did I have no paternal business to aspire to—I also had pretensions to the intellectual life.

Dad called often, usually from a phone booth or between steams at the New Orleans Athletic Club, to sermonize. *Don't let those liberal Yankees brainwash you, son.* Having been forced to pay for my schooling, he wanted to protect his investment. Plaintive calls on the dorm pay phone to my mother resulted in her same refrain, *your father's set in his ways, you'll never change him.*

But my radicalization had begun. The root cause was not Yankee liberalism but watching heads busted during the 1968 Democratic National Convention in the Grant Park Chicago police riot the summer before I went to American. I grabbed my Nikon F to record what I saw on the TV screen. There was little need: the images were etched on my memory. Part of my turmoil in freshman year was the cognitive dissonance experienced as an Ayn Rand enthusiast as I digested and tried to make sense of such images. I had dragged my best friend, Ricky, to see her speak that summer when we passed through New York. Rand's talk took place in the bowels of the Empire State Building, hardly the lofty setting one would expect for the creator of Howard Roark. Listening to her throaty drone, I began to wonder.

Still, I went off to college at least half a southern conservative. On the one hand, had I had the right to vote in November 1968, as eighteen-year-olds do now, I would have voted for Nixon. His promise to end the war helps explain my support. At the same time I was marching through the streets of Washington giving voice to the frustration I felt. The moratoria marches, candlelight vigils, teach-ins, and tear gas convinced me that the world, and I, had changed irrevocably. Even before he took office, I couldn't believe I had even considered supporting Nixon. We learned later that his secret plan to end the war involved sending Henry Kissinger to Hanoi to threaten nuclear attack. He wanted to convince them he was just crazy enough to do it. Dad loved him. If Dad could have thrown him a birthday party, he would have. Mom might have attended.

Meanwhile, my intellectual pretensions had little bearing on my study habits. I earned a D in freshman English—I stopped attending—and did only a bit better in my government course, my declared major. Worst of all, it took some fast-talking with my Thai instructor to get my grade point average high enough to stay in school. Since I'd been to Thailand, I signed up for Beginning Thai—although I had shown little aptitude, and even less application, for Latin, French, or Spanish in high school. The teacher was the exquisitely beautiful daughter of the Thai ambassador. This might have inspired hard study; instead it inspired only a rich fantasy life. By the end of the year, I had slipped so far behind that I stopped going to class.

At semester's end I approached my professor with a novel argument for a passing grade. Freshmen with failing grades could erase them by retaking the course in their sophomore year. "If you give me a D rather than an F," I explained, "I promise not to take your course again." She was happy to oblige, saying that I might have better applied my cleverness to my studies. *Sawaddi Krap, and I'm out of here.*

I also made a decision that, during the Vietnam War, almost had life-altering consequences. In 1968, every young man knew the rules governing the draft. It was generally understood that draft boards considered twelve hours of coursework per semester "full-time," meriting the 2-S student deferment. What I didn't know was that each draft board determined its own criteria. The New Orleans board demanded fifteen hours—five courses—to retain a student deferment.

Before learning this I had dropped my philosophy class. I had read Camus and Nietzsche in my untutored way in high school. If God was dead, what was the point of learning Aquinas's medieval proof of his existence? I decided that this course was not *doing* philosophy and that I was cleverer than my adjunct philosophy professor, a middle-aged rabbi. On the day of the exam, which I was unprepared to *do*, I approached the professor's desk with a drop form. *Are you sure you know what you are doing?* he ominously intoned.

That summer my draft notice arrived: I was no longer 2-S and should be prepared to take my physical. The next fall, I spent long hours at the American Friends Service Committee draft counseling office near Dupont Circle. But I did not act upon their advice. When the notice to report for the physical arrived, I had not secured any paperwork from physicians or psychiatrists declaring me unfit for duty. I boarded the military bus. We rode silently to a military base in the Maryland countryside. The building was situated on the corner of Counter and Intelligence streets, an ominous sign indeed.

My plan was to claim every possible disabling condition. I had no supporting paperwork, but maybe I could convince them with quantity. *My bedwetting. The scar on my wrist? Yes, I tried to kill myself. Yes, I do like boys! Drugs? There isn't anything I haven't tried!*

A psychiatrist in a starched white coat looked at me with some measure of sympathy and then turned to the paperwork on his desk. I read upside down as he wrote in large block letters: "Psychoneurotic complaints—1-A." I wasn't sure what the first phrase meant. The second was crystalline.

It was a long ride back to Washington, D.C. But I had signed up for six courses. My best chance to recover the 2-S deferment was to make up the hours I'd lost the previous semester. Maybe I'd cut Uncle Sam's "Greetings" letter off at the pass.

The semester flew by. Political Theory was taught by a brilliant woman who asked us to call her Ruth and who ran us through scintillating discussions of political thought from Plato's *Republic* to Marx's early writings. Ruth welcomed creativity; I wrote a short play in which Ayn Rand builds a time machine. She goes back in history to thank Aristotle for the principle she redeployed in *Atlas Shrugged*: that "A was A." But, in my play, Aristotle has been reading Heraclitus and announces he has rethought that first principle: A isn't A but only *becoming* A. Ruth gave the paper A+ and included a quote from Ezra Pound:

> I have oft been as a tree
> Among the wood,
> And many a new thing understood
> That was rank folly to my head before.

Ruth got it that I got it. But Ayn Rand's "rank folly" came back to haunt us all, channeled by devotee Fed Chair Alan Greenspan, who during the financial meltdown of 2008 expressed surprise that self-interest was not the economy's most trustworthy guide. Nonetheless, as far as my intellectual development was concerned, Ayn Rand was history—progress. I switched my major to English.

I earned eighteen hours of A's that semester but it turned out I didn't need to. In November 1969, I came up with a lifesaving 272 in the first draft lottery. According to the new dispensation, numbers 1–150 could expect to be called when their deferments were finished. But books had worked their spell by then. Applying myself, I discovered that I had a calling to read, to write, and to teach. My life's lot was cast. Graduate school and teaching lay ahead.

And that's how, because of the Vietnam War, I came to look at life through the lens of books and ideas.

The next summer Dad and I traveled yet again. This time we went down to the Yucatán, walking the colonial streets of Mérida, visiting the Mayan ruins, and enjoying the beaches and waters of Isla Mujeres, the Isle of Women, an odd choice for a man that hated women. As always, we went our separate ways. I spent as much time as I could walking out to Garrafón at the southern tip of the island where the snorkeling was right off the then-deserted beach—this was long before hotels and sculpture gardens invaded.

On the way back to Mérida, as I walked to the Observatory at Chichen Itza, a tropical thunderstorm blew up. As I ran for shelter, a lightning bolt struck, just on the other side of a stand of trees. It was so close that I felt the electricity buzz in my teeth fillings. That was an appropriate symbol for the sixties—my awe at the immensity of events swirling around me, of being fully alive, and of fear: I could be next.

My conflicts with my father now had a new political dimension. Having dropped out of high school, Jerry received his draft notice. By then, Chris Steak House was well on its way to becoming *the* political hangout. Thanks to some of her loyal customers, Mom had the clout to get Jerry out of the draft, and keep him from the Vietnam War. Although she supported the war, she saw no reason to give her son to it. Nonetheless, Jerry's friends were going and so would he. In part, Jerry's choice was in support of his buddies; in part, it expressed his deeply ingrained distrust of authority, which the war exacerbated. My brother was in boot camp preparing himself for the jungles of Southeast Asia. As my father and I wandered through the jungles of Mexico, he wanted to know, "If you're drafted, will you serve?"

My high lottery number—272—mooted Dad's question, an answer that didn't satisfy him. But it was the sixties, a decade when truth-telling was a political act. Finally, after days of this hectoring, I told him, "No, Dad, I will not serve in this war."

We were driving the main highway that crossed the Yucatán Peninsula west to east, from Isla Mujeres to Mérida. We were almost to Villahermosa.

Dad stopped the car and told me to get out. "You can find your own way home." Only more fast-talking saved me from joining the tarantulas on the side of the highway.

Dad was classified 4-F in World War II. Now he was charged up about his elder son's fighting in a far more morally and politically ambiguous war and adamant that I join him. Had he had dreams of heroic action that he imagined we would now fulfill?

Dad was a lifelong athlete, which did little to explain his 4-F status. How to square the two? While he urged me to the current war, I asked my mother about how he'd avoided the war, and her answer was a stunner. "Your father had syphilis. He told me on our honeymoon."

Her tone was not one to invite follow-up questions. But the episode casts light on the misery of my parents' honeymoon: a trip around the world, a man grown taciturn, trouble at an African port—no visa—the trip home. How had Mom responded to this revelation? Had she feared for her own well-being? Even as a trained scientist, she probably lacked knowledge about the social disease that no one mentioned socially.

Still, if Dad contracted syphilis, it need not have affected him long-term, just long enough to get him out of the war. Before the time of Mom and Dad's honeymoon, one shot of the new drug penicillin usually knocked out the spirochete.

At the time, I imagined that this news offered an explanation for my father's long history of odd behaviors. I wondered if "The Great Scourge" was the source of my father's craziness. Was he psychologically unfit?

Uncle Barney's lawyer was probably wrong in this regard. The spirochete's ill effects on the brain emerge only after many years. Discovered in 1928, by the mid-1940s penicillin was widely available. There is no reason to believe that this miracle drug didn't cure him of the great pox.

And yet what trace effects did it leave behind? Was the mythology of syphilis an element in Dad's misogyny: did he imagine that syphilis was *done to him* by some woman? Did he contract syphilis from one of the girls that he brought up to the General Semmes Hotel in Mobile? Was syphilis the source of his pursuit of living forever: the healthy foods, the mineral baths, and the fetal lamb cell shots? Was this part of his attraction to Hot Springs, where Camp Garrity, just north of town, was at one time the largest syphilis treatment center in America?

Were there positive gains? Did syphilis humble him to life's fragility and his own mortality that he shared with all around him? Sadly, I think not.

• • •

In the early seventies, Jerry served in the Parrot's Beak area around Tay
Ninh, a perilous place where the Cao Dai, a religious sect, fought for the
United States and where the enemy forever slipped back and forth over
the border wreaking havoc on our troops. He was part of the "Cambodian
Incursion," the cross-border invasion that led to the campus protests, the
Kent State massacre, and the Khmer Rouge killing fields. A member of his
platoon wrote me years later, trying to get in touch with Jerry, "He was the
best medic we had, and an even better card player." I didn't doubt either.
Jerry was loyal to his friends. And crazy enough to face hot lead for his
buddies without a second thought.

Mom kept his medals in her drawer, and she showed them to me once—
at least one Purple Heart and a bronze star. But like many of that war who
saw hard duty, Jerry never told a combat story. The closest we came was
his tale of Dad's pulling strings to get him R & R in Hong Kong. Unable
to get in to see an important army general, Dad set up a perimeter on the
general's office steps. Finally one day the general stopped to ask for an explanation. Perhaps Dad threatened to attack the guerillas with gorillas. Or
maybe Dad's charm did the trick. Next thing, Jerry's first looey was getting
radio messages about Fertel getting R & R—only three months into his tour
of duty. A helicopter air-lifted him from Cambodia. From Ben Hoa Jerry
called Mom. She was on the next plane. When Jerry got to Hong Kong, Dad
announced they had rooms at the YMCA. *Well, I'm going to stay with Mom
at the Hilton.* Dad was hot. Dad's only reward was to take credit: *Saved your
brother's life.* Dad finally had a war record.

Jerry did tell me of some hell-raising while on another R & R, an all-
night poker game, a bar fight. We were in Palma de Majorca in the fall of
1971. I was studying French at the Sorbonne in Paris in my last year of college. Jerry and Dad were returning from a trip around the world after Jerry
completed his tour of duty. After their estrangement during most of Jerry's
teens, the war had reconciled them.

Jerry tracked me down by phone in Paris. Although Dad and I had not
spoken since our disastrous trip to the Yucatán, I relented. Majorca was too
tempting to pass up.

Dad and I immediately started bickering and, strangely, that brought
Jerry and me closer. This was the first time we were spending together
when we were not throwing punches. Jerry had met some young French
sun worshipper and, while we walked together on the beach, wanted me to

teach him enough French in an afternoon to seduce her. "Tell her, *tes yeux sont trés beaux*," I recommended (about as adept a seducer in French as I was in English). I wrote it out phonetically in the wet sand with my toe. Another afternoon, as we shared fried squid sandwiches at a counter in Palma's open market, Jerry came as close to wisdom as I ever heard from him. "The thing you have to remember, Randy," Jerry ventured, "is that Dad never found anything he liked to do."

As usual, the visit to Majorca ended badly between Dad and me, so Jerry came alone to visit me afterwards in Paris. I took a week off from my studies and showed him the city I had come to love. It's the most time we ever spent together, the most effort we ever made to get along. The war had taken some of the fight out of Jerry. I could see he was amongst the walking wounded and needed kid-glove treatment like when he had childhood migraines.

But, most of all, we seemed to inhabit different planets; there seemed little point in fighting. At the end of the week, sitting in a cafe just below the Sorbonne, I asked him: "Well, Jerry, what do you think of Paris?"

He thought a moment. "The French bread is better at home," he replied, repatriating chauvinism to the land that invented it.

After the war, Jerry seemed to drift and his behavior became odder. Home that first summer after his return, I spent a few evenings at his apartment smoking pot and playing chess. I had found pot in my dorm rooms and he in the jungle. It was stoned and over chess that I heard the few R & R stories he was willing to recount.

The next summer Mom asked me to fill in for a couple weeks for Jerry in the pizza parlor she had bought for him, *he needed a break*. Jerry had asked for help in naming it. I offered Dante's Pizza, keeping to myself that I had the poet in mind and infernal pizza ovens. It was next to his buddy Tank's pool hall, the Golden Cue. Tank got his name from his size, which the pizza parlor helped maintain. I took courses in German and French in the mornings. In the afternoons I made dough in a huge Hobart mixer, spun pizza dough in the air, and made half-pound hamburgers from Mom's leftover tenderloin tips that people were crazy for. Six weeks later there was no sign of his return. Mom didn't understand how I could desert him. I was on my way to graduate school in Oregon. The pizza parlor didn't last much longer and Jerry went to work for Mom turning steaks.

Like many vets, Jerry seemed to carry Vietnam with him, his emotions frozen into a defensive crouch, fairly well camouflaged by his Rodney-like bluster. After Jerry had been back for several years, he was living with Rosemary in Lafayette, two hours or so west of New Orleans deep in bayou country.

One day Jerry went off for his early morning breakfast. Like Dad, he was an early riser, a habit from his racetrack days and confirmed by his tour in Vietnam. But he neglected to close the gate behind their sweet boxer, Prissy. Later that morning, Rosemary sat down to the daily restaurant paperwork. Like Ruth, she kept her desk in the middle of the dining room. Opening the drawer, Rosemary was horrified to find two bloody dog's ears. She slammed the drawer shut, then sneaked it open again: *yes, Prissy's two severed ears.*

She asked Jerry about "those ears."

"Prissy got out and was killed on the highway," Jerry explained. As for the ears, "That's what we did in Vietnam. To remember."

Jerry longed for his buddies and he longed for good parents as much as I did. The army is no better than academia in issuing trustworthy fathers. The Vietnam era's father figures all disappointed: JFK, LBJ, Nixon, McNamara, and Westmoreland—each promised much and delivered worse than nothing. Jerry lived in a more black-and-white world than I. Even more than I, he needed a parent he could look up to. To Mom he was like an errant puppy. Her lap was the gravitational center of his life around which he circled at some distance, never coming to rest. A restless life.

After he left Lafayette, the restaurant, and Rosemary, Jerry ventured widely and erratically, criss-crossing the country. Mom could tell where he was by his VISA card bills that she paid for him with his allowance. He worshipped her but couldn't quite do her bidding. It helped that she didn't expect much, perhaps expected and wanted just what she got. Dad was his model for being *crazy like a fox,* the best compliment Mom and her friends could muster for Jerry. That role helped him fulfill the other, the role of being no challenge to her.

I have spent more than twenty years studying and teaching the Vietnam War. But I have had no longings for war's often hollow promise of manly fulfillment. Nor do I feel any guilt for not serving. It was a bad war and I got lucky—draft lottery number 272.

The guilt that I do carry, that in some measure fuels my teaching the war, is that I never wrote Jerry while he was in-country. One thing you learn reading the memoirs and novels that came out of the war is how important mail from home was. I could try to excuse myself by saying that we were so

12.1 Back from Vietnam, Jerry wears a gold woolen suit, made in Hong Kong during R & R. I wear my war protesters' uniform and demeanor. Between us, Mom holds Trouble and beams for the camera, untroubled.

thoroughly estranged by that time that I had nothing to say. I could claim that we were on opposite sides of the war. But our opposing views confirmed rather than caused that estrangement. Writing was the right thing. I didn't do it.

Jerry has never said a word about my not writing. I'd like to think that his sharing those squid sandwiches with me in the Majorca marketplace was his way of expressing forgiveness. I wish, too, that he had found something that he loved to do.

In that regard, I was blessed.

Jerry doesn't spend time with his nose in books. But he never had any trouble deciphering the *Daily Racing Form* or the morning line on the sports page. The only book he ever told me he read and *almost finished* was Thomas Berger's *Little Big Man*, a veiled anti–Vietnam War novel. Jerry may not have penetrated the veil, though perhaps he connected with the book's idea that the White Man in charge wasn't what he promised. It might have helped Jerry make sense of his feelings about the betrayals of authority.

Not being much of a reader, Jerry was not much of a speller. "Rien" was Jerry's spelling for Ryan, his firstborn. He grew up in Lafayette, the American city where such a name was best calculated to mean "nothing" to the most people. *What's troubling you?* might ask friends of some complaining Cajun Cyclops. *Rien!*

Jerry named his third son in honor of our grandfather but spelled the name "Author." Mom insisted he go to the trouble of legally changing it to "Arthur." Maybe his son would have become a writer like his uncle, or will still. Jerry named his racing stable after the earlier incarnation: Author's Stable. Because of the paperwork, the name stuck; my friends come back from the track having read the *Racing Form* and wondering why Jerry named his stable after me. Jerry's fourth son, Janatahan, responds to a sound that you and I would spell Jonathan. Mom by that time had thrown up her hands and so, I imagine, Janatahan is still legally his moniker.

While Jerry was searching for something he liked to do, golf, the race-track, and the betting parlor would do for the while. He also spent time helping his buddies. One of them, a commercial fisherman, was out in the Gulf for days at a time. Jerry would return with stories that made his eyes sparkle, of exceeded limits and dodged game wardens, of selling hundreds of pounds of pompano through the kitchen door at Galatoire's and Antoine's. Twenty years later, a Galatoire's manager asked me with a smile, "Are you Jerry's brother?" He remembered the ice chests of pompano at the back door. Such smiles, like those that accompany memories of the Gorilla Man, are always at once gleeful—charmed—and knowing. Jerry's other buddy was an air-conditioning installer. At dinner, Jerry would recount hoisting AC units onto rooftops and the hilarious disasters that often ensued. Once, one of their customers told me how he met my brother. "This guy in greasy clothes had just walked through my home. The air-conditioning contractor pointed to Jerry and said, 'You know who that is? That's Ruth's Chris's son.'"

Later in life, Jerry's occupied himself with lawsuits against Dad. In the first of these, in the early nineties, Jerry was living in a house he owns in Hot Springs with Sophie, his new girlfriend and the mother of his two younger sons. Dad moved in with them because his house on Whittington Avenue had been destroyed by neglect. Soon after, Dad had "words" with Sophie and tossed a closetful of her shoes onto the lawn. Jerry got mad.

"You can't treat Sophie that way."

"Yes I can."

"No you can't. Get out of my house."

"You can't throw me out," Dad reminded Jerry. "Remember that paper you signed?"

"I didn't sign any paper."

"Sure you did. At the lawyer's office. You signed a contract that says I can live here 'til I die."

Dad would later pull the same dodge about shared real estate in Las Vegas. He bought some worthless desert property and gave Jerry a share. Las Vegas exploded and Dad sold the property for six figures. Jerry asked for his share.

"What share?" Dad asked in disbelief. "Remember that paper you signed?"

"What paper?"

"That contract giving me back your half of the property."

The litigation went on for years. Jerry was hell-bent on making sure that Dad would do time in the pen. He swore that his signature was forged even when his own expert witness, a handwriting specialist from Los Angeles, confirmed that the signature was in fact Jerry's.

When all was said and done, Dad and Jerry were housemates again. They certainly seemed to be soul mates, even when—or especially when— they were fighting or holding grudges.

I loved Paris and was determined to learn French. After graduating I returned to my studies at the Sorbonne and taught English in another part of the University of Paris. Linda and I met in line at the American Express office around the corner from the Paris Opera, each waiting to get a money transfer from home. She was picking at the split ends of her shoulder-length brown hair and seemed depressed. Not usually one to be forward, nonetheless I ventured, "You okay?"

Her response, *not really*, left me not much else to ask but, "Where you from?"

"New Orleans."

It wasn't quite true—she was from Berwick, on the Atchafalaya River across from Morgan City—but it was enough to get us started. Linda and I went for a cup of coffee and talked about how we had both spent the year in Europe—she had studied art and Italian in Florence and I had just left my part-time teaching position in the Paris suburbs because my colleagues teaching conversational English were just that: English speakers. I wasn't learning what I had come for. We were both leaving Paris to travel in the south of France and talked vaguely of meeting again.

Hitchhiking through Provence, I once again ran into Linda in the American Express office, this time in Nice, both picking up our mail. A marriage made in Amex! Another ominous sign.

We fell in together and took the steep Train des Pignes up into the Basses Alpes to Digne-les-Bagnes where Jean Valjean got his miserable start on his long journey to redemption. Hitchhiking the next day, we got separated. Stopping in a café for *une bière à la pression,* I was taken for the first and only time in my life as a Frenchman. This is why I had come to France. Of course it is also true that almost any accent was more Parisian than Provence's Italianate French: *je suisa alléa ce matinga.*

Meeting up again, Linda and I hitchhiked over to Aix, lunched at the famous café Les Deux Garçons that Hemingway frequented on Cours Mirabeau, and hiked to the Cezanne family mansion the Jas de Bouffan near his beloved Mont Sainte-Victoire. We made love for the first time in Arles after watching the sun set over van Gogh's Rhone where both currents and colors swirled, then hitched back to the coast. When I went off to Corsica, we talked of getting together again that summer in New Orleans where I would be studying German and where her family kept a house Uptown.

That fall I drove off to the University of Oregon for graduate school in English. Linda soon followed.

I spent two years in Eugene but feared that a doctorate from the University of Oregon wouldn't help me land a job in the tough market for college English teachers. Master's degree in hand, I applied to transfer to more prestigious universities back east. Soon I was faced with a hard choice between the University of Virginia and Harvard. My Oregon professors were unequivocal and unanimous: Harvard's English Department was coasting on its reputation; the University of Virginia was a coming powerhouse in the field. But how could I turn down Harvard? Echoing in my ear I heard Ms. Guichard's laughter about my aspiring to Harvard. How could I turn down an opportunity to thumb my nose at Ms. Guichard and Ben Franklin High School where I had achieved so little?

Linda was at my side, a brilliant woman of manifold, if not well-focused, interests. When we met, Linda had been studying art; at Oregon, she pursued linguistics and folklore. At Harvard, she studied psychology and got a master's degree at the Graduate School of Education. Linda seemed so unlike my mother. She was adept at analyzing people. She could talk about emotions. She cared about art and languages.

And we would always have Paris. In 1975 we decided to get married.

Linda and I had chosen for the wedding the least Catholic of Catholic churches in New Orleans—Our Mother of Perpetual Help Chapel. It looked more like a Garden District mansion, which it once was. After the service, we walked to Commander's Palace where James Booker, a New Orleans piano legend, played the reception.

Arranging for the music was the one task Linda gave me for the wedding. Having been away for many years, I had asked Vontel, the Ruth's Chris grill master, for help. "Call this number," he said. "Booker'll play your gig." James Booker sits alongside Jelly Roll Morton, Professor Longhair, and Dr. John in the pantheon of New Orleans piano greats, but at the time his career was in eclipse. I was unaware of him. I called. Booker was willing but insisted on a union contract. He had no car. Could I pick him up? So I drove my mother's red El Dorado—I had named it Ruby Dick—to a shotgun near the projects on Melpomene, one of the nine muse streets in the Lower Garden District, a legacy of the Neoclassical Revival period in the early nineteenth century, but pronounced Melpo-MEAN. A short wiry man with an eye patch that sported a glitter star opened the door and hustled to the car.

The eye patch helps explain Booker's need for a union contract. A legendary studio musician in his day, Booker had played the opening riff on the Beatles' "Lady Madonna" and then been roughed up by some goons when he insisted on his fee (some say he had already received it). He lost an eye in the encounter.

Driving to the union hall on Esplanade, not truly trusting Vontel, I found myself pumping James Booker with questions a suburban white boy might ask: "So, do you know who Jimmy Buffett is?" When we got there, he offered his answer. "Come with me, you don't think I'm any good." He took me to a room, sat at an upright piano, and laid his hands on the keys forming a chord so rich and blue that I begged him to stop, forgoing as penance the intimate recital he was offering. James Booker, the black Liberace, the Bayou Maharajah, played for the Beatles, and for our wedding!

It was an early high point. Lows would follow.

"What's the matter, Linda? Why are you crying?"

"I . . . was . . . just . . . thinking about what it will be like when I'm sixty."

"You're thirty. Why are you worried about sixty?"

"Well, I just know that I won't be hearing the patter of my grandchildren's feet."

What Linda *was* hearing was her biological time clock. But, at twenty-six years old, I was deaf to such matters. I had just finished my first year at Harvard. I had another year to go and then the dissertation. *Why hadn't I heard anything about this pressing timetable when we talked about getting married?* And fatherhood? *Shouldn't I have a job, not just a teaching assistantship?* Still more potent: *Can I be a better father than what I grew up with?*

After many months of her crying, I relented. In a fundamental way, Linda was just like my mother: certain matters were not negotiable. It was all too easy for me to adapt to such familiar territory. Besides, I was determined to stay married. In my mind, to walk away was to become my father. This determination was set for good when my first son, Matt, was born in 1978, followed by Owen in 1981. Those boys were the joys of my life. But I wasn't quite ready for them.

I had boxed myself right in, clueless as to how I'd gotten there.

I hadn't seen Dad for years but, at the time of the wedding, I wrote to introduce him to Linda and her family. Linda's father was a successful merchant from Berwick, Louisiana, an orphan who had been delivered from a New York orphanage to immigrant adoptive parents on a "baby train" in the early years of the century. Now he owned a bank—an American success story. Always doing his best to hurt, my father wrote back: "Sounds like you're marrying her for her money." I did my best to shrug it off. He wanted Jerry to be my best man. I put Jerry in the wedding but, unaccustomed to getting into a suit, Jerry made us twenty minutes late to the chapel, a big hit with Linda.

I next saw Dad in 1977, two years after my wedding. One morning in Cambridge, he called out of the blue, at 5 a.m. I'd been up till 3 reading. "I'm coming to Boston to sign a million-dollar lease for the W. T. Grant building." He wanted a ride: "Do you wanna pick me up?"

I immediately fell into my old habit of splitting hairs. "Do I want to pick you up at 8 a.m.? No, but I will." As always Dad's inevitable grudge was triggered from the get-go.

Linda was home in Louisiana. Dad stayed in a hotel. One day as we were driving, suddenly he announced, "Cows have it so easy. Don't you wish you could just graze all day and have no worries?" There are no cows at Fresh Pond in Cambridge, but it wasn't the off-the-wallness that gave me pause. It was the wish itself. It wasn't as if he was loading sixteen tons everyday. As a graduate student certainly I felt I was a better candidate for the chore.

I cooked dinner for him. A fellow graduate student, a woman, joined us. I guess I needed someone from the graduate program to witness this man and this relationship. In many ways it was a typical encounter: Dad preached and got angry. He left Boston without a word of goodbye.

A year later I received a flurry of letters and packages, all emblazoned "GORILLA MAIL" and addressed "c/o Harvard English Department." Dad got a charge out of the Harvard connection—I often heard secondhand that he boasted about *my kid at Harvard*.

After a few of these letters, I wrote back, expressing my objection to the way he blew hot and cold. I had heard how he walked out when my brother, Jerry, and Rosemary told him they were expecting their first child. "Just as you've walked out on our lives so many times. . . . Jerry needs all the support and all the guidance in his new role that he can get. Your walking out is like a child's pouting because he didn't get his way or enough attention."

I wrote that I had no desire to be his crony. I upbraided him for preaching to me, in my teens, never to marry or have kids, sermons that shamed both my mother and his sons. "I know that your advice came out of the pain of your own failure in marriage, but I don't see why you had to make your individual pain and failure into a universal rule. I pity you for your shortsightedness and for the loneliness it has created for you."

I got a bitter response, which should have been no surprise. But still it surprised me. The letter came in yet another envelope announcing *Get the Gorilla* along with a message, in block letters: "Are you still cheating on your wife?" He meant with my colleague. Friendship with a woman was alien to my father. There were no Paulettes among the Pauls in his circle. Even though I got along well with the English Department secretaries—far better than I did with the stuffy professors—it was humiliating to retrieve these envelopes from the department office. They handed them to me as if with three-foot tongs. *Here, I think this is for you.*

Inside on yellow legal paper Dad quoted King Lear in red ink: "'How sharper than a serpent's tooth it is / To have a thankless child!'" and the Bible: "'Judge, ye not least, ye be judged'[*sic*]. . . . You have Judged me. Be careful someone does not Judge you!"

As an English graduate student, I noted his misuse of the quotation from the Gospel of Matthew. It is wise to remember, Christ reminds us, that we have all sinned. We are none of us perfect. We all have a beam in our eye. "Judge not, that ye be not judged" is not an invitation to give up moral judgment. It is an admonishment against arrogance.

But to me, the idea that we are beyond judgment, unaccountable, was the very height of arrogance. That was my dad to a tee.

The family dance was hardly over. Five years later, in 1983, I attended a summer seminar at the elegant Huntington Library in San Marino, California. I was a few years into an assistant professorship at Le Moyne College in Syracuse. I fell in with two other professors. We often talked long into the night over scotch, not always about the fine points of the visionary poetic tradition we had come to study. One evening, a member of our trio told of hunting down his father in the Canadian woods and how they were reconciled before it was too late. I demurred, "It's just not going to happen with my father. He's just not that kinda dad."

But the seed had been planted. Telemachus-like, I took the southern route home at the end of the summer so I could pass through Las Vegas where I tracked down in his trailer his high school friend, the craps dealer Sam West. He thought Dad was in Hot Springs. I made Ft. Smith, Arkansas—thirteen hundred miles—in a day, exhausted. Hot Springs was just south.

The house on Whittington Avenue, once owned by his grandparents Sam and Julia, then Annie, was about ready for the bulldozer. There was the front porch where I had my earliest memory, at age three or four, of a woodpecker's echoing tap-tap-tap, of bright green trees rustling, of cool and fragrant mountain air, of crystalline light.

I found the front door open but no one home. At the door a full-length mock gorilla barred the way, perhaps his homage to Dalí's stuffed bear. I picked my way through piles of the *Daily Racing Form*, mounds of plastic jugs for mineral water drawn free from the spigot at the town center, and boxes of plastic gorillas from the Gorilla Man campaign. Dad had bought five hundred gross, seventy-two thousand, half-black, half-white, in Hong Kong. No lights. No running water, except what had coursed through the five-foot hole in the roof in the next room, damaging everything in sight including the floor beneath where a dark chasm gaped. I backed out quickly, avoiding rotten floorboards.

The open door convinced me Dad was in town. My search took me first to Oaklawn Park. The horses were not then running, but there were people to ask. *No, they hadn't seen the Gorilla Man.* Not at the racetrack, nor at the golf course, nor at Red's Health Food Center, which had replaced Hammons in Dad's culinary firmament, nor in the dining room at the Arlington Hotel, which also had seen better days. I stayed there, finally, now, on my

12.2 Mom reels in a big bluefish in Massachusetts Bay.

own dime, but its glory days were clearly over. I went to the Buckstaff Bath House. No, they hadn't seen him. But I found one attendant who could explain the open door. "I haven't seen your dad in a few days, but he left the door open for me to fix the roof."

Discouraged, I passed again by the house for one last try. An elderly woman, frail and European, was outside the house next door. I approached her. No, she hadn't seen "*that man*. He's a terrible man. He's mad because my tree fell on his roof. I offered to fix it. But he cursed me. He put up this barbed wire on the fence between our houses. I feel like I'm back in Auschwitz. I told him that and he laughed at me. What kind of Jew is that?"

I decided on the spot to leave my car and fly down to New Orleans to touch base with my mother. I recounted my search. She wanted to explain it all away.

"Well, you know how your dad is. He's not gonna change."

Nor was Mom. One summer—*the three great things about teaching are June, July, and August*—Linda and I rented a house on Cape Cod and Mom came to visit for a week. I took her deep-sea fishing in the bay for blues

12.3 Mom wobbily exults on her first bike ride.

and we cooked together and had a good family week. Matt was eighteen months and they built sand castles on the South Dennis beach—very large sand castles that would have won any competition. One day Linda and I decided to take a bike ride.

"Come on, Mom, we'll rent you a bike and take a little jaunt on these country lanes. Piece of cake."

"No thanks."

"Come on, Mom."

"No thanks."

But finally we got her on the bike. She was pretty shaky at first but soon seemed to be proving the adage that "you never forget how to ride a bike."

When we got home, she plopped down on the couch. "You know, in Happy Jack, all the roads were shell roads and there were no sidewalks, so we didn't have bikes. That was the first time I ever rode a bike."

Mom was so competitive, she couldn't just say, "I don't know how."

I hadn't found Dad that time in Vegas or Hot Springs but eventually his letters again found me where I was teaching in Syracuse, New York. In 1984 during my Thanksgiving break I agreed to journey with him to Zurich, Switzerland, where Dad took the cell shots. After a blood workup, the doctor would decide whether, for example, the patient's liver needed to be

12.4 The Gorilla Man takes Zurich.

stimulated by cells from a fetal lamb's liver. Pope Pius XII took these shots, as did Churchill and Onassis. Somerset Maugham swore in his memoir *The Summing Up* that the shots at the famous *La Prairie* Clinic in Geneva had given him new skin. My father had found a bargain basement cell shot clinic in Zurich where the weeklong treatment was a mere $5,000. Though the shots were prescribed once every five years, my father went every year. *If you know what's good for you, you'll be on the next plane to Zurich*, he would say to any chance acquaintance, even those who might not know where their next $2 for a chalk bet was coming from.

At thirty-four, I sought neither eternal life nor a new skin. I was trying to rescue my academic career. What I sought was enough financial help from my father to stay in a low-paying career and an expensive marriage.

My mother liked to say, *If you love what you do, you'll never work a day in your life*. But to make this wisdom work, Linda and I had to live within our means. I had completed my doctorate and started my teaching career. My salary at Le Moyne College in Syracuse had grown from $15,000 to $21,000 after three years of teaching. With two kids and expensive tastes, we weren't managing. Linda had many virtues and was becoming an accomplished, if uncommercial, portrait painter and watercolorist. But she lacked a willingness to negotiate limits.

I felt hemmed in, desperate to keep the profession I loved but couldn't afford if I stayed in the marriage. My continuing motivation was not to be crazy like my father. In my book, that meant staying married and not deserting my kids. Although I had not seen my father in six years, I found myself in Zurich, desperate for a small stipend that would enable me to maintain my life. Dad had the wherewithal. Would he have the generosity?

We converged on JFK International Airport for the transatlantic flight. As so often happened, Dad was content to pick up where we had left off, which meant forgetting (but not forgiving) the last time we quit speaking. This always left me with a sense of unfinished business. It doomed us to repeat the last disaster in some new form.

In Zurich, Dad opted for a trolley ride to the small hotel, the Vorderer Sterner, a long walk from the clinic. *Walking's good for you. You should walk three miles every day.* The tiny double room with two twin beds overlooked the noisy trolley substation. For luggage, Dad toted a woven plastic burlap oats sack, picked up from the track where lately he stabled his half-dozen Thoroughbred racehorses and where he had been sleeping in the tack room: *got to learn to rough it; it's good for you, son.*

As we unpacked, my father pulled out of his oats sack a worn plastic baggy full of Rolex watches. "Best watch in the world, completely waterproof, like an oyster."

"Coals to Newcastle?" I wondered to myself.

"Las Vegas," he knowingly explained, "the best place to pick up pawned Rolexes—all those gamblers needing a new stake to get back in the game. Would you like one?"

There were more than a dozen. Abashed, I chose the simplest, a stainless steel Rolex Oyster Perpetual. He pulled out a Datejust with a blue face and announced he would have the luminescence renewed while we were there. Later he decided that the newly luminescent watch was not to his liking and gave it to me.

Before the week was out, I had taken the fetal lamb shots and wandered the streets of Zurich, taking my lunch alone and feeling very literary at the James Joyce Pub. I made my case for my father's generosity. I came away from Zurich with two timepieces and no stipend. Linda was astonished at my new skin. It glowed.

In the end, it was not finances but fear that triggered my exit from teaching.

One year after the Zurich trip, I jumped at a position teaching at the University of New Orleans. I would make $20,000—I took a pay cut to come home—and yet I was still paid more than many more senior colleagues. UNO's English Department was deeply demoralized. We were required to teach brutalizing numbers of courses in facilities that were barely a step up from public secondary schools.

Teaching freshman English to students who came out of the New Orleans school system presented challenges for which I was not trained. I myself was a product of the New Orleans public schools, but during a different era and from the system's first and best magnet high school.

In my freshman English class, I had a student who wrote his papers in longhand, in block letters, without commas or periods. If he failed the exam at semester's end, he would not be allowed to continue at the university. Built like a fire plug, the student approached me about the importance of his passing grade, adding, "I was a Navy SEAL in the Vietnam War and they taught me how to tell who was on my side and who wasn't, and what to do about them." I knew the kind of men the SEALS attracted and the trauma of their duty in Vietnam.

"That sounds like a threat."

"You can take it any way you want."

The university dean removed him from my class, but soon after I noticed a hole in a window in my house. The two events were probably unrelated but I imagined the worst and feared for my family. While I felt a liberal's sympathy for my students, I had neither the training nor the talent needed to teach remedial English or provide clinical help. In sum, I didn't believe in the product that I was offering my students.

Ruth's Chris was, however, a product that I could believe in. More and more I was feeling an obligation to learn the business that I would one day in part own.

By the time I went off to American University in 1968, Mom had three restaurants, all in the New Orleans area. By the time I graduated, there were four, still local. By 1981, when Mom came to my Harvard graduate school commencement, there were seven restaurants, two of them franchises. By 1986, when I left teaching, there were fifteen restaurants in the system, six of them franchises.

When I returned to New Orleans in 1985, Mom asked me to join the corporate board. I taught that first year back, but not only was I growing tired of teaching four courses a semester and freshman English to students unprepared by the public school system, but also, the monthly Ruth's Chris board meetings began to worry me. The liquor flowed before business commenced and I watched the monthly scene: Mom surrounded by advisors who kowtowed to her but each with his own agenda. I found myself unable to trust that my mother was in good hands.

Ralph Giardina, then vice president of franchising, had always made clear his contempt for the teaching profession. A few years Mom's junior, Ralph had served in the military after graduating high school, young enough that the war ended before he shipped out. After the war, good with figures, he had risen through the ranks from bank teller to bank president. Ralph had been asking me, *When are you gonna quit that useless job and come into your mother's business?*

One night, as the end of my first year teaching at the University of New Orleans approached, I surprised him.

"How about now?"

Ralph's sizzling steak could be heard over his stunned silence.

CHAPTER THIRTEEN

RUTH'S CHRIS STEAK HOUSE

AFTER THE FIRE AT THE ORIGINAL RESTAURANT, RUTH HAD RE-CREATED her world in seven days and was back in business. But the original sales agreement said that if she moved, she couldn't call the new location Chris Steak House. Ever direct, Mom added her own name, and the flagship Ruth's Chris was born. Besides, she had grown to hate being called Chris or, worse, being taken for Chris's wife. Customers angling for a table on a packed night sometimes claimed that they *knew Ruth before she married Chris*.

Ruth's Chris Steak House. A mouthful and hard to say, but also an asset because once learned, it was hard to forget. One food critic announced it should be used as a sobriety test, a test many happy customers were likely to fail.

As business grew, Mom added more waitresses: Lou Dufresne (under five feet), Carol Held (Boston-Irish and called Yankee), brassy Theresa Arena, tiny Lois Oxman, Shirley Barlett, and Faye Pastrano.

Faye, a feisty redhead who cruised the floor, had once been married to flashy light-heavyweight champion Willie Pastrano who fought for the Mob. Lois—pronounced "Loyce"—unaccountably called everyone "Big Booby" or "Little Booby" and just as unaccountably got away with it. Theresa raised dogs on the side. Her daughter and granddaughter would later make careers as waitresses on Broad Street, too. Shirley was famous for her endless stream of jokes. "One customer," she quipped, "liked Pierre

13.1 Imperial Ruth.

martinis—so dry all he did was pee air." Once, when Louisiana governor Edwin Edwards came in with his entourage, Shirley eventually acceded to his appeal for a joke. Edwards was a well-known philanderer, famous for once declaring that the only way he could lose the next election was if he "was caught in bed with a dead woman or a live boy." Diabetic and rail-thin, Shirley came over with a doggie bag and asked him to place his hand inside. With the bag on the governor's hand, Shirley just stood there.

Finally, Edwards succumbed: "Well, what do you want me to do now?"

"See," she smirked, "it's just like I told them in the kitchen: once I got you in the sack you wouldn't know what to do." Sneaking peeks at the governor, who took it as homage, the Edwards entourage collapsed in guffaws.

Shirley got away with her fresh jokes. Ruth's Chris's success started with fresh, unfrozen steaks and fresh marketing—the "Home of *Serious* Steaks." Early on, Mom realized that she needed to educate the marketplace.

13.2 The Prime House temporarily becomes Chris Steak House.

Quarter- and half-page print ads explained why only 2 percent of the beef raised in America was good enough for Ruth's Chris customers. No less a personage than Arnie Morton, founder of Morton's Steak House, her chief competitor, once told me that "Ruth Fertel *created* the prime steak business"—this despite the fact that his father was selling steaks in the 1920s. She created *the market* for prime steaks, now a significant and ever-growing segment in the upscale restaurant market. All the red-meat scares seemed only to incite the carnivores. If they *were* going to eat less red meat—and many talked a better game than they ate—when they did, they wanted the best.

In the very early years, it was Lana Duke who convinced Mom that advertising could work for her. Lana started out in her early twenties selling ads in the local Catholic weekly the *Clarion Herald*, but aspired to start an ad company. She used Mom's restaurant as the springboard for Duke Unlimited.

Mom put her entire year's advertising budget in Lana's hands—about $20,000. Lana invested it all in making one TV commercial and broadcasting one flight of ads. This was an audacious strategy; Mom had been placing little ads here and there. Now she let Lana run with it. The copy for the first television ad read under a loudly sizzling center-cut, three-inch-high filet, "The Steak that Speaks for Itself." The sizzle was born.

Lana made my mother's hot plate the Ruth's Chris signature. It had been part of the original Chris Steak House—to put the platter on top of the broiler for a minute or so before plating the steak and serving it with butter and parsley. The butter bubbled a bit, and Lana pushed that to its logical conclusion, taking supersalesman Elmer Wheeler's 1930s adage to its literal conclusion: she sold Chris Steak House's *sizzle*, not its steak. In fact, the idea wasn't original to Lana. Sizzler Steak House was serving its choice steaks on a hot metal platter and their ads showed the sizzling steak. But now the image was coupled with a prime product and Lana knew how to milk it. The close-up of the sizzling steak in Lana's first TV ad made you salivate. And the customers trooped in the door. Not too much later, Lana worked out a deal with the Saints to play the spot at the Superdome on its big screens at quiet moments between quarters. As part of the deal, they turned the sound up to eleven. Years later, long after we'd quit running the ad, customers still trooped in after the game talking about how the sizzling ad had brought them in. Thank you, Dr. Pavlov.

As Mom broadened the marketplace for prime, her client base expanded, and the numbers started to work as economies of scale set in. Ruth's Chris also flipped the normal economic structures. Restaurant Biz 101: food costs in a fast-food restaurant run 40 percent and labor costs 20 percent. In a fine-dining restaurant, with expensive, trained chefs—chefs, not "steak turners"—and ever-changing menus, the reverse percentages apply. The genius of Ruth's Chris was to wed the food quality of fine dining with the economics of fast food. Despite her high prices, her well-marbled (and perfectly turned) piece of meat gave the impression of value. Mom used to say that she made "a buck a steak." Her real profit was in liquor and side orders.

Ruth's Chris also thrived on its exclusivity. Ever price sensitive, Mom kept steak prices as low as possible to gain market share. But the goal never was to be accessible to the multitudes. Let the multitudes eat at Sizzler and other *chains*. Ruth's Chris was a *family* of fine dining restaurants—a distinction we insisted on. Mom's goal was that Mr. Deep Pockets should eat prime steak often; those who could barely afford it would save up for special occasions. The goal was to make the sizzling steak "top of mind"— when Mr. Deep Pockets got hungry or when the less solvent were ready to splurge.

Yet Ruth's Chris was not exclusive in its bearing. Mr. Deep Pockets dined in his business clothes or casuals. In May, high school kids came in their tuxedos and gowns. Tourists and Chalmatians—those working-class folk from downriver in Chalmette—arrived in jeans, cutoffs, and tank tops. We tried to seat the cutoffs discreetly, not too close to Rex—the king of Carnival—or the bejeweled exes of ex-Rexes.

One momentous decision grew out of Mom's expansion in the marketplace, the decision to switch from dry-aged to wet-aged prime beef. In aging of any sort, but more so in dry-aging, natural enzymes in the beef break down the protein strings and connective tissue. In dry-aging the primal cut, short loin or rib loin, is hung or stored at thirty-six to forty-three degrees in fan-cooled cold storage for two to four weeks. Some aficionados hang it longer. Ruth's Chris called for twenty-one days, three weeks. Dry-aging tenderizes but also dehydrates and inevitably shrinks the beef, concentrating its flavor and, as most agree, its beefiness.

Dry-aging presents two problems. Not only are you paying for the cold storage but also for the shrinkage. What might have been a forty-pound loin arrives weighing thirty pounds, part of which you lose in cutting off the aging, an eighth or quarter inch of crust where the muscle that has been open to the air and has turned black, or, because of a quite benign mold which forms, white or even green. If, say, the prehung loin was worth $10 a pound or $400, now you are paying more per pound, $13.50 or $14.00, plus whatever the meat packer adds for the trouble and expense of storing meat in the proper conditions for three weeks.

Another problem involves a kind of loss besides shrinkage. Sometimes dry-aged meat "goes over," goes beyond beefy to gamey. Mom weekly lost a few steaks to such taint when customers turned up their noses. She never questioned the complaint, but just explained it was a function of *a little too much aging* and promised a replacement as quick as possible. The order would be conveyed, *steal a ribeye medium rare for table 81*. The danger was not just the write-off of a pound of steak, but perhaps of a customer who didn't buy her explanation and thought not just his steak, but the restaurant was tainted.

Sensitive to price point and to customers' consistent pleasure, wishing to expand and worried that meat packers wouldn't have the space to dry-age the amount of meat her growing empire needed, Mom made the momentous decision to switch to wet-aged. Wet-aged beef is Cryovaced, placed under vacuum in plastic. Hugh Fearnley-Whittingstall, in his magisterial *The River Cottage Meat Book*, speaks of "the dreaded vac-pack favored by the supermarkets." In wet-aging, some measure of the enzyme action takes place. Taste and tenderness improve somewhat. Shrinkage and the likelihood of gaminess is much diminished.

I wasn't around when this decision was made, but I'm sure that, given my mother's commitment to quality, she agonized over it. As always decisive, however, she rarely looked back except when, every once in a while, she or I would be served a strip or ribeye with the old flavor. We'd always offer a knowing look when we said, *taste this, it's like the old days.* We'd eat it as if we'd been returned to paradise.

Even slightly diminished by wet-aging, the product was exceptional. I was proud to be even peripherally part of it all. But not all her deals were smooth sailing.

In 1975, despite a decade of notable restaurant success, Mom was facing personal bankruptcy. A real estate deal had gone south. Mom needed to hide her assets. She put 80 percent of her corporation in trust, naming Jerry and me as beneficiaries, and retained 20 percent. She put her banker and friend Jim Queyrouze in nominal control of the trust, even though he had brought her into the failing real estate deal; the other trustee was her lawyer Phil Brooks, who had drawn up the deal.

The trust was a highly successful act of estate planning. Mom paid $200,000 in gift tax while estate tax on the 80 percent put in trust was completely avoided. Like so many of her successes, it was a happy accident. But this decision would later shape the course of our lives. The Ruth's Chris empire was in my name and Jerry's, but it was not ours. The trust was my mother's, to do with as she wished. Not by law, but that hardly mattered.

The real estate problem successfully dodged, the business thrived. By the late 1970s, Mom had four restaurants in New Orleans alone. Other locations followed, continuing the oil patch connection in Lafayette, Baton Rouge, and Houston.

As the restaurants expanded in New Orleans, Mom promoted her waitresses and other female friends to run them. Ruth's college roommate Gloria, not her brother, Sig, shared half-ownership in Chris II across the river in Gretna. Betty ran "Vets" on Veterans Highway in Fat City, a booming area of Metairie—until she was caught with her hand in the till. When Mom reopened four blocks up at Broad and Orleans after the fire, Myrtle ran the restored original at Broad and Ursuline. Upon Myrtle's death, Doris took over until her hand, too, was caught in the till. She spent some years in the wilderness and then was forgiven.

Ruth trusted her girls. And didn't. She kept a tight rein on bills, inventory, and receipts. The manager opened and closed, counted her bank and made her deposits, hired and fired front- and back-house staff, and ordered all inventory except the meat. Mom ordered the meat, a biweekly ritual. Steaks were counted as they were cut and counts were checked against steaks sold. Counts were taken before and between shifts. A lot of money was tied up in that meat, and it had a habit of *growing legs*, as she'd say, *and walking out the back door.*

When Mom had to open up the new Broad Street in the Prime House after the fire, word got around that she had taken the broilers with her. That explained the consistency: *the taste is all in those stoves. They're seasoned from years of use. That's what makes the steaks so good.* In fact, like the restaurant's simple menu, the stoves were easily duplicated. Mom worked with Montague Stoves to increase the heat output of their hottest broiler. After a few days the new stoves were well-seasoned. As she expanded further, the talk was about how Ruth could never repeat the original's quality: *She's going to ruin it. It'll never be the same.* They came to check—and stayed.

When she moved to the Prime House after the fire, the decision was made never to duplicate the original look and ambience. Each restaurant would have its own character. The owner of the Houston franchise near the Galleria decorated his restaurant throughout with oil company logos. A sign above his dining room door read, "The worst oil field trash in the world has passed through these doors." Loving to see themselves as veterans of the wildcat drilling days, the oilmen flocked in. Around the country customers got used to their local Ruth's Chris. Many believed theirs was the original and were surprised to hear of the New Orleans connection. We had no desire to disabuse the sense of ownership that kept customers coming back to *their* clubhouse.

Years later, when renovations were needed in the new flagship on Broad and Orleans, customers inveighed against the very idea that Ruth would change anything. The Empress of <u>Serious</u> Steaks never closed to renovate; she was <u>serious</u> about not losing a day's receipts. The work was done after the dinner service, through the night, the restaurant put back together sometimes just moments before the front doors opened for lunch. Despite customers' anxieties and anger, sales soared during construction: they came even more often to see the latest step in the renovation. Jim's bank held their annual Christmas dinner for seventy-five of his best customers one year when the front wall of the restaurant temporarily consisted of a sheet of plastic. A cold snap gripped the city. People warmed their hands above their sizzling steak plates. Mom's determination was on everyone's lips.

The renovations completed, people rejoiced in their new luxurious home away from home. Instead of linoleum, there were carpets. Instead of board-and-batten, dark redwood, now lighter cypress wainscoting and original local artwork graced the walls. Instead of acoustic tile, there were cypress-coffered ceilings. Leather booths with blue velvet curtains paid homage to the infamous green-curtained booths. Mom spared no expense. Acid-etched windows with double, reversed Rs that could be seen from either side welcomed you in the foyer.

Customers joked that the double R meant "Ruth got you coming and going," expressing their discomfort about how big their monthly house accounts could grow. Others wondered if it stood for *Ruth and Ralph* and some added, *what does she see in that guy?*

I was proud of what Mom was creating but frightened at the team she had chosen. Jim Queyrouze, Philip Schoen Brooks, and Ralph Giardina lunched every day at the original Chris and stayed afterwards to play gin rummy. They became her banker and lawyer and future CEO, all members of her corporate board. Curiously, the key performance criterion seemed to be their willingness to while away long afternoons absent from banking jobs and law practices.

Ralph Giardina had left his bank presidency under a cloud. Rumor had it that he floated unsecured loans to his bookie. The FDIC frowned on such commerce and, the story went, had offered him a choice between prosecution and retirement from banking. He then earned his only credential in the food business. Mom staked him in a once-Mafia-owned restaurant across Lake Pontchartrain. Within a year he had driven it into the ground and closed the doors. The one sweet thing to come out of that sour deal was the heavenly, garlicky remoulade dressing that Ralph brought back with him. It is still a Ruth's Chris signature.

As Earner often said, Mom had a weakness for Ralph. Some believed they had been lovers for a short time. It might explain a lot. Round of face and paunch, favoring polyester shirts and jackets, Ralph was always ready with a story or joke to smooth the way. He was such a dead ringer for that great Boston Celtics general manager Red Auerbach that he was often mistaken for him in airports. Even at five foot ten, Auerbach had a couple inches on Ralph. But he had some of Auerbach's charm and Mom was his best audience. After he failed in the Northshore restaurant, Ralph wanted to try his hand at training horses. Mom bought the horses and financed his failure as a trainer.

Finally she brought him into the restaurant. One afternoon Mom couldn't resolve a few cents discrepancy in the daily restaurant sales. It was keeping them from their daily gin game. *Ralph, if you find those thirty-two cents, I'll hire you.* Child's play for the former bank teller turned bank president turned railbird. Ralph was her new manager on Broad Street.

Philip Schoen Brooks, Mom's lawyer and chief advisor, was white-shoe Uptown through and through. Except for being indicted along with Governor Edwin Edwards on Racketeer Influenced and Corrupt Organizations Act (RICO) charges in a nursing home federal corruption case (both he and the governor were acquitted), his principal accomplishment was that his family once owned Schoen Funeral Home, a landmark on Canal Street beloved for its Spanish Colonial architecture and its elaborate display of Christmas lights that drew revelers from across the city. He also served as city attorney for a period, a political appointment.

Jim Queyrouze, Mom's banker, a dark Frenchman, was proud that an ancestor had served Napoleon on Elba and received a land grant in Erwinville near Baton Rouge. Like Phil, Jim had faced RICO charges (he, too, was acquitted) for conspiring in an insurance fraud case with state senator Michael O'Keefe (who, found guilty, was sent to his own Elba). The rumors about Jim's Mob connections were so strong that, discussing the career of Frances Pecora, the *Times-Picayune* tried to show that *she* must be mobbed up *because Jim Queyrouze was among her known associates.* Pecora's husband, Nofio, was Carlos Marcello's number two. He ran Marcello's headquarters, The Town and Country Motel on Airline Highway. The phone call Nofio Pecora received from Jack Ruby just before he killed Oswald was part of the evidence that the murder was a Mafia hit. Rough company in her own right, Frances Pecora did two and a half years for conspiring to kill a traffic judge who had jailed her son for drunk driving. She spent long boisterously drunken afternoons on Broad Street with refugees from the casting agency. So, it was stunning to see the local paper of record treat Jim as a clinching piece of evidence, rather than the other way around— Frances Pecora wasn't Mobbed up, she *was* the Mob, or what was left of it.

13.3 Jim Queyrouze.

Mom's response was not denial but concern for Jim's wife: "Gayle must feel awful."

What are the chances both men Mom chose as trustees would face RICO charges?

Perhaps the Mob connections help explain the conversation I had with Jim when, newly returned to New Orleans, I went to see him at his Merchants Bank on Williams Boulevard in Kenner where Mom was board member and part owner. After wondering aloud *when was I going to leave teaching to come help my mother*, he explained that his bank *didn't have the cheapest mortgage rates but that you could count on his Loyalty.* In his mouth the word seemed laden with meaning. I half expected to hear next about Our Thing—*La Cosa Nostra.*

I didn't trust what these men were doing for, with, and to my mother. Outwardly the epitome of normality—bankers and lawyers—they were the latest in a long line of disappointing father figures. Oddly, though, they were also my counterparts. They, too, were looking to be washed in Mom's charisma. They, too, were trying to make their way up the same dry stream, with little in the way of a paddle, and little in the way of water to float their boats. They, too, were destined to go home thirsty.

Not that they weren't charming in their own way.

Las Vegas, 1974: my future wife, Linda, and I came down from graduate school in Oregon to meet Mom and her growing entourage. In Las Vegas for a gin tournament, she spent her nights playing high stakes baccarat and craps. *Sleep? Who needs it?*

We stayed at the Dunes where, thanks to her New Orleans bookie, everything was on the house for Mom and her group. Linda and I had been living on $600 a month. Now we could order breakfasts of eggs and whitefish or sturgeon. I was going through a short country phase—Willie and Waylon and the outlaws sang to me deeply—and I made a special trip downtown to hear Waylon on a small stage on the Golden Nugget casino floor. He was just feet away.

But the real show—from an outlaw in her own way—was Mom at the high-stakes tables, her purse crammed with $100 bills skimmed, tax-free, from the receipts on Broad Street. In craps, Mom's method was to wait it out, betting steadily, winning a hand now and then, doubling that win, then losing it back. The goal was to stick around until Lady Luck—in whom she believed—turned her way. When the luck turned, she could win back all her losses and plenty more. In craps there were so many possible simultaneous bets that when the luck turned she'd be rolling in green.

Over the course of her lifetime, no doubt she lost more than she won. But once, she had to be escorted to her plane by two armed guards—she was playing with tax-free cash, so had to take her winnings in cash to leave no trace. For that thrill, she was willing to lose a few times.

Part of the fun was the entourage. Mom put up Ralph's stake: they were "in cow" and would share his winnings, she alone suffering his losses. Mom liked him around and was willing to pay for the company. Earner hinted more than once that she paid his gambling debts. In return, he greased the skids, always ready with a joke, a snide remark, or a $20 bill precisely placed when it was dinnertime. The tab was always on her.

Each player had a different way with the dice. Ralph showed a banker's precision, setting the dice on the numbers he needed, blowing on his fingers then rubbing them on the felt. He then lofted the dice so they bounced just before the far wall, then tumbled softly back. Mom nonchalantly grabbed the dice and threw. *Gimme that 5!*

Mom and her pals liked a boisterous table where players jeered and cheered amongst themselves till a crowd gathered. *Make that hard 8 for me, baaaaby!* They couldn't stand an uppity table too cool to act up. When a number was made after a long run, the table broke into loud cheers. *At-taboy! You ma man!* If a player made a series of successful numbers, he was toasted and feted: *You da best!* If he lost, everyone visibly sank: *Awwww!* But they took their lumps. After a long night, win or lose, they tossed around their highest boast: *we're such degenerates!*

I hung around, betting as small as the table allowed, just to witness all this. I was at their side long enough that even I earned their mark of approval: *Ran, you're a degenerate, too! I never woulda guessed.*

At the baccarat tables, the large, uniquely rectangular chips came in dominations starting at $100, marching up to $5,000 and $10,000. Mom glowed behind her stacks of gleaming rectangles, pushing them forward and raking them back with glee. The stakes were too high for me. I just sat watching and enjoying the exquisite beauty of the shills the casino brought to the table so players wouldn't play alone. True pros, seeing I was no player in any sense of the term, they never met my eye. Mom cried *banco!* with gusto when the dealer's shoe came before her and she symbolically became the dealer. The croupier was usually Marcel Taylor, a tall, charming Chalmatian with a chewy accent that out-Y'ated the Y'ats back home. He would later own two Ruth's Chris franchises, in Las Vegas and Denver. Even if Mom lost at baccarat, she was laying the foundation for her monthly 4 percent franchise fee for years to come.

The restaurants multiplied. Mom's table-desk in the Broad Street dining room couldn't support all the work, so bookkeepers were added to the mix. Her first, Dotty Perez, needed the work because her husband was doing a jolt for bookmaking. She had *plenty* experience with numbers. Mom set up a barebones office in a former storeroom, out of sight of customers. Several metal desks were arranged into one big rectangle, with the bookkeepers and Mom facing one another. Simple plywood shelving held years of paperwork. But Mom still kept a desk out front with her calculator at the ready and she made a point of working there during busy hours. Customers loved to see her looking up over her half-frame glasses balanced on the tip of her nose. They enjoyed displaying their juice when she nodded their way or the extra juice if she visited their table.

Mom was so busy with the paperwork generated by her swelling empire that food and service began to slide. Ralph's management style, honed in his banking days, did little to improve things. He issued edicts from his inner sanctum for the girls on the front lines to follow. This put their teeth on edge. They had long been running the restaurants largely on their own. Besides, Mom joked that Ralph was *the last person to troubleshoot a kitchen since he enjoyed everything he put in his mouth.* To calm the waters, Mom eventually promoted him to vice president of franchising. That got him out of their hair and into the dining room, where he wined and dined prospective franchisees.

As more executives joined the business, it was time to expand the corporate office. A new second floor was built above the Broad Street kitchen, camelback style. In the new offices, my mother's conservative tastes gave way to Ralph's notion of splendor. He decreed mahogany desks, woodwork stained a too-red oxblood, wall coverings blood red. *I feel like I'm in the cool red center of a rare filet,* Mom joked and decreed a coat of slate blue paint. Ralph and Dan Earles, the new vice president for operations, located their offices behind heavy doors. Ever unpretentious and determined to be in the thick of things, Mom occupied the office center, an open space without walls or doors. The bookkeepers' and secretaries' waist-high partitioned cubicles surrounded her, in easy reach of her voice.

New Orleans is a city of aristocracies, both competing and intertwined. The first of these, the Creole aristocracy, descend from the French and Spanish colonial settlers—though their ancestors may have been transported convicts. Then after the Louisiana Purchase came the Anglos, whom the Creoles called Kaintucks wherever they hailed from. Despised by the Creoles for their ruthless business acumen, the Kaintucks created modern Mardi Gras in 1857 to answer the Creoles' nativist claim with a display of their newly minted royalty, trying to beat the Creoles at their own aristocratic game. Meanwhile, in the *plaçage* system of common-law marriages, the mixed race offspring of the Creole planters became a parallel aristocracy also called Creole, and, eventually, largely usurping the name. Finally came that special, culinary aristocracy whose stature came not from bloodlines but from sweat. Their power to feed and water made the other aristocrats forget, at least while they were dining, their imagined superiority. All bowed, when hungry and thirsty, to the three queens of New Orleans cuisine: Ella Brennan of Commander's Palace, Leah Chase of Dooky Chase's, and Ruth Fertel of Ruth's Chris, my mother. Only these three women, earthy and hard-working, seemed not to care hardly a whit for such pretense. Which increased their power.

You need to talk to Miz Ruth? Well, here she is.

People were pounding on the door to open a Ruth's Chris franchise. Old friends and customers begged for franchises in Dallas, Las Vegas, Philadelphia, New York, Los Angeles, and Scottsdale. Mickey Rooney, in town for a run at the Saenger Theater, became a regular and suggested that Ruth sell him a franchise. *I can see it now*, he proclaimed rising from their dinner table, gesturing their names into lights:

MICKEY ROONEY'S CHRIS STEAK HOUSE!

That ended the discussion. They had almost been an item.

Now, in part so Mom could avoid such personal confrontations, it fell to Ralph Giardina to anoint the happy few, many of them his old friends with little restaurant experience. Leona Clade had been a bank teller for Ralph. An exception to the amateur rule, after her banking days she owned a restaurant, the Black Orchid, the Mafia were said to favor. Ralph sold her the rights to Dallas. Marsha Brown had been Ralph's secretary at the bank and then at Ruth's Chris. She took Ruth's Chris to Broad Street in Philadelphia. Marcel Taylor was the Chalmette boy who had done well as their favorite croupier in Vegas. David Cory, born Corigiano, of New Jersey, Ralph's *paisan'*, got Weehawken right before David's well-insured shipboard restaurant in the Hackensack River mysteriously sank. Only the wine cellar could be saved. Ralph threw in Manhattan for a song. That cost us plenty millions to buy back later. David now lives splendidly on the banks of the Arno in Florence. Those thirty-two cents Ralph saved cost Mom millions.

Ralph's notion of deep marketing research was to declare that, if a city had an NFL team, that was good enough for Ruth's Chris. Such marketing metrics as a city's "propensity to dine out" were Greek to him. At $10,000 each—his cut from the $35,000 franchise fee—Ralph was more interested in selling franchises than in vetting and guiding them to success. Annual meetings of the franchisees became obstreperous. Mom had a serious illness before one such meeting; the franchisees announced in all seriousness that they needed a guarantee Mom wouldn't die and leave Ralph in charge.

Lana Duke meanwhile despaired that the lag in professionalism our growth spurt created would chase away new customers her advertising brought in. Her job was to make Ruth's Chris "top of mind"—the first thing that came to mind when you got hungry. But if lousy food and service came to mind, Mom's advertising dollars would be wasted. In 1986, Lana made the case for hiring Dan Earles as vice president of operations to strengthen the company and its ability to expand. Dan brought an accountant's mind to the task, but his skills had been honed on the fine grit wheel of Ella Brennan's restaurant empire across town. The Brennan family had established a classic French Quarter restaurant and then split in two, Ella taking her clan over to Commander's Palace in the 1970s and creating a separate restaurant empire.

The New Orleans culinary scene suffered from bad press in the 1980s, unfairly described by John Mariani as "a thousand restaurants, ten recipes," a list that began with gumbo and ended with bread pudding. (Our menus are no more repetitive than French bistro menus, Tom Fitzmorris points out.) Ella had begun to change all that, creating the concept of the *new* New Orleans cuisine: the best local ingredients in updated and supercharged Creole recipes (e.g., Commander's white chocolate bread pudding soufflé with warm whisky cream poured on at the table as your mouth waters). With Chef Paul Prudhomme at her kitchen's helm, Ella garnered raves in the national press and added luster to New Orleans's reputation as a great food city. When Chef Paul left to open K-Paul's, she discovered Emeril Lagasse, who took his place.

Dan brought Ella's rigorous standards to the Ruth's Chris table, at each of her sixteen restaurants. First he wrote new manuals to systematize every aspect of the business company-wide. Then he "fixed" the flagship, installing his new systems and firing longtime workers. Staff—front house and back—cringed when Dan showed up. As did the managers. That reaction was just what he wanted. Dan pored over profit-and-loss statements, noting any line that didn't meet targets he'd set, ignoring the many goals met. His main role was to hover, looking for mistakes.

Dan once described my mother as a "great gut-player." Who would not be charmed seeing Ruth cut a wiseacre meatpacker off at the knees? Twice a week, Mom ordered all the meat for each of her restaurants, and she knew that the best prime beef was secured by means of constant vigilance. A great steak is all about fat cover—the layer of fat on the outside of the loin—and marbling, the fat laced through the muscle itself. Fat cover is an index of the degree of marbling. The meatpacker in the Chicago slaughterhouses had to be vigilant to pull the best lots, and Mom had to be vigilant to ensure that his best lots came to her, not her competitors. Mom's toughness got her customers the most tender, flavorful steak on the planet.

Chicago meat purveyors are a tough lot themselves, and one of them had gotten on Mom's bad side. Carl Ruprecht was a character with street savvy and a mouth to match. He had come to town to talk his way back into the Ruth's Chris account after some years in the wilderness. Before meeting with Ruth, he had to jump through some hoops with Dan.

Dan invited me to sit in. In his Chicago Loop accent, spoken from the side of his mouth, the meat man defended himself, choosing to defer to me. "Yer mudder got mad at me when I slipped. I took my eye off the ball. I was diddling the secretary. I know. I know. But now I've married her and I can do the job. The meat's gonna be right from now on."

Dan and I were eating this corn up when my mother walked in. She listened for a couple of moments, then cut him short. "You screwed up once, you'll screw up again."

Gut player? Her friend Joe Segreto, an associate of the Marcellos, once remarked, "Yer mother had balls like zeppolas." I heard *zeppelins* at first but the St. Joseph Day donuts in Greenwich Village street fairs offered image enough. With friends like the ones she surrounded herself with, zeppolas is exactly what she needed.

Mom shared a large and well-appointed houseboat with Jim Queyrouze. Using it to go hunting and fishing out of Happy Jack Marina where they kept a fishing camp, they called it *Floating Prime*. After a year or so, I had to point out the pun. Mom saw it as a joke about banking's "prime rate." She didn't also hear "prime beef" in the name. Metaphor was not her forte.

One day, a knock came at her door behind the restaurant.

"Do you own a thirty-four-foot houseboat named *Floating Prime*?" The man in the dark suit and tie showed Mom his federal ID. He stood at the door of her house behind the restaurant.

"Yes. No. I mean I used to. I sold it yesterday. The banker Jim Queyrouze co-owned it with me." Mom was wearing her ratty pink housecoat.

"You sold it yesterday?"

"I did."

"Do you have a bill of sale?"

"I can tell you how much. The gentleman paid me $48,000. Cash."

"Miz Ruth." The man paused. "You thought that was normal—$48,000 cash?"

"Well," my mother said, "green is green. It was okay with me."

"Ma'am, are you aware that your houseboat was employed yesterday evening to run drugs up through Barataria Bay? They gave us quite a run for it. That houseboat is fast."

"It sure is. It does forty-two knots. We used it for duck hunting, and when the duck are flying you don't want to spend all day getting to the blinds. And no, I didn't know what they were going to use it for. None of my business."

"You know, Miz Ruth, we could confiscate that $48,000 cash."

"You could?"

"But we won't. But, please, ma'am, be more careful who you deal with...."

"And tell me, Miz Ruth, are your steaks as good as they say...."

CHAPTER FOURTEEN

CORPORATE AND OTHER CARNIVORES

LEAVING MY ACADEMIC NICHE FOR RUTH'S CHRIS IN THE SUMMER OF 1986, I was put to work as assistant manager. At Lana Duke's suggestion I was given an inflated title, vice president of operations. Lana placed a piece in the *Times-Picayune* business section trumpeting my entrance into the family business. It was impolitic. For training I was put in the hands of Dan Earles, who had been hired just a few months before, also as vice president of operations. As a family member, I had listened to and supported Lana, Mom's advertising and PR guru, as she made the case for his hiring; as a board member, I had participated in the discussion that finalized it. Now, the VP ops role was crowded, at least in name. Dan himself was not promoted nor his title changed. I would report to him. No one seemed to notice the conflict it set up.

Dan showed me the front- and back-house operations and what my daily routine should be. His training was largely anecdotal, stories in which he cast himself as hero, always delivered with a patronizing smirk. According to Dan, Ruth's Chris was an unsophisticated mom-and-pop operation that he was transforming into a professional fine dining establishment. He loved to tell the story about the time he was walking through the Commander's Palace pantry (where salads were made). A tiny Vietnamese woman, a hard worker, approached him.

"'Salad station too high. Salad station too high.'"

"Well, okay," he told her, "we'll get a taller salad girl."

"Never heard again about that problem," he boasted.

14.1 Randy enters the fray.

He'd also boast about the money and goods he'd cadged during the Vietnam War running a PX in Khe Sanh. One of our more costly blunders in the war where the NVA regulars had the 9th Marines besieged for several months, a feint to set up the disastrous Tet Offensive, Khe Sanh was a lucrative affair for Sergeant Earles. His characteristic gesture, when he was asked to consider a new idea or something important to you, was to lift his open palms and shrug his shoulders. It was a kind of "what, me worry?" without the Alfred E. Newman smile. Smiling was not in Dan's vocabulary. When he hovered in the dining room, customers wondered aloud who that dour, hard-faced guy was.

Dan was a counterpart to Jerry. They shared the cynicism and distrust of the world that they'd brought back from Vietnam. Both had something dark and secretive around the eyes. But Dan was effective in what he set out to do, not the fall guy like the ever-generous Jerry could be to his friends. Dan seemed to have no friends and he wasn't generous. He was a ruthless version of Jerry, a similarity that perhaps gave Dan power over Ruth.

For training, Dan gave me a full half-hour of his restaurant expertise. Then he cut me loose to flounder about on my own.

Dan loved to manage by displays of power, and he expected me to model myself on him. The luckiest day of his life, he said, was when Lillian, working sides—the station for side orders—refused to stop smoking on the line and walked out and up to Mom's office. Lillian was the common-law wife to Vontel and had outlasted him at Ruth's Chris. Lillian's demeanor was cool and her pace a tad nonchalant. Her Lyonnaise potatoes were legendary. Heavy-lidded, Lillian rarely ashed her cigarette, and it sometimes drooped ominously above her cast-iron skillet. The running joke, at which Lillian herself guffawed with her raucous laugh, was that her cigarette ash was what made her Lyonnaise so ambrosial. Mom was herself a lifelong smoker and had set the tone in the kitchen; everyone smoked until Dan laid down the law. Everyone thought he would cave in and let Lillian have her smokes, or wondered if Mom would allow her termination. Proving them wrong was just the power play Dan was seeking. Mom supported him. Lillian, who had been with us since 1965, was out. Broilers could be duplicated, but not Lillian.

I once overheard my mother say over the phone, "I think I'm getting screwed, and at least I like to get kissed when I get screwed." There would be no kissing during my tenure at Ruth's Chris. Always colorful, she once echoed a song from long ago: "hey grease monkey, get ready for a long slide." It would indeed be a long slide.

I was faced with performing managerial jujitsu, teaching my staff as I learned myself what both they and I needed to know. Any slip and I felt I might be down for the count. Two weeks into my job, Dan called me into a meeting and announced, "Randy, you don't have the character for the restaurant business."

He had a point. I am quickly bored by repetition, and the restaurant business is nothing if not repetitious. I loved to learn and needed *to understand*, not just by rote *to do*. As a teacher, I wanted to nurture, not bully. And I had a temper, especially when frustrated. Given so little instruction about how to make things work, I was often frustrated. "Dan," I came back at him, "if that remark is the way you treat people who work under you, one day we're going to have a problem."

Dan danced that misstep directly upstairs. From that day forward, Randy was *the guy with an authority problem*.

14.2 Ruth and Ralph in high cotton.

Still, Ruth's Chris was in my blood. I loved our commitment to quality; I loved the buzz and sexiness. Ruth's Chris was the place to be. I cared about the workers, many of them my surrogate mothers, sisters, and brothers. And nothing made me feel better than a fat and happy customer. I was good at catering to the Uptown crowd whose many demands for special attention drove us nuts on Sunday evenings. I had grown up with many of them, or their children. Customers liked having a Fertel serving them. Ralph liked to tell the story of overhearing a patron say, "You know why Ruth's Chris is so good? There's a Fertel in every restaurant." As the number of restaurants grew—entirely his doing, in his telling—Ralph had more and more trouble keeping the bitterness out of his laugh as he delivered the punch line.

After much trial and error, I developed my own philosophy of management: I worked for my staff. It was *my* job to make sure they could do *their* job.

Salesmanship was one key to improving the bottom line. For example, wine sales were one way to upgrade the quality of the dining experience *and* the bottom line. Having had my share of five franc Côte du Rhone and Beaujolais in Paris, I had a head start on the waitstaff. And since Ruth's

Chris was one of the more productive outlets for red wine—a big steak loves a big red wine—our wine merchants were happy to bring me samples. I proceeded to teach myself and the waitresses about the varietals, starting with California: merlot, pinot noir, and cabernet. The girls enjoyed them and didn't mind beginning the evening service with a bit of a buzz. They sold the hell out of merlot, which they came to love. One wine purveyor offered us a special on 1985 Beaucastel, which we were able to sell cases of at $5 a glass. I wish I had a case of it now.

The real key was convincing our waitresses to sell, not just take orders. But they mustn't oversell. We served potatoes and vegetables family style in generous portions; it was important to warn people not to over order. A table for four didn't need two Lyonnaise, even if they were Lillian's. On the other hand, appetizers, desserts, drinks, and coffee would add to their dining experience and our totals. Since servers earned increased gratuities from these add-ons, it would be a win-win all around.

Disdaining the mom-and-pop order pads the waitresses had always used, Dan put in a computer system. I used it to keep track of sales by customer, category, and server. We put in some contests: highest wine sales, most desserts. I bought elegant silver asparagus pins from a *New Yorker* ad and offered them as prizes for the most side orders per customer. The girls immediately dubbed it the "Silver Penis" for its shape and wore it proudly.

Tracking sales helped convey to the staff that they were sales personnel, not just servers. Suddenly Sally, our dizziest server, surged ahead. She'd been letting the other servers carry her on the floor and in the tip pool for fifteen years. Now that she was focused, her individual check averages rose from $35 to $40. At three hundred covers daily, that added up to an additional $36,000 in the till monthly, and an extra $7,000 for the servers to split.

Which was timely since the New Orleans economy, in the mid-1980s, suffered from the downturn in the oil industry. There was talk of restaurants *you could shoot a cannon through and not hit a customer.* But Ruth's Chris was one of the few safe havens: customers trusted they wouldn't find an empty and melancholy dining room. Restaurants were closing and we were thriving. After all, there *was* a Fertel in the kitchen and it was the flagship's kitchen right next door to corporate headquarters. Some of the staff, back- and front-house, had been with us twenty years. They were dedicated to my mother and, the truth is, they saw that I was between a rock and a hard place. They helped me improve the food and service. They carried me.

I didn't at first know the recipes but I knew what they should taste like. For example, the julienne potatoes, one of our biggest sellers, were not right: soggy instead of crispy and brown. Made from scratch, the fresh-cut potatoes were first blanched in 250-degree oil, then switched over to 350-degree grease. Following Dan's advice, we experimented, changing the grease more often, trying potatoes with less water content or less sugar. No change. They just weren't right.

One day, musing about my days in Paris and a *stek-frites* place near the Sorbonne where I studied, I suddenly remembered that the *stek-frites* lady— a blonde and earthy Parisian with a quick and surly mouth—always pre-blanched her *frites*. Not right before the hot grease, but earlier that morning. They had a chance to cool before hitting the hot grease. After that Proustian moment, the fries on Broad Street were perfect—crispy and golden.

Some challenges went beyond the food. Maple was the broiler cook at lunchtime. She was heavy in body and slow in her ways. Beside her worked Diane, as quick as Maple was slow. It was my job to ensure their stations were prepped and that, when we opened, food flowed in a timely fashion from the kitchen. Maple readied the mushrooms stuffed with crabmeat and prepared the potato, broccoli, and cauliflower gratins, mixing vegetables with béchamel sauce and spooning them into dark green ramekins. After being heated till they bubbled on the flat top above the broiler, the ramekins were topped by a slab of sharp cheddar and placed under the broiler to bubble and brown. Diane prepared all the other potatoes, slicing and preblanching the steak fries, juliennes, cottage fries, and shoestrings, sautéing the Lyonnaise, steaming the "baked" potatoes (our secret to our much-prized baked potato). She prepped Uncle Martin's creamed spinach in double batches, its "cream" made of pounds of butter, flour by the cup, and quarts of half and half.

Maple did everything at one pace—slow—and sometimes forgot to prep an item. If I commented, her retorts were sharp. One lunchtime, after many such back-and-forths, I watched from across the kitchen as her first order for stuffed mushrooms came in. She looked in the reach-in: no mushrooms. She shrugged her shoulders and told the waitress, "Eighty-six the mushrooms."

I fired her that afternoon, my hardest moment as a manager. Maple had been with us for two decades. For once, Mom backed me up. Maple moved over to Crescent City Steak House, a much smaller operation. Once a competitor, they hadn't given us a run for the money in decades. I was relieved that Maple found a place where she could keep up with the level of business.

Replacing Maple, I was able to achieve one goal Dan set: to get lunch customers in and out in one hour or less if they wanted. (Of course some spent the day.) When the ticket hit the line, the first course was on the table in fifteen minutes at lunch, twenty minutes at dinner. We started doing more than 100 covers a day at lunch, sometimes 150. Meeting Dan's goal was ignored. I was second-guessed almost every time Dan or Ralph or even Mom walked down the stairs from the corporate headquarters on their way to lunch where I could have them back at their desk within the hour.

At the end of each shift, the servers usually would "marry"—combine— the half-empty Heinz ketchup bottles. (We chuckled when customers underscored their sophistication by asking for ketchup *for the fried potatoes*.) To save on cost and labor, I purchased a Heinz dispenser for refilling them. Walking through the kitchen on her way to lunch, Mom ripped the new dispenser off the pantry wall without a word and, before a half dozen employees, tossed it in the trash.

And it's me that has an authority problem, I thought to myself.

I did have some successes. I counted Troy among them.

A mountain of a man in his early thirties, Troy showed up unannounced for a job interview. "I worked for Miz Gloria at your mother's place across the river, Ruth's Chris II. I promised her I wouldn't leave to work here while she was still open. But she's closed now."

Mom's best friend since college, Gloria Dallas was taller than Ruth and more outgoing. When Mom switched to the bouffant in the early sixties, Gloria's hair followed. She had a chewy New Orleans accent, I'm not sure from which neighborhood. When Mom came to visit me in Paris in 1971, she brought Gloria along and we careened around the city for a few days. They stayed at the Hilton on the Seine near the Eiffel Tower. One night Gloria was in a huff.

"That cabbie knew where I wanted to go. 'Eiffel Tower. Eiffel Tower,' I kept saying. He knew. These Parisians!"

"But Gloria," I tempered, "Eiffel Tower is as foreign to his ear as *La Tour Eiffel* is to yours, as far as his *Chartres* is from our Chart-ers Street in the French Quarter. If a Frenchmen tried to get from *la rue Borgogne* (what you'd call, BurGUNdy) to *la rue Chartres*, his pirogue would get nowhere."

"I don't care how they say Chart-ers. He knew where I wanted to go."

When Ralph came on, suddenly Gloria could do nothing, let alone pronounce a single syllable, right. *That man be jealous*, Earner would stir the pot in my hearing. *He don't want nobody close to your momma. He can't get rid of Lana, but he gonna get rid of Gloria.* Lana, who had by then ingratiated herself into being not just the Ruth's Chris advertising agency but Mom's new best friend, sided with Ralph. Before long, Gloria was made an offer. She declined. She bought Ruth's share and hung out a new sign, Dallas Steak House. Gloria was exiled from Mom's world, and her restaurant did not survive without the Ruth's Chris marquee. Mom and Gloria never spoke again, which visibly pained Mom but she wasn't going to swallow her pride. With Gloria's exit, a part of my mother that I loved, earthy and sassy, left, too. Ralph and Lana seemed to become Ruth's surrogate family, which was just fine with them.

Now, Troy told me he had always had two dreams. The first was to play NFL football, but "I got hit by a car and the doctors botched my knee." He gestured toward his bowed left knee. "I walk crooked but I work fast. My other dream is to work for Ruth Fertel." I hired him on the spot to replace Maple. No one prepped or cooked more steadily and efficiently.

But one day Ralph walked through the kitchen on his way from the office to a lunch meeting. He noticed Troy's crooked leg and limp. "Randy, we have potential franchisees coming through this kitchen, and I can't afford for them to see Troy. He makes such a bad appearance."

Ralph had let it be known that I was heartless—I think his term was "spoiled brat"—for firing Maple and for hiring dishwashers at minimum wage. He was right about the latter but Dan, to whom I reported, always had his eye on my labor costs and the bottom line. His bonus depended on profits in all the stores he oversaw. Not Ralph's bonus, which depended on franchises sold. It was odd to receive this lecture about the working poor from such an archconservative.

I was tempted to quote the EEOC laws at Ralph but instead told the story of Troy's dreams, his loyalty to Ruth. Ralph relented. Troy was my rock star at lunchtime.

Working the kitchen could be fun. Once, Shirley shared a joke circulating among the staff, a sheet of number-coded restaurant curses. It was good for a chuckle. That day while I was expediting, Troy announced with a grin: *five.* I remembered what that meant, something to the tune of *I hate this fucking job.*

Without skipping a beat, I replied, "Nineteen." *Great. Fucking great.* My stock in the kitchen went up.

There were other high points. One Saturday morning I came in to check the dining room and dinner prep. Saturday lunch was invariably slow. To my surprise, the accordion door to the back small dining room was closed. I went in to check. There, with an air of expectation, sat Fats Domino, whose "Walking to New Orleans" and many other hits still fill jukeboxes and clubs.

"Fats, you don't have to sit back here. There are plenty of tables. You can sit anywhere you want." (As if he couldn't if we had been busy!)

"Oh, no," he replied in his rich Lower Ninth Ward accent, "you don' undastan'. I'm meetin' a young LAdy, and if my wife find out, I'll be *running from* New Orl'ns."

It was a line he probably used all the time, but I knew I would dine out on it for years to come. I brought them some blueberry cheesecake on the house and hoped he got the musical salute.

At our level of business—300 covers a day, close to $400,000 a month in sales—the restaurant should have run with two or three managers, maybe four. When I served as Doris's assistant on weekend evenings, we had two. But as sole lunchtime manager, I oversaw all the ordering, prep for both lunch and dinner, service in the front of the house, and flow of food out of the kitchen. Dealing with 350 covers on a busy day, I would be on my way to solving one problem when another problem would crop up. By the time I'd solved the second problem, I'd forgotten the first. I found the pace dizzying and unrelenting.

As tickets piled up on the line, the most pressing challenge was to get the food out of the kitchen. I would jump in as expediter—as Mom still did in real crises—arranging steaks, sides, and bread on the trays, sending the runners out when all was ready.

First, I'd call the orders, based on the time printed on the ticket: *sides, table 81 coming; get ready.* When the short order cook was ready: *rib, medium-rare; double, rare, extra butter; filet, black-and-blue.*

The hot platters came down on the napkin-covered tray I placed before the broiler cook, then the steaks, sizzling as they hit. Simultaneously I called for the sides: *Lyonnaise—crispy; julienne—extra crispy. Gimme-a-creamed.* When all was ready, I would ladle an ounce of butter on the steak, garnish with chopped parsley, and push the runner out the door, a pair of napkins beneath the tray to protect his hand against the heat. Trays were Dan's addition, his way of moving us away from the mom-and-pop hand carrying—a big improvement to service. If the plates weren't sizzling the customer might send them back. *Gimme-a-hot-plate.* They were heated now in a convection oven—another Dan improvement. In the dining room, the trays were set on stands, and any free waitress, in the spirit of gang service, might help serve the steaks: *hot plates, hot plates. . . .*

Sometimes I served as butcher, too. I could call on my experience back in the 1960s. The porterhouse or steak-for-two required the band saw to slice through the T in the T-bone which gave you the sirloin on one side and the filet on the other. For filets, our biggest seller, the challenge was to get as many large filets (fourteen ounces) and small filets (eight ounces) as we could from the whole tenderloin. The tenderloin—which now to keep up with demand came broken out from the short loin in a Cryovac bag—tapered from the butt to the narrow tail, going from ten-to-twelve-inch circumference down to almost nothing. Too small to make a steak, the tapered "nothings" were used to fill out, or "stuff," the porterhouses—and for Earner's heavenly, fork-tender steak stews. Because of the taper, each slice needed to be a different width, so the weight was always got by guess, the right weight by luck or years of practice. Cut too large (nine or fifteen ounces) and you lose money. Cut too small (seven or eleven ounces) and you *crap out*: disappoint and lose customers. Harry Peters, a wiry little guy with a distinctive soul hitch in his giddyup, had been at Chris's since the sixties. Harry worked his way up from porter to butcher in the seventies and could steadily nail the proper filet weights all day long. When I managed to do so, I'd look around for the ticker tape shower.

The boned-out ribeye loin, with neither bone nor taper, was easiest of all. But the first night we needed ribeyes cut, I went next door.

"Mom, I need a little help. We had a run on ribeyes. You didn't have ribeyes back in the sixties. I've never cut them. Could you come and watch while I cut?"

"Sure, Ran. . . .

"Now, set the loin straight on the board. First you slice off this inky nub with the USDA prime mark. Now weigh it. Hmmmm, a little over ten pounds. What you want to do is get ten ribs out of this loin. Easy. Score it . . . like this. . . ."

Mom lightly scored the rib loin's fat cover halfway down, then lightly scored four marks within each half. She hadn't bothered to put an apron on over her white silk blouse.

"Then you just cut 'em."

I threw my tie over my shoulder, sharpened the long butcher knife on the steel the way Vontel once taught me, and settled into cutting steaks. Mom settled in just behind my shoulder.

I cut the first steak—a knife that sharp cutting through prime this good is like the proverbial hot butter knife. I weighed the new ribeye and placed it on the butcher-paper-lined aluminum tray: sixteen ounces, a perfect ribeye steak. Piece of cake!

On the next slice, Mom reached past my shoulder and pulled the steak away as I sliced. She grabbed it. Next to the first perfect steak, this one seemed out of kilter, higher on the left side than the right. It weighed eighteen ounces, not sixteen.

"Randy, be careful."

"Sure, Mom, okay."

On the next one, she again reached past my shoulder and pulled the steak away. This time the angle was even more extreme.

"Can't you keep that knife straight, Randy?"

"I'm trying, I'm trying." I was sweating.

Halfway through the loin, I realized what was happening. When Mom pulled the steak away, she took not just the upper sliced part but also dragged the lower part with it. The muscles were attached.

"Mom, it's you. Stop pulling the muscle."

"It's not me. You just can't cut straight."

"Okay, Mom."

"Randy, just don't cut any more meat."

"Good night, Mom."

My office was down a short corridor from my mother's office, close enough that we could hear each other on the telephone. After a long, friendly conversation with one of our suppliers, she stopped in my doorway.

"You have the worst laugh," she said.

It is true that I have quite a guffaw, loud and boisterous. To my friends, my laugh is endearing and infectious. "If you can't like my laugh," I replied, adapting Danny Barker's famous remark about New Orleans dance music, "there's something wrong with you."

Or maybe that's what I wish I had said. What I did tell her is that I would have none of her put-down. But I understood that, however well I did my job, I couldn't overcome my laugh. My guffaw was my father's.

Well, it was hardly all laughs. Whenever I worked as expediter or at one of the line positions, I was sure to be drenched to the skin by the intense heat of the kitchen and likely to be stained by grease. But after the rush was over, I would put my suit jacket back on, take the end of my tie out of my shirt and walk the dining room asking, table by table, how their dinner was. I did this even if Doris had already done it.

Shocked faces often greeted my query. I can now see how clouded my judgment was. What sense did it make that a guy straight from one of Dante's rings in hell came dripping to your table as you festively enjoyed the last morsels of your steak dinner?

But it's clear what clouded my judgment: I had to prove myself; I had to go all out. Not only was I visibly working my heart out, by walking the dining room I was playing the one card I almost uniquely could play. It was my only hope of a trump card. Although Mom never acknowledged it, showing a Fertel face to her customers was something I alone—apart from Jerry—could contribute. Since she had moved the office upstairs, Mom was less of a presence in the dining room. She was missed, visible only when she occasionally dined or played cards. My presence in her stead was like ordering a melt-in-your-mouth filet and getting chewy Boston butt, but at least it was Boston butt off the same prime steer.

And of course to Dan, Ralph, and Lana, my trump card was exactly why they had to trump me.

Years later I heard Doris explain how Mom preferred her hard-working women servers to men, and I ventured, "Maybe that's the source of the trouble Mom had with me?"

Doris said, "No, Randy, you tried too hard. You just tried too hard."

I guess I forgot the rule *don't look, just carry.*

Watching me try too hard, Doris Brouillette, my immediate boss, decided to move back closer to home to run the Mobile store. Doris had been my mother's first hire and was the last of the original crew. The move was explained as a return to her native Alabama. But I discovered later her retreat was in part to escape the conflict that swirled around me on Broad Street. Her leaving made me general manager, but until I found an assistant manager to replace me, I would need to work split shifts: 9 a.m. to 3 p.m., 5 p.m. to midnight or 2 a.m., depending on business. This would mean covering the restaurant on busy weekends (350–400 covers) alone when Doris and I would have run it together. Dan insisted I cover every shift, staying until the money was counted and dropped in the floor safe.

I spent many of my afternoon breaks interviewing applicants to be my assistant manager.

After a few weeks, I needed a break and asked Dan for *a day, even a shift off?* I got the shrugged shoulders: *What, me worry?*

That Friday night, Dan came in for dinner. After he had eaten his steak, Dan announced with a chuckle, "This is that night off you were asking for." It was already 10 p.m., but I was glad to get off early even if by then my kids were in bed.

I had a ten-year-old and a seven-year-old at home who hardly recognized me any more. Any intimacy in my marriage was long gone. I fumed, but Dan held all the cards and Mom listened to him. I was *the guy with an authority problem.* Any objection I raised would prove Dan's point.

I needed allies but I knew Lana was an unlikely one. Duke Unlimited, her advertising firm, had all Mom's business and needed to keep it. Ruth's Chris's advertising program—and dollars—dominated and sustained Lana's firm. Dan oversaw the advertising budget and made decisions about the program.

Besides, Lana was not in the corporation, but she made herself a corporate player like the rest, part of the ongoing power struggle. In the cutthroat competition to be anointed by Ruth's charisma, Lana had two special cards to play. She laid fair claim to having helped create the brand with her early advertising campaigns, and she was Ruth's best friend. Or more. An orphan who grew up in foster homes in Ontario, in her mind she was family, Ruth's family. She was willing to defend her family turf ferociously. As with Mom's executives, so with Lana: I was an intruder. To me she was always at once ingratiating—big wet kisses on the lips—and supercilious. It was always *honey this* and *sweetheart that.* Just a few years my senior, at best she treated me like a clueless baby brother. I might be clueless but I had her number and she knew it.

Lana shared with Ralph another special hole card, that card you turn over to show you have not just the two pair showing but a full house. Mom had all that charisma and everyone loved her, but what many didn't realize was her country girl's shyness. That's where Ralph and Lana came in: they greased the skids of social discourse. They were the life of Ruth's party. Ruth was the belle of the ball. They made sure her dance card was full.

A couple years before, 1986, the ball moved en masse to Las Vegas, where Ruth's Chris Steak House held its annual meeting for franchisees. I was invited. Every night, the casinos invited her with her guests to their gourmet dining rooms, expecting she would stick around after dinner to play. She knew the game and was happy to oblige, willing to trade a fine meal for her spending a *nuit blanche* at the craps or baccarat tables. *I'll sleep when I'm dead*, one or another of them would say. Dinner might cost her $10,000, but it got her not only dinner but a night's worth of action.

One night we traveled from the Strip to dine downtown in the high-end Italian restaurant at Binion's Golden Nugget. We were a group of eight at a large round table. It was a slow night and Las Vegas wasn't yet the dining destination it is today with its legions of Wolfgang Pucks and Emeril Lagasses. Across the room only one other table was in use. There urbanely sat Cary Grant and his former wife Dyan Cannon.

The liquor and wine flowed and Ralph began his jokes and stories. One was about driving back from the Ruth's Chris franchise in Shreveport, 350 miles from New Orleans, and seeing a man trudging in the heat along the highway.

Damn, that looks like Jerry. It was. Ralph stopped and offered a ride. Jerry, who had had a bad day at the Louisiana Downs track, accepted nonchalantly as if they had met on North Broad Street or Seville Drive. The table generally agreed: *That Jerry!*

Then Mom asked Lana to tell her famous "bladder infection" tale. Lana Duke sometimes played the clown's role and this was her cue. She told a vivid story about the time she sat on the potty smoking as she did her business. Finishing the cigarette, she threw it in the toilet. Suddenly she started feeling a burning sensation and thought to herself, *Wow, I've never had a bladder infection come on this quickly. Wow, this is going to be a bad bladder infection. Wow! Ugggh! Argh!* And then, she explained, she looked down and realized that the cigarette had landed on toilet paper that hadn't gotten wet. *The toilet paper and she were aflame.*

The presence before us completed the vivid picture she painted. Lana is a big woman. On that hot seat, picture the Pillsbury Dough Girl in a gauzy nightie.

The hilarity knew no bounds. Except that, whenever we laughed uproariously, and we did often, it was impossible not to remember the sedate table across the room. Grant's incredible shock of white hair and elegance didn't slow us down, but his presence added spice to our hilarity. More than once, as we dried our tears of laughter, someone would remark, *My god,*

14.3 Lana and Ruth.

what that other table must think of us. . . . All the same, we felt a pride that we weren't put off our game. Who was Cary Grant to get in the way of our letting *le bon temps rouler*?

Grant's party had gone when we filed past his reset table. Lana suddenly broke rank, pulled out his chair, sat on it, and rubbed her once-singed and still very large bottom over the chair's tufted, cushioned seat. Guffaws all round were followed by every woman in the group—including Ralph's very demure and very Catholic wife, Linda—sitting one by one in the newly hallowed chair and wiggling in the same manner. Ruth went second which gave everyone else permission.

That's Lana Duke. She didn't need permission. She knew no boundaries. She had named her company well, Duke Unlimited. She was always the first to bring crazy ideas to the table. Most important, she brought to the table things that loosened Mom up. Mom loved her for it.

Ralph served a similar function. But Ralph's hostility toward me was hardly veiled. *You know*, I'd hear, *most people in my situation would be upset to see a family member come into the business—but not me.* Even more direct: *Just remember, I'm gonna run this corporation for five years after your mother dies. Your mother's promised. So have the trustees.*

And yet, sometimes he also displayed an element of sympathy. *I don't know what's wrong with your mother. I spoke to her about her inability to say anything positive to you.* I was grateful for the gesture. If even Ralph can see it . . . ?

A couple times over drinks, Ralph also confided how tough his job was. *Ruth,* he complained, *expects me to play gin with her every night.* For years, he would put in his day at the office, then head next door to Ruth's house for a drink and Earner's pork roast or spaghetti with red gravy. They would play gin for hours. If Earner was at bingo, they might break for a steak after a few sheets of Hollywood, the tray sizzling across the parking lot to their table. Meanwhile his wife sat home awaiting his return. *Do you think I enjoy all those nights,* he wanted to know?

As Ralph's underling I had to let these things roll off my back. But as a member of the Ruth's Chris board I had a fiduciary duty to the company's welfare. While struggling to learn the business, I attended the board meetings held in the private dining room on Broad Street. After the call to order, the drink order was always the first item on the agenda. Ralph conducted the meeting. Mom didn't like to run meetings. Agendas were rarely circulated in advance.

Since Ruth's Chris drinks are famously stiff, these were by no means sober deliberations. One night, after dinner had been served and the meeting was breaking up, Ralph announced that he had almost forgotten an important agenda item. He had put together a deal in St. Louis with a group of investors, young lawyers who spent long afternoons at Ruth's Chris. They wanted to buy a franchise with Ralph, who, putting up no money himself, would own 51 percent and serve as general and managing partner. He would manage St. Louis from his mahogany desk upstairs on Broad Street. "Does the board approve?"

Shock registered on every face. Even as drunk as we were, there wasn't a person in the room who didn't see through this cunning and self-dealing. Everyone was scandalized—but no one dared speak up if Ruth didn't. Including me. Ralph was given the go-ahead.

Mom's head bookkeeper, who was the widow of Ralph and Mom's late bookie, took me aside and whispered that Ralph had exercised his normal deal as vice president of franchising, taking his $10,000 cut for selling a franchise to himself. She issued the check. She seemed to think that wasn't the appropriate vigorish.

The St. Louis franchise closed in a hurry. The location was ill-chosen, the restaurant badly run, and St. Louis's propensity to dine out back then leaned toward hot dogs rather than prime steaks. The Ruth's Chris board bought it back, dollar for dollar. Ralph and his associates failed, but they didn't lose a dime. As always, Mom was covering his gambling debts.

Meanwhile I was losing my grip, depressed by an overwhelming sense of powerlessness. One day the pressure was too much. I found myself in tears at my desk. I took refuge in the kitchen's bathroom. My faucets staunched, I was returning to my desk when Ralph walked by and caught my red-dened eye. He was visibly stunned. What registered first was his concern. It turned quickly to glee: *just what I need to bring to Ruth.* I looked at him and shrugged my shoulders as if to say, *what can I do, you'll use it as you will.*

A poet friend with a lighter touch than I perfectly captured the absurdity of my tenure at Ruth's Chris Steak House:

the learned host

> *like a canterbury tale retold*
> *our host, a scholar, being bold and*
> *determined not to be outwitted*
> *by educating, he summarily quit it*
> *to eke from life the very most.*
> *i present to you the learned host*
> *whose education, i attest,*
> *categorically was the very best, and*
> *silly though it seems, 'tis true—*
> *he's serving crackers on broad avenue.*

Still, I hardly looked back. Because my academic background was such a demerit in the eyes of the corporate bosses, I made a point of never bringing a book to work. There were many long afternoons after busy lunches when I could have used one. Besides, although I missed the classroom, I had also realized that teaching, no less than slinging hash, was sales. What counted was how much you believed in what you were selling. I loved books, the play of ideas, and watching students grow. But I also believed that by *serving crackers on broad avenue*, I had the best shot to make a difference and to leave my mark. I liked the *idea* of working for my mother, the legacy she had created and put partially in my name.

More important, the business was in my blood. I had worked as a teenager clearing and setting tables, helping to serve, washing dishes, helping my mother butcher the huge loins, making late-night emergency bread delivery runs. Although I was ensnarled in a nest of vipers, it wasn't just a job. My name was on the front door.

Meanwhile, even as Dan was making my life miserable, he would bend my ear about how Ralph was threatened by him, and how my mother didn't appreciate what he could do for her with his restaurant and accounting skills. I listened and decided that, while he was making me miserable, he did have skills the company needed. Quality was sliding around the country. I went to my mother: maybe Dan was being underutilized; maybe his role should be expanded.

The conversation took place in her home behind the restaurant. Dan had schooled me that the way he got what he wanted from Ruth was to approach her, not at her restaurant desk where, girded in her armor, she gave a virtually automatic no. Instead, he made his pitches at her dining room table at home, preferably on the weekend without Earner around, with the football games droning in the background as Mom lounged in her housecoat smoking cigarettes. *That's why I come to work Saturday mornings*, he explained.

Apparently I didn't benefit from that special dispensation. Mom's response to me was a withering look and one bald statement: "As if I didn't create this restaurant. . . ."

The response suggested a fragility that few glimpsed. It helped me gauge just how deep was the slough I was in. But what could I do to dig my way out?

Mom had a saying, *to be a glutton for punishment*. It came to mind as the waitresses and I watched in awe as Jack Parker ate himself to death.

Mr. Parker was an insurance broker who had cornered various city accounts. In New Orleans, where almost anything can be bought for the right price, Jack knew the game. He daily commanded table number 81, the best, most visible table in the house.

Lunch began with BBQ shrimp swimming in butter to the brim, mopped up with loaves of French bread. Then a pork chop, *the thickest and fattiest you have* with apple slices caramelized in brown sugar and butter. Jack added four extra pats of butter to Uncle Martin's au gratin spinach, creamed spinach with cheddar bubbling on top. He ordered *extra everything* on his baked potato. He drank multiple triple vodka martinis in an iced tea glass: *hold the vermouth, extra anchovy olives.*

Dinner for Jack, sometimes the same day, was *our fattiest ribeye.* He didn't trust us to remember *extra butter.*

Jack Parker often lunched or dined alone although his ostensible reason for being seen at Ruth's Chris was important meetings with city leaders. He arrived at 11:30 a.m., usually our first customer, and often stayed through dinner. He'd drape his coat on the chair and loosen his tie beneath his pink cascading chins—his collar no longer buttoned. Sweat beaded on his forehead and poured down his cheeks; if there was still pork or beef fat on his plate to be consumed, he couldn't be bothered to wipe his brow.

The waitresses and I felt we might be assisting in a suicide. When Jack Parker died, we all breathed a sigh of relief, even the waitresses who would miss out on his $100 tips at Christmastime.

While Jack Parker, starved for affection or respect or self-regard, gorged himself to death, I convinced myself in turns that *if only. . . . If only I achieved the right numbers this month; if only I found the right words; if only I figured out how to get her ear; if only I could get her out of Ralph's grasp; if only I worked an extra shift a week; if only I could stop all this crazy rumination. . . .*

But still our attraction-repulsion dance went on, a perfect reflection of those black-and-white Scottie magnets in Dad's bar so many years ago.

One day a call came from Orlando. Linda had taken the kids for spring break to Disney World and Matt was having chronic asthma attacks so bad, in and out of hospitals, that Linda was losing it. I knew the irrational streak that sometimes gripped her. She faced a long drive home with the kids, ten and seven, at one another's and at *her* throat. Didn't sound safe to me.

"Mom, here's what's happening. . . . I'm afraid I need to go down there to help her out. I know Linda can't handle it. I'll be back in a couple days."

"You can't do that."

"I'm sorry, Mom. I have to."

For my mother, family was a weakness, not a strength. Its demands constricted. Rather than providing an opportunity to continue her legacy, my presence cut her options. In her mind this weakened her in the eyes of others. She couldn't fire me for running down to Orlando. She might have understood the need in someone else. But coming from me it was unforgiveable.

I felt trapped. I left a tenure-track teaching job to enter business. Academic jobs were so hard to get that my time outside academia had killed any tenure-track possibility. If at Ruth's Chris my academic background was considered proof of my uselessness, academia would value my business experience just as low. I didn't know what to do.

Still, it was important that I survive this gauntlet and that the business thrive. Forty percent of the company was in trust to me. Another 40 percent was in trust to my brother. Jerry, traipsing around the country, was less of a threat to Mom's executive team. Ralph's running joke was that Jerry was paid his allowance to stay *out* of the business.

Jerry had barely held a job since Vietnam, first running a pizza place financed by Mom and then cooking steaks at the restaurant for a couple of years in the early eighties. When Rosemary, a Ruth's Chris waitress, gave birth to Jerry's first child, she was promoted to manager of the Lafayette restaurant. Jerry worked for a while in the kitchen as a steak turner. Then word got back that he was firing everyone. Jerry left and Rosemary stayed and thrived for decades as the restaurant's manager. Per capita, the Lafayette restaurant was one of the most successful in the chain.

Jerry wanted to get involved again. Jerry was just as skeptical as I about Mom's circle of advisors. Ralph in particular had him muttering under his breath. But Ralph had his number. He hit on the idea of having Jerry report on every Ruth's Chris around the country. *That'll keep him busy.*

Within the week, Jerry was confronting the Houston manager, a woman who had risen to the position from waitressing in New Orleans. He bunked on the dining room floor. From that vantage point, he got a glimpse of the dirt on the chair rails. Scratches he noticed inside the cocktail glasses outraged him. He put two chairs and a bagful of glasses in his Crown Victoria's trunk and rushed back to New Orleans.

The Houston manager's account of his behavior beat him back to the office; Jerry's report was not well received. After hitting a brick wall upstairs he came to me for support. I sympathized, but support was hard to muster. I showed Jerry how all our cocktail glasses, nested one on top of the other, had the same scratches. Since hundreds of glasses are needed to keep the liquor flowing and the space for them was only so large, what else could we, or the manager in Houston, do? Jerry looked at me in exasperation.

His return to the business as an extra pair of eyes was dead on arrival. That he had been given no instruction or criteria for troubleshooting restaurants killed it before his Crown Victoria hit the I-10 on-ramp.

Ralph, Dan, Phil, and Jim didn't need that incident to demonstrate there was no danger of Ruth's favoring her kids. They watched my mother call me on the carpet in her no-walls office before the entire office staff for each blunder and offense. I couldn't convince her to dress me down in private—a request that was further proof of my authority problem. To speak up was to invite Mom's displeasure and their subtle and not-so-subtle vengeances.

After several years of these conflicts, I approached Mom with an idea: *maybe we could hire a family business consultant.* I'd read that our problems were typical of family businesses. Mom, the visionary entrepreneur, had hired executives who now felt cheated of the inside track to power as the entrepreneur's children got involved in the business. From the executives' point of view, all the children offer is the right last name, and yet they end up with the lion's share, the executives' sweat equity; passed over. They needed reassurance, I argued, and a piece of the future action, but not at the expense of my present well-being.

"This isn't a family business," Mom said.

"We're not a family business?"

"No, Randy, we're not a family business. That's not the problem. You just need to change your personality."

I was stunned into silence, but over the next week, I drew out of Mom and Ralph exactly what "family business" meant to them. To them it meant that a consultant would come in and say, "Randy's family. He's in. If you're not family, you're out." They were singing the same tune. Mine came from a completely different hymnbook—Greek to their ears.

In her memoir, *Family Affairs,* cousin Audrey, ever innocent, speculated from a distance about my career on Broad Street: "Randy is manager of the restaurants in New Orleans. I know she is happy about this, because now she has someone to take over when she is gone. It would be a shame to build up this empire with no one to keep it up. Besides, it must be easier for her now that she has someone to take over some of the work."

Isn't it pretty to think so?

Meanwhile, with the long hours I worked, I drifted further and further away from my family. Linda spent much of her time painting in the studio we built for her behind the house in Lakeview. In the absence of a family life, Matt and Owen became best buddies and lived in their own world, sharing a love of Atari video games, Marvel comic books, and Lucas and

Spielberg movies. Matt began to have nightmares; Owen's disturbances we couldn't get to the bottom of. They would eventually develop a plan one day to become the next Wachowski Brothers, the team that made the Matrix trilogy, perhaps to make their own version of a Matrix world where nurturance was equally spurious and self-regarding. Our family hadn't provided much modeling or guidance for healthy closeness. Eventually, too enmeshed, Matt and Owen had to learn they each needed to find their own way. As adults they are struggling to find their way separately into the difficult world of moviemaking.

I had felt determined not to be like my father but, however well-meaning, had nonetheless stumbled into my own way of deserting them.

CHAPTER FIFTEEN

BREAKING THE NAPOLEONIC CODE

THE FIRST TIME MY MOTHER FIRED ME WAS IN 1989.

After too many years in too near proximity to the corporate headquarters on Broad Street, I moved to Florida to get away. We had just bought back the Florida franchise group and they needed a general manager in North Palm Beach. More than eight hundred miles would separate me from my family until the end of the school year, but, for the sake of my own sanity, I had no choice. Ralph gave his blessing: "Randy needs to show what he can do on his own without us hovering over him." Dan was put in charge of the transition. "As a *formality*," he emphasized, I would report to Bob Gifford at the Fort Lauderdale restaurant. Dan came down with me to make the introductions.

Bob Gifford had helped to grow Ruth's Chris in Fort Lauderdale into a sexy, successful restaurant, his tables turning two and even three times most nights of the week. At first I found him refreshing, a New York operator with many years experience in a number of great restaurants like legendary Joe Baum's Water Club and River Café. Unlike Dan, Bob sat me down and talked to me at length, telling me what he wanted, what I should expect, and the problems to be addressed, starting with the quality of the French bread. But the biggest problem was sales. Unlike its Fort Lauderdale counterpart, North Palm Beach was not a mature restaurant. Its business was uneven and suffered especially in the off-season. Bob gave me my marching orders: *Run the restaurant as if it were your own.* We shared a grin about the irony. His grin had a familiar edge to it.

I had arrived just in time for the snowbirds, northerners who come south for Florida's warm winters. Business was good. After a few weeks, I found an authentic French bakery and ordered their bread for a week to see if the quality was consistent.

When Bob came up to North Palm Beach for our next weekly meeting, he entered fuming. He had heard from my assistant manager about my *changing the bread.* Bob was an Irishman and when he was angry, he ranted. *Who do you think you are, changing the bread without my okay?!* Bob had an Irishman's delight in hearing himself roll out all the permutations of an idea, its causes and consequences—in this case, the idea that I thought I was something special. He was a teetotaler, a dry drunk whose new drug of choice was anger. The rant went on for an hour.

I reminded him of the marching orders he'd given me. How could I run the place as if I owned it if I couldn't make basic decisions? I learned that this was restaurant lingo for if the place is on fire in the middle of the night, meet the firemen at the door. It didn't mean that I had license to make my own decisions. *Randy, who do you think you are?!*

The obvious answer was: I am a Fertel who has been eating at Ruth's Chris since the day it opened and before. I come from New Orleans, I've lived in Paris, and I probably have some notion of how French bread should taste and crunch. I've been sopping French bread in butter and steak drippings since I was old enough to fight my brother for the porterhouse T-bone. To say any of that, however, would be seen as a refusal to accept Bob's "authority." Dan, I now learned, had warned him about me. Bob knew all about my authority problem.

I resolved to make the best of it. I might be under Bob's thumb but he only had two of them, compared to the fistfuls that Ruth, Ralph, and Dan deployed at my expense. Sales and profits soared as the snowbirds flocked south. I would try to grit it out.

Then I was faced with a surprising dilemma about Bob's way of doing business. Bob was supervising the build-out of a new Ruth's Chris in North Miami. When I came to Florida, he had told me all about my predecessor, the ne'er-do-well who, before we had repurchased the franchise, had built the North Palm Beach restaurant from the ground up, but with huge overruns—unbudgeted expenditures—that the manager took the blame for;

Bob had fired him right after the opening. North Palm was Bob's demesne, no matter who ran it.

Now the same scenario seemed to be happening in North Miami. Maybe it was Bob who overspent in North Palm and needed a fall guy? Bob's oversight was so tight it was hard to imagine my predecessor had the room to overspend on his own. Did I have a responsibility to call attention to this potential problem? Or would this be seen as more insubordination?

I queried our North Palm Beach bartender who had been on the opening team. Yes, she confirmed, Bob had used that other manager as the fall guy for his own cost overruns. But she warned me, "If you do something with this, you're on your own."

Within a few days, while I was still worrying out what to do with this information, Bob had learned about my conversation with the bartender. Corporate headquarters back on Broad Street knew, too. They waited till I returned to New Orleans to move my family down to North Palm Beach—we had been separated for the school year. I was called into a meeting with Ralph and Dan in Mom's living room. She was not in attendance. *Wheel of Fortune*—Mom's favorite—blared in the background. Earner was sent out of the house while her red beans simmered on the stove.

Ralph and Dan sat at Mom's dining room table. I contemplated the LeRoy Neiman painting behind them that Mom prized. It pictured a duck hunt: a wintry day, men hidden in a duck blind, black Labs eagerly awaiting the call to retrieve the ducks that were about to fall from the sky after decoying down to their death.

"Randy, when will you grow up?"

"What about my fiduciary duty as a member of the board? How could I just watch as he wasted money in Miami?"

"That's none of your business, Randy."

The kangaroo court lasted three hours. I was offered a plea bargain. In exchange for admitting my insubordination, Ralph and Dan would give me my job back on Broad Street. "This is your mother's wish," they said. They would prefer just to show me the door.

It was a hell of a message to bring home. Linda and I gnashed our teeth and bickered but in the end decided that, job or no job, it was time to leave Ruth's Chris. Refusing the guilty plea, we packed up and moved the family down to Florida.

So she didn't actually fire me, at least not literally. That time.

I spent a year licking my wounds. I had worked hard and sacrificed much, in return for what? My kids were bewildered, yanked from school to school—three in five years.

It was 1989. I was on the cusp of turning forty. I played with my kids' Gameboy till my head buzzed. Listlessly I walked the beach. As they had for eons, great loggerhead turtles came ashore to lay their eggs. The surf crashed. I was a stranger in a strange land.

I found a job as development director for a nonprofit theatre. Six months later, my mother visited us in Florida. She wanted me to come back to New Orleans to work for her. No apologies and no admissions, but she hinted that she didn't trust her key people. *Life is not worth living*, she complained, utterly confusing and dumbfounding me. How do I broach my mother's inner feelings when she has never expressed one to me her entire life?

I agreed to return on two conditions: that we see a family business consultant and that she assign me a role that would employ my skills. Like marketing. Communications was my strength. No one had believed that my skills in academia could transfer into the corporate world. All I wanted was a chance to prove otherwise.

The meetings with the family business consultant in West Palm Beach were frustrating and soon petered out. Mom awed the consultant. She was not reflective by nature, nor could she admit any mistakes or failings. The location in North Miami, after large overruns in the build-out, had failed. Bob had been shown the door. But this did not cause Mom to rethink the sequence of events that led to the kangaroo court. Even if she didn't trust her key people, that still didn't give me the right to question their authority.

It didn't?

But, like my dad, Mom was set in her ways. And, she had her imperial throne to protect. I was willing to accept her pride if I could get my life and my family back on track even though it meant I would again be separated from my children so they could finish the school year in Florida. I returned to Ruth's Chris as vice president of marketing. I would still report to Dan, vice president of operations.

But I also insisted that I spend part of my time troubleshooting restaurants around the country. I had been schooled by Lana: no use getting customers in the door with my marketing efforts if the food would chase them away. This meant I would be going into kitchens that Dan had visited and whose food he had signed off on.

I knew that conflicts were written into the job description. Every problem I found in restaurants Dan had inspected would be another act of insubordination. But I knew that quality control was sliding. And I cared.

Part of Louisiana hunting lore is the infamous *dos gris*, the gray-back duck that is so stupid that even after you shoot at it once and miss it circles around and comes back to give you a second try. And so, *dos gris* down to the pin feathers, I circled back around. Maybe those LeRoy Neiman hunters were grinning because they had *dos gris* in their sights.

As head of marketing, I oversaw the advertising and public relations for Ruth's Chris. I was the company's link with Lana and her creative team at Duke Unlimited, and with Primavera Public Relations. My first suggestion was to make the logo consistent so that there were no longer as many Ruth's Chris emblems as restaurants—something neither the corporate executives nor Lana had thought to do. I created the restaurant's *Prime Time* newsletter. Even my mother grudgingly admitted, I heard indirectly, that I was good in the communications role. True to form, she never told me directly.

Lana Duke and I worked on a new Ruth's Chris billboard campaign. She showed me the mockup: the word *Sizzling* with just our logo in the lower right corner. The brand's coupling of the iconic steak with the sizzle was so well established that we could skip the icon and go straight to the sizzle. What came to me in a flash was the power of onomatopoeia. *I'm seeing four or five Zs*, I said. Lana called in her art director. Now we had a new billboard image:

SIZZZZZLING

That day I experienced an alluring aspect of business. I saw five Zs in my mind's eye and weeks later, they were on billboards around the country. The new look had been accepted not only by corporate—Mom and her executives—but by many of the franchisees. It was used nationwide for a decade. I was two months into the vice president of marketing job. I was proud.

But there was another aspect to my satisfaction. Teaching is an ephemeral pursuit. A class discussion—good or bad—is a performance that leaves no tangible record. Maybe I would see my influence in the work my students produced; maybe not. As a graduate school colleague had once put it, our job as teachers was to be around when the light goes on. But the alchemy is more complex than that: the light may ignite years down the road, invisible to you.

Teaching may offer deeper satisfactions, but in business, the results were immediate and tangible. The numbers showed success or failure, tracked on a daily, monthly, quarterly, and annual basis. With the numbers, you knew where you stood.

Sales figures were soaring but other numbers were in the air, some of them disturbing—like 25,000, the number of cash dollars Ralph handed over in a paper bag to a Chitimacha Indian chief, in a parking lot in the dead of night. Mom and her fellow "investors" meant to "purchase" an option in an Indian casino that promised to be highly lucrative. They were *going to make a fortune.*

The Chitimacha Indian chief took the paper bag and bought a Cadillac. That sudden display of opulence sent smoke signals throughout St. Mary Parish, a rural parish a hundred or so miles west of New Orleans. Bribing an Indian chief is a federal offense. Indian-head nickels were dropped to the Bureau of Indian Affairs.

I was summoned to my mother's living room. Mom and Ralph were going over their story. The idea had been that the Indian chief was acting as the tribe's representative, not as a lone wolf. Mom was the picture of haughty innocence. "How could the U.S. attorney think this of me? How did I know the chief would buy a Cadillac?"

"A paper bag?!" Ralph asked with a smirk. "$25,000? In a parking lot? What did you think was happening, Ruth?"

It fell to me to accompany Mom to the Hale Boggs Federal Building where U.S. Attorney John Volz held court before the federal grand jury. Volz had been the man who convicted Mafia don Carlos Marcello on RICO charges (which were later reversed). He had indicted Mom's banker, Jim, and her lawyer, Phil, on RICO charges. Now Volz had set his sights on Ruth Fertel.

I had never seen Mom so scared. She'd brought a book as she always did, but was unable to concentrate.

"Miz Fertel."

But when Mom came out of the grand jury room, she was laughing. She recounted the end of the session.

"I have one last question that goes to your honesty, Miz Ruth," Volz had intoned, with a pregnant pause. "Are you telling the truth in those ads about how good your steaks are?"

"Absolutely," she replied, triumphant. She knew she would skate from the moment he said, "Miz Ruth." Volz dismissed her.

My mother's reputation for scrupulous fair dealing doesn't square with such episodes, nor with her comfort in surrounding herself with sycophants whose reputations would make many squirm. A part of her seemed to thrive on that dark dynamic. Something of a *dos gris* herself, she kept returning to the high stakes table looking for more action. She shared the gambler's penchant, that money was just a way to keep score. She was in it for the game—and the adrenaline rush.

Her love of the game explained some of it. But Mom's environment helped influence her comfort level with that way of life. "Half of Louisiana is under water," it's been said, "and the other half is under indictment." In Louisiana, the definition of a crooked politician is one that won't stay bought. Earl Long, who reigned as governor during my parents' young adulthood, liked to distinguish between honest and dishonest graft. Dishonest graft meant bribes. Honest graft meant using the patronage system to reward friends and relatives. Uncle Earl's predecessor, Governor Richard Leche, went haywire and then to jail, but not before delivering the quip for which he is remembered: "When I took the oath of office, I didn't take any vow of poverty."

But even in a state where corruption was de rigueur, Plaquemines Parish held the distinction of being called "America's only unconstitutional monarchy." Mom was raised under the imperial sway of Judge Leander Perez, who took power in the 1920s and hung on until his death in the 1960s. If you did business in Plaquemines Parish, you did business with—and gave a cut of your earnings to—Judge Perez.

Perez made one fortune during Prohibition when the bays and bayous of the Delta were almost impossible to police. It's been said that under the Volstead Act, the wettest spot in America became the "wettest" spot in America. Perez made a second fortune in 1932, when sulfur was discovered at Lake Grand Ecaille, and the Freeport Sulphur Company created an entirely new technology to build "the mine that couldn't be built" because it lay under a tidal marsh. He made his third and largest fortune when the oil and gas industry came to Plaquemines.

Judge Perez's Plaquemines was a world of ruthless, unscrupulous power politics. To gain and maintain power, Perez stuffed ballot boxes, controlled the rolls, or just bought votes outright. His power and influence filtered down to all levels of parish life. He put everyone (every white, that is) on the payroll. This one was surveyor of levees, that one was head of mosquito or alligator control. How could you buck the system once the system buttered your bread?

In his public pose as the benevolent "Father of Plaquemines," Perez ensured that the parish coffers were enriched by severance taxes. Meanwhile, behind the scenes, he gobbled up oil leases on lands to which he had no right and sold them to the oil companies at astronomical margins.

And then there was the matter of his racism. The adage during Perez's reign was, "If you're black, stay back; brown, stick around; white, you're all right." That my mother managed to avoid the influence of this bigotry was a signal victory. I attribute it, but I'm just guessing, to her Missouri-born father. I'd like to think Nan' Jo' had that kind of backbone, too.

When Perez wasn't attacking the feds, parish business took Judge Perez up and down the highway, from Venice at the river's mouth to Belle Chasse, now a suburb of New Orleans. From time to time, Perez would stop and wander into the kitchen of Uncle Sig's restaurant in Happy Jack. If Aunt Helen was cutting the dry-aged prime loins she acquired from Mom's back door, the judge liked to grab the loin's first quarter-inch slice of green mold–encrusted dry-aging, destined for the garbage. He'd throw it on the grill to have himself a treat.

"Christ, Lea," Aunt Helen said. "At least scrape off the potash" (the carbon on the grill).

He grinned. "Helen, a little potash is good for the soul."

But facing charges for bribing Indian chiefs wasn't Mom's only problem. Once again other disturbing numbers trickled down from the corporate level. My mother had again become involved in another bad real estate deal, separate from the restaurant empire, and needed cash to bail herself and her partners out. As in 1975, her banker, Jim Queyrouze, had brought her into a deal, and again, the deal had gone south. Mom faced bankruptcy. Again.

The partners in the real estate deal—Jim included—were equally responsible for the $3 million—*in solido* was the legal term I kept hearing—but there was no talk of pooling assets to retire the debt. Mom had to fund the bailout because everyone knew that if the project failed, the lawsuits would descend on *her*. Ruth Fertel had the more visible assets, even though they were in trust and therefore not technically hers, and not liquid at all. She would have to produce $3 million or be forced into personal bankruptcy.

As a child of the Great Depression, Mom dreaded bankruptcy. Since her personal assets included some of the restaurant buildings, the plan was to have the corporation purchase these buildings. This would yield the $3 million needed to pay off the debt. However, since the company didn't have this kind of cash, it would need to pledge corporate stock for a bank loan.

Mom didn't own enough Ruth's Chris stock to collateralize the loan, given that the Jerry and Randy Fertel Trust owned 80 percent. To get the $3 million in cash, the trustees would be required to sign the trust over to Sanwa, a Japanese bank, as collateral.

All this was taking place in the months after the 1991 Gulf War. Our business had fallen off by a third as people stayed home to watch the first televised war. The effect had been short-lived, and the bottom line rebounded quickly. But Saddam had not been ousted and President George H. W. Bush, bent on correcting that blunder, was rattling his swords. No one knew how long a second war might last. If we failed to meet the performance ratios written into the loan agreement—ratios that assumed ambitious sales—Sanwa could seize Ruth's Chris, on the principle that their collateral was in jeopardy.

In 1991, the Japanese were America's biggest economic rival and worst nightmare. All over America, the Japanese were buying up prime real estate, like Rockefeller Center, and their aggressive acquisitions were the subject of intense media coverage.

To Sanwa, Ruth's Chris must have seemed a tasty morsel. For Japanese businessmen and tourists, American prime beef was the nearest they could get to Kobe beef. Compared to their legendary beer-fed and hand-massaged Kobe, our prime beef was dirt cheap even though prices were soaring because the Japanese were importing so much. In the worst-case scenario, Sanwa would get 80 percent of Ruth's Chris Steak House for $3 million. It was worth tens of millions. The Empress would be divested of her empire. Jerry and Randy Fertel and their heirs would get exactly zilch.

I tried to convince my mother that surely there was another way to get the money she needed, in a way that wouldn't put everything in jeopardy. I asked that we run the numbers with a possible downturn in mind; if the possibilities were as dire as I and my CPA imagined, we had to find another way to get $3 million out of the company.

Mom's response was threefold. First, I should trust her. Second, she had always been a gambler; it was hers to gamble away, not mine to prevent her throw of the dice. Third, my questioning her sounded like a power play.

This was a term I was hearing elsewhere. Phil, my mother's personal attorney, corporation attorney, corporate trustee, and franchisee, had expressed his fears to me. "I hope power plays aren't being done." He explained that there might be an effort by one of the corporate executives, Ralph or Dan, to wrest control from Ruth or the trust.

For his part, Dan recounted a board meeting I had missed in which he had offered his counsel concerning the Seattle franchise owned by Jim Queyrouze the banker. Jim, our real-estate whiz, had settled for a bad location and business reflected it. Dan had been offering his pessimistic view of the market in Seattle. Ralph pulled Dan out of the meeting. "Don't you ever cross me again! If Jim goes under in Seattle that will cost us less than our taking it over. From now on, we'll have a meeting before the meeting so you can say what I want." Hearing this from Dan—*why do they all confide in me?* I wondered—did little to increase my faith and trust that my mother was in control of her own fate. I began better to understand the anxiety Mom had expressed in Florida. Mom was at the center of a Byzantine maze of her own making.

I met for lunch with Jim and Phil at the tony Metairie Country Club— "neutral turf" except that it was their turf, not mine—to express my fears for the trust. It was the first time in almost twenty years that my trustees had invited me to dine with them. As they enjoyed their martinis, I hit a stone wall. *Randy, there are no problems. No, there is no conflict of interest. That Jim was a partner and his exposure would be reduced by $3 million was just one of those things . . . a coincidence.*

Jim's *Loyalty*, for all his promises, lay elsewhere.

I felt Mom had a moral right to remove capital and value from the company she created, but she didn't have the right to gamble it all away. I felt I had a moral duty to prevent this roll of the dice—a responsibility to my sons who were too young to speak up and to my brother who was not in the game.

I paid thousands to an accounting firm (whose name ominously was DeRouen) for an analysis of the deal. They reported that the required performance ratios were the "most onerous" they had ever seen. If we failed "to make the ratios" we could lose the company. Mom refused to read their report, claiming that the corporate accounting firm had approved the loan document with all its performance ratios. *Why go to the extra expense of more accounting analysis?* To me, Mom seemed penny-wise and pound-foolish—millions were at stake, as well as her legacy—but I agreed to talk

to the accountant who led the recent company audit. If the corporate accounting firm had signed off on the loan document, or would sign off, I
agreed to calm down.

But when I questioned the audit team's head about the loan document,
she said they had never seen it. This was a surprise to Mom and astonish-
ing to me. We met together with the auditor who left with my accountant's
analysis.

Later, when we spoke, the auditor said her firm declined to look over the
analysis. Pressed about why, I learned that Mom had told the accountant
she wouldn't pay for the additional analysis of the Sanwa loan. I offered to
pay the fee.

"No," she replied, offering the real reason. "The firm doesn't want to be
put in the middle between your mom and you."

I was out there all alone.

Stonewalled by my mother, the trustees, and the corporation's accoun-
tants, I sued the corporation to stop the loan. I sued the trustees for conflict
of interest and failure to do their fiduciary duty. My legal team got a temporary restraining order to prevent Ruth's Chris Steak House from firing me.
In contempt of the restraining order, Ruth's Chris fired me the next day.

I told Jerry what was happening, and he joined me in the lawsuit. For
one day. Then someone got to him, I don't know who. I imagine my mother
was too upset to make the case against me but the case was made. Jerry
went over to their side.

Before the switchover, Jerry had brought Dad in the loop. After years of
silence, Dad now called to egg me on: *Got to fight for your rights, son. She's
got no right to do that to you.* Maybe he would finally get his vengeance on
Ruth. In his mind, Ralph was a good stand-in for Joe. I listened. I wasn't
averse to allies, however ineffectual. But I had crossed the Rubicon long
before he weighed in.

Technically, I sued the Ruth's Chris corporation and the trustees over-
seeing the 80 percent of corporate stock that was "beneficially" mine and
my brother's. Suing *Ruth's Chris*, and not *Ruth Fertel*, is a small distinction
with a big difference under Louisiana's Napoleonic Code. In the original
suit we got that correct. But in the temporary restraining order lay the Napoleonic rub. After I was fired, my legal team asked the judge to respond to
the corporation's contempt for his restraining order. My lawyers mentioned
my mother *by name* in the brief. That put her in play. Which helped me

fulfill my genetic destiny. I am a Fertel. In effect, I, too, have sued a family member.

My mother's legal team called her to the stand. If she was found *personally* liable for contempt of court, she could be sent to jail. Jail time was the furthest thing from my mind. I was just trying to protect my paycheck while I protected my rights. But this was theater, and Mom was writing the script.

Our motion was denied. How could I have imagined a fair day in court in a state where Ruth Fertel fed and watered just about every judge?

As we left court that day, Phil approached me. In an ominous tone, he told me that, having put my mother in jeopardy, I would lose the trust unless I ended the lawsuit.

I laughed nervously. "Phil, the trust is irrevocable. You don't know what you're talking about."

"You'd better look into it."

I shuddered.

My faith shaken, I moved to a new law firm, known for their intellectual rigor. They found an obscure paragraph in the Napoleonic Code: if someone is given a gift and then puts the donor in jeopardy, the gift can be rescinded. *The Ruth's Chris trust* was irrevocable; the *donation to the trust* was not.

My case for the trustees' conflict of interest was open and shut, prima facie, they agreed. But I could be defending an *empty trust*.

My new lawyers had done the research: the only cases that invoked the Code's obscure paragraph were both named *Fertel v. Fertel*.

This information was conveyed to me in an elegant conference room lined with pictures of New Orleans from the turn of the nineteenth century. The room faced Rampart Street, two blocks from where the Fertels once ran their pawnshop. It seemed that I was playing out a Greek tragedy written into my genetic code. If character is fate, my worst nightmare confronted me: my genes had formed my character. Thinking I was standing up for myself, I was, in fact, falling into well-worn family grooves.

Which Fertel had sued which Fertel to rescind a donation? That paragraph had been at issue in Julia's succession. Later, my father used the same paragraph to sue my mother—*Joe's brandished pistol*. Mom must have remembered *Fertel v. Fertel* and brought that obscure paragraph to the lawyers' attention. It was our family legacy, now deployed by a brilliant woman.

In the midst of the legal battle, my internist called. For a year I had been seeing doctors about anemia and low energy. The paleness of my skin once caused a customer to remark, "I've seen barroom pallors before, but yours is ridiculous."

"Randy, I have great news," my internist said, proud of his diagnostic skills. "I know what's wrong with you. You have a brain tumor."

I had a pituitary tumor; my pallor and lack of energy stemmed from having no hormones in my system. Without an operation to remove the tumor, I was told, I would soon go blind as it grew and encroached on the optic nerve.

Mom and her corporate team used even this information against me. Phil said that if I didn't back off, I would lose the health insurance that I needed to pay for my operation. COBRA (the federal law that extends health benefits after job termination), he explained, would only be a temporary solution. *Who knew what my medical future would demand?*

Bad enough that this threat came from a man who, as my trustee, had agreed to fiduciary care, the higher legal duty to act in my best interests. Still worse, he was a messenger boy, bearing my mother's coup de grace.

I had failed. I lost my job, and our trust was put in hock to a Japanese bank that, fortunately enough, would find no cause to foreclose. In Mom's eye, this showed that I had been wrong all along. Iraq's second war awaited a second generation of bad leadership.

This Lear, having given her empire away, had managed to control it.

After the lawsuit, the head accountant was rewarded for her loyalty, hired as comptroller of Ruth's Chris Steak House. Jerry received a new Buick Roadmaster, the equivalent perhaps of the $100 Annie offered to suborn my father's testimony regarding Julia's diamonds. Phil's second franchise opened a year later. He got Birmingham. I didn't hear from Dad again for many years.

When I came back from treatments at M. D. Anderson in Houston, Linda asked me to leave. *She'd had enough of the Fertels.* I couldn't blame her. I had had enough myself.

CHAPTER SIXTEEN

THE EMPRESS OF STEAK

FOLLOWING THE DEBACLE OF 1991, MOM AND I DIDN'T SPEAK FOR A year or two. She made few inquiries after my health struggles. We lived in different parts of the city, me uptown, she behind the restaurant in Mid-City.

Slowly I made my way back to teaching, as an adjunct at Tulane University. I taught a course on the literature of the Vietnam War, a literature filled with disappointing authority figures and the abuse of power; although I had managed to avoid the draft, these were subjects not far from my experience. I learned that Ron Ridenhour, the soldier and journalist who blew the whistle on the My Lai massacre, lived in New Orleans, and I invited him to my class. He was a mesmerizing speaker with a life-altering story to tell, and we became friends. In 1994, I directed an international conference on the twenty-fifth anniversary of the My Lai story. Whistle-blowing—speaking truth to power—was something I could understand.

In the mid-1990s, Mom and I began a peacemaking process. I tried to explore the theme of reconciliation. *We had both made errors. I regretted mine. What about hers?*

What errors?

It was clear I would have to leave a lot unsaid if we were to have a relationship. It would be a relationship on her terms. In the middle of one of our emotional tangles, Mom and I got around to comparing our strengths.

241

I was better at feelings, she admitted; *she could learn a lot from me.* I imagined this might mark the beginning of a change. I was wrong.

Perhaps this was an element in my mother's discomfort with me: where do feelings figure on the *Daily Racing Form* or the monthly P&L? Yet, in some ways, I was no better at feelings than Mom. I had my own difficulties with the life of the heart.

When Earner's mother, Pearl, died, taking her spectacular talent for crawfish bisque with her, I went to her funeral at Our Lady Star of the Sea Catholic Church on St. Roch Avenue. Nearby stood the St. Roch Chapel, where petitioners bring representations of their suffering to an altar in hopes of being blessed with St. Roch's healing intervention, as he had done in the yellow fever epidemic in 1867. The altar is filled with legs and arms from dolls, braces and crutches, even a pair of concrete eyeballs, an effort to cure someone's blindness.

I sat in the rear of the church, to be far from my mother who sat with Earner's family. The service was intoned by an earnest priest whose heart was big with a sense of personal salvation and of community. Pearl's community filled the church.

I found myself weeping, then heaving with tears.

Yet I hardly knew Pearl. I cried for the mother who for me had died, not just because of the family business fight but somehow long before. I cried for what, given the outpouring of community I was witnessing, I now sensed I had never had, that pearl of great price, love. I should have left a plastic heart on the St. Roch altar.

And yet still I wanted to know my mother and to be close to her.

In the mid-1990s, Mom and I began to share some time together. One night we dropped in on Emeril's newly opened Delmonico's, his high-end homage to the great nineteenth century Creole table d'hôte restaurant, complete with formal tableside service.

As usual, Mom was dressed in slacks. "Do you think they'll let us in?" she wondered.

"Yeah, Mom, maybe. . . ."

When the Empress of Steak entered, they all but bowed and kissed her ring. Emeril himself emerged from the kitchen to carve our classic Roast Chicken Bonne Femme for two. All eyes in the packed dining room were upon us. Mom glowed.

For my forty-eighth birthday, Mom took me to the Napa Valley Wine Auction. Robert Mondavi, Jack Cakebread, Dan Duckhorn, all princes of

16.1 Ruth, Robert and Margrit Mondavi.

wine, paid homage to the woman who sold more of their red wine than any other restaurateur in the world.

On occasion, I cooked for Mom—she loved my Chinese cashew chicken and even admitted grudgingly that my smothered snap beans with ham—a family favorite that we eat over rice in New Orleans—were better than Earner's. We found a kind of peace although it was a peace filled with silences. In the time we shared, I settled for our breaking bread together, long the family's stopgap cure for trauma.

On my own I did what I could to make sense of what I had experienced and to explain my mother's actions. It was hard to understand how a person I experienced as so powerful was unable to admit any weakness or fault. Unlike our famous live oaks, she could not bend.

Were my efforts to explain Mom just another version of the "smart attacks" to which I had resorted since childhood, trying to apply my brain in an effort to adapt to the difficult world presented by my parents? With Ruth, I had been vigilant, anticipating her caustic wit while craving her love. With Dad, I had been hypervigilant, trying to stay sane as I imagined he could not. I had avoided my brother's unbridled violence by keeping my nose in a book. Books would civilize me in the midst of an uncivil household.

Despite his economic advantages, my father lived in an economy of scarcity, the land of never enough. For Dad, haunted by death—how else to understand his determination to live forever?—and obsessed with revenge, life was a gamble, a zero-sum game he was determined to win and, if you won, was prepared to make you pay. By contrast, Louis Armstrong, whose spirit—like my father's—haunts South Rampart Street, was, according to his own delighted account, born into a depraved and sordid world of hookers and gamblers, violence and racism. Yet, despite this impoverished upbringing, Louis lived and entertained within an economy of abundance. The world was not only wonderful but a cornucopia, a brass horn no doubt, which the artist's transformative art helped to brim over with joy. Dad was king of an island that stood alone in a vast sea. Longing to become an individual, I needed him to be less wildly so. Unfair to him? Of course it was.

Mom, too, operated in an economy of scarcity, always out to show her father had been right, she *did* hang the moon, bigger and higher than anyone else. She *was* a radiant presence, but if push came to shove, if there was competition in the room, in the end she shone for herself alone. I was proud of my mother and often equally abashed. Like Sig, I was used to giving in. Coming in second was a survival technique. The game was zero-sum and nonnegotiable. The one time I hadn't given in, I came in on the short, red-ink side of the zero.

Trying to survive my mother and father and schooling myself with books, I sought my salvation trying to be the good and rational son and citizen. Trying to survive my corporate battles with Ruth's Chris, perhaps my embracing an amorality equal to my opponents' immorality—doing not the *right* thing, but rather *the thing that works*—might have served me better. To bring morality to bear in an immoral battlefield is not to be Lear's wise Fool but to be just plain foolish. The trick—which I had failed to accomplish—was to distinguish between Dad's arrogant and hurtful Trickster and Earner's true Trickster. The true Trickster doesn't seek to hurt. The true Trickster is never taken in by another's high horse, but never mounts one herself. I mounted one, the high horse of Truth and Law, and managed to get myself dumped from the saddle and trampled.

In the 1990s, as the Ruth's Chris brand spread nationwide and around the globe, the restaurant industry recognized Mom with every award it had to give—The Silver Plate from the National Restaurant Association; Best Chain from *Nation's Restaurants News;* Executive of the Year from *Restaurant and Institutions* and their Ivy Award of Distinction; Woman of the Year from the Roundtable of Women in Foodservice; Entrepreneur of the Year from Ernst & Young and Merrill Lynch; and many more.

16.2 Ruth shares the stage at Ford's Theatre with Coach Don Shula for Horatio Alger Awards, 1995.

By 1995, we were reconciled enough that Mom invited me to attend the Horatio Alger Awards in Washington, D.C. The awards, presented during a glitzy weekend of events, honor those who succeed despite adversity. The awards also have a charitable dimension, with a hundred college scholarships given to worthy high school kids from severely challenged backgrounds.

Mom joined nine others who had pulled themselves up by their bootstraps. Former winners in attendance included Quincy Jones, Colin Powell, Maya Angelou, Oprah Winfrey, and Chuck Yeager. When I asked the former test pilot if he still flew and what they let him fly, he gave me a look that said, *whatever the hell I want.* Colin Powell grew two inches when I mentioned that I had gotten to know General Walt Boomer—great name!—at the My Lai conference I had directed: *There's a real soldier!* averred Powell. I didn't venture to ask Powell about his own little-known role in the My Lai cover-up.

The one event where Mom had to perform was held at Ford's Theatre. One after another, the awardees stood center stage, recounted their rags-to-riches stories, and then fielded questions. It seemed like a contest to see who had made the most of their early strife.

My mother was not one to fuss about her many accolades; she didn't set much store by such honors. Although she was always nervous before audiences, her unassuming manner put everyone in the palm of her hand. She told the gathering that, when she grew up in the Depression, her father *eked out a living, but there was food for the picking, so I never knew that we were poor.* Asked about her role as a model for young women aspiring to the business world, this reluctant feminist icon said, *I succeeded because I worked hard, and seeing how I worked, people—men and women—wanted me to succeed.*

As the 1990s came to a close, Mom decided that it was time to cash in. She had replaced Ralph with a new CEO whose charge was to prepare the company to go public. Ralph quit, angry that this first "outside" CEO was not a figurehead who would do his bidding. *Doesn't he know I built this brand?* After due diligence, the new CEO announced that selling the company outright was the best way to go. Although this CEO was later terminated for cause, the next CEO also determined that an outright sale was best, and the board gave him the go-ahead. It was time to cash *out.*

In 1999, the company was sold to Madison-Dearborn, a financial concern in Chicago. They promised that Ruth's Chris would be kept *just as "Miz Ruth"* wanted.

I resisted the sale. Although the payoff to the trust would be handsome, I doubted that my mother's legacy would be respected. But no discussion of my carrying on her legacy got past my bringing it up. I knew I didn't have many of Mom's strengths, particularly her decisiveness that had served her both well and ill. But I thought with my willingness to hire people stronger than myself, I could build a team that could bring Ruth's Chris back to its founding legacy, its commitment to quality and to people. Mom pressed on. *I'm tired. This is the right moment in the market. I want you boys—*I hung on the word—*to benefit from my success.*

As usual, the unreliable men with whom Mom surrounded herself made out like bandits.

I was concerned about those aspects of the sale, but I was also concerned about the consequences for Jerry and for me. I didn't have to look far for examples of the ill effects of windfalls of money. I took Mom to dinner at Bayona one night.

"Mom, I've been talking to private banks that I think will help me handle this money intelligently, but I've also learned that some are prepared to handle not only investments but also the day-to-day business of wealth. Jerry relies on you quite a bit to take care of his bills and his affairs. Maybe you might urge him to look into a bank like this to help him. They might help protect him from all those friends of his he is so generous toward."

She thought a minute.

"Maybe he will grow up," she offered.

I thought about that awhile.

"So what you're saying is that Jerry is about to make fifty and is about to come into a lot of money and that's when he's going to decide it's time to grow up?"

We muddled through the rest of our dinner.

As the sale of Ruth's Chris approached, Phil, the sole remaining trustee—Jim had died of a heart attack—approached the board for his "payoff" for serving as trustee. *All those years I never took a fee.*

Created because of one of Mom's real estate debacles, the trust had been a passive instrument, except when it was used to bail out her next real estate debacle. It owned 80 percent of the corporate stock, and until the sale, had no liquidity. Thus, the trust contained no money to manage. While Phil was called upon to do none of the business transactions that trustees usually perform, he had reaped significant benefits from the insider position his trusteeship gave him, earning fees both as Mom's personal and as the corporation's attorney. However often she might roll her eyes at his incompetence, she could not easily fire him. And he cost us more than the fees he was paid. He wrote franchise documents that confused radius with diameter in defining the area of geographical exclusivity, a blunder that would cost millions in legal battles with franchisees. He obligated the trust to pay a local investment-banking group to monitor his efforts in the sale—to cover him as trustee. He promised them $3 million for what we were later told should have cost $300,000. He felt no need to negotiate the fee, it wasn't his to pay. His biggest personal payoff had come from the franchises he acquired. When the corporation hired its first outside CEO, he set a moratorium on the opening of new franchises. Phil approached the new CEO and said, "Of course that doesn't apply to me, right?" Phil was entitled.

As a board member, Phil would reap hundreds of thousands of dollars in stock options when the company was sold. But he wanted extra payback for his years of loyalty and service to Ruth Fertel—a million dollars to sign his name to the trust dissolution that would allow the sale proceeds to flow to Jerry and me. Phil announced that he would fight us in court rather than relinquish control. We refused. Mom sided with Jerry and me.

Now on the outside but ever the dealmaker, Ralph tried to intervene. He asked me to lunch. We met at La Riviera, his favorite Italian restaurant, where he ravished a plate of their famous crabmeat ravioli in cream sauce. Ralph urged me to settle with Phil. "A million dollars is reasonable, Randy. Have I ever given you bad advice?" he asked, dabbing at the cream dribbling down his chin. Laughing to myself, I wondered what his cut of the cool million would have been. *How stupid did he think I was?*

The legal battle began with depositions. Because the trust paid for Phil's "defense of the trust," I was paying for all six lawyers around the long table. His legal team's line of questioning surprised me. For more than an hour, they led me through my academic career, inviting me to recount my years at Harvard, Le Moyne, the University of New Orleans, and Tulane: my publications and teaching awards, my advancement toward tenure.

"So, basically, what you're saying, Mr. Fertel," I remember them saying, "is that you've never done anything practical in your life." They had revealed their cards. Phil's hole card was to demonstrate that I was unable to fend for myself. I needed his benign and competent protection. I hadn't known that anti-intellectualism in America ran that deep. I should have. Along with my last name, my Harvard degree had always been my worst demerit.

After the deposition, Phil's lawyers must have seen that this strategy wouldn't play well in a court of law. The case, and Phil's million-dollar demand, went away.

Jerry hired a Lafayette lawyer to manage his affairs. They met through a golfing buddy. Allan "Sprinky" Durand, who earned his nickname the first time his father changed his diaper, stepped down from the managing partnership in his law firm to have the time for Jerry. Their contract stipulated that, given this sacrifice, Sprinky would be compensated if Jerry terminated their relationship. A few months later Sprinky resisted Jerry's plan to build a golf course. He fired Sprinky and a judge upheld the penalty Jerry was required to pay. Jerry hired a lawyer to file ethics charges against Sprinky and Sprinky walked away from the judgment in his favor. I don't know who now manages Jerry's money. Ranches in New Mexico, restaurants in Covington, Louisiana, stables with a hundred Louisiana-bred horses now crowd his portfolio. Judy Agular, the manager of his stable, who was in my class in middle school, would tell me, *he's more like your daddy every day.*

Within weeks of the sale, Bill Hyde, Mom's sweet-talking and well-named CEO, kept on by the new owners, sent signals that Ruth's Chris would not be business as usual. Rosemary, the mother of Jerry's first sons, was retired from managing the Lafayette restaurant. Lana and Duke Unlimited were replaced by another ad agency. Similar gestures followed, making it clear: Mom's people were out; she was no longer needed. At one point Hyde boasted to Bill Primavera that he had cleaned out the Ruthian stable, forgetting that Primavera Public Relations had been on the hit list.

Mom fumed mostly in silence.

CHAPTER SEVENTEEN

EMBRACING PAHRUMP

MY FATHER'S STREET-PERSON REGALIA HAD PROTECTED HIM FOR DECADES. But one time in the late 1980s, the costume failed to work. Dad was accosted outside a Reno casino, robbed of his gold Rolex and his thick roll of greenbacks. The thief struck Dad and put out his left eye.

The emergency room doctor presented Dad with a decision. The eye would never again serve him; the doctor could leave it in or take it out. It was Dad's call.

Dad sat upright in the hospital bed, his left eye heavily bandaged, and, misquoting the Bible again, replied with a bitter grin: "If thine eye offend thee, pluck it out." So instructed, that's what the doctor did. After Reno, Dad wore an eye patch that conformed well with his desire to shock. By Jerry's account, he had a bit of trouble on the golf course from loss of depth perception. But, according to Jerry, he was generally unfazed.

I rarely saw Dad for a decade or so and I didn't seek him out. The next time I heard from him was in 1995 when he called, looking for Jerry. He needed a ride to Las Vegas from Hot Springs. *Did I know where Jerry was?*

Of course I did: as always, *Jerry was out of town*. The bad joke didn't slow him down; I could hear Dad edging toward asking *me* for the ride. Usually at such moments, I would remind him that I had a job—I was teaching the literature of the Vietnam War at Tulane at the time—and unlike him couldn't take off for parts unknown. This time I skipped such small change: "What can you be thinking asking me for a favor? When I had a brain

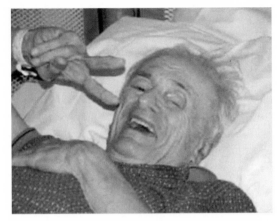

17.1 One-eyed and raring to go—
the Gorilla Man on his deathbed.

tumor and lost my job and family, you disappeared. Not a word. This is the first time we've spoken since 1991."

"I thought that's what you needed," he offered, his version of tough love, I suppose.

That was the end of that conversation. Soon after that call, he called at five in the morning. "The hotels in New Orleans want too much money." He had heard about my new house on Audubon Park.

"I don't think that's a good idea, Dad." It wasn't right turning away my father, but I wasn't sure how I would ever dislodge him. Maybe this time it would be my shoes, not Sophie's, on the sidewalk and my house signed away.

A year or so later, Jerry showed up in Florida at Mom's condo on the beach. She had decided to hold Thanksgiving dinner in Destin. Rosemary had brought Rien and Tommy and I brought Matt and Owen, all young teens. Jerry had Dad in tow—but had sense enough to install him in a nearby motel. One afternoon Jerry took all the boys bowling. When they came back they told me in hushed tones about their one-eyed grandfather at the bowling alley. They had met him only once before.

"When we were leaving, Dad," Matt explained, "he asked Uncle Jerry who 'those boys were?'"

"Yeah, Dad," Owen added, "he doesn't even know who we are."

Now, in Las Vegas, 2003, it was time to pay my last respects. I was on my way to a sustainable food conference in Napa, California, when I got a rare call from Jerry: Dad was in a coma. Besides losing an eye, Dad had taken a fall in his Hot Springs bathhouse that had required drilling his cranium to release the pressure of the bleeding. The present seizure was probably a long-term result of that injury. Jerry had found him after this new seizure. Actually he found him twice. The first time Jerry found Dad lying on the floor, he and Sophie assumed he was taking a nap. He had been playing with the kids. Jerry wanted to wake him; Sophie said, let him sleep. Three hours later, returning from the movie, they found him still lying there, still unconscious, but now, humming and murmuring. They couldn't wake him. Jerry called 911. The ICU and the ventilator's rhythmic whoosh followed.

I finished my talk—about Mom's presence—and rushed down to Vegas filled with anxiety not just for Dad but for myself. I hoped to make him more comfortable but I also hoped I would not let him get to me.

Las Vegas seemed a figment of Dad's dreaming. You didn't even need to travel to develop new prejudices. There the wide world was, lining the Strip, pasteboard masks of world travel, prejudices hardened into clichés hardened into Lake Como, Paris, Rome, Manhattan, Istanbul, Cairo, and of course the Wild Wild West. But it was a Jewish gangster's dream, Bugsy Siegel's, so it included gambling, which was just fine with Rodney. Sam and Julia had saved every penny dreaming of bricks and mortar paid for with hocked diamonds and, then, in some of the most expensive real estate in the world, Annie, and then Rodney, and then Jerry (and sometimes me), would put those pennies grown to dollars on the Pass line in hopes that our dreams would come true.

But now it was nightmare time. I sat at his bedside. For an eighty-one-year-old with one eye and suffering from seizures, he looked pretty good. From all those years of fetal lamb cell shots, his skin was almost wrinkle-free. Somewhere in his peregrinations he had lost his prosthetic eye, so there was only a dark cavity beneath a lifeless lid. Unaccommodated man. King Lear on the heath. But this Lear wasn't just unfazed, he was still totally himself. He still exuded his zest for life, never suffering a moment of self-doubt, nor ever a moment's hesitation about just what you needed to fix your ill-informed way of life.

Finally he awoke, happy to see me. Not especially surprised. Like we had talked not a decade ago but just the week before.

That first night before he woke, his nurse shocked me with her bluntness. For four or five days, she'd been dealing with Jerry and his family, Sophie and their kids. Jerry came often to the hospital but stayed outside Dad's room, gregariously chatting up the nurses as the kids ran the corridors.

"Why do you bother?" the nurse asked.

"Well, he's my father."

"But they're Pahrumpsters, all of them," she replied, as if this fact should reset my moral compass. Pahrump is a town up in a mountain valley above Vegas where Dad and Jerry often played golf.

"Pahrump," she explained, "is filled with wooly old coots like these two. The whole town is nuts. Some people can't be helped. It would have been better if your brother had just left him there," she concluded.

This came from a bright-eyed, intelligent nurse. Perhaps it was the end of a long day. It was as if she had taken my measure and decided I didn't belong to the same nest as these two Pahrumpsters. Hers was an odd and surprising perspective, but I felt grateful. Despite her harsh stance, her professional care never flagged.

I would do what I could. I would act on my good feelings while inwardly honoring my darker feelings. This man had never really been a father to me. But, then, no one had showed him how.

Jerry, good caretaker or not, held the high ground. He had been in charge of this difficult man for some time. If he disagreed with me, he felt he had the right to say, *Randy, where have you been?* The best I could do was stay out of a lawsuit, and finesse getting Dad the best care we could.

Over the next weeks, Jerry and I mirrored the baby-boomer generation in microcosm. I was the one-time hippie and antiwar activist trying to work *within* the health care and legal system. Regardless of the 1960s, I now saw that the system was not my enemy; in this case, it was my only ally. Jerry, who had gone off to war trusting the system and refusing his mother's political leverage, now denied anyone in the system knew what he or she was doing. He was hell-bent to sue the moment he had something to blame them for. And the hospital knew it.

Jerry also knew, what I didn't, that in the will drawn up by Jerry's lawyer, Dad had disinherited me, true to family form. I would soon face the challenge of fighting the impulse to contest it, a signal victory for a Fertel. (At least he wouldn't claim I had tried to kill him in France. But he didn't need to: the Napoleonic law of forced heirship had been rescinded.) For the moment my ignorance saved me from the difficult choice—would I let my anger get in the way of my doing the right thing for my father? I'd like to think I would have overcome that impulse.

Dad became difficult to handle. Unable to walk on his own, he would not allow the physical therapists near him. His doctor transferred him from the rehab hospital to the lockdown geriatric-psychiatric unit. Jerry and I trailed his ambulance in separate cars to the new hospital across town.

When we got there, for a too-long moment, Dad was lost in the shuffle of paperwork. Anxious, Jerry speculated, "When we were leaving that last hospital, they told him he was going to see the movie *Chicago*. Maybe they did."

I reminded Jerry that the nurses had heard us talking to Dad about how he loved that movie and had seen it five times. "They were making a joke, Jerry. Sometimes people make a joke."

"Well, they shouldn't."

Jerry was determined to transport Dad to Hot Springs. They both believed that only the baths could cure him. "It's all he needs," Jerry insisted. So, Jerry coached him. Calling on his experience as an army medic, he urged, "Dad, you're in a psych ward. Tomorrow they're going to ask you some questions. They'll want to test if you know where you are. You got to remember to tell them you're in Las Vegas."

"Las Vegas. Okay."

"And they're gonna want to know what day it is."

"What day is it?"

"Tuesday. Tomorrow is Wednesday."

"Wednesday. Okay."

"And Bush is president."

"Yeah, he's going to war . . . okay . . . wait. Can you write this down?"

Jerry took the morning line—a sheet with the point spreads for all the day's games—from his front pocket and, not wanting to lose the record of his bets, tore off a thin corner strip. "Las Vegas, Dad. See? Las Vegas. Can you read that?" he asked, putting it up to Dad's good eye.

"Yeah. Las Vegas."

"2003, Dad."

"Yeah."

"Tell them you're in Las Vegas."

" . . . I'm in Las Vegas? . . . I thought I was in Hot Springs." Jerry turned away in exasperation.

The next day, examining Dad, the new rehab physician turned to me. Without even stepping out of Dad's hearing, he asked, "How long has he been suffering from onset dementia?"

Dad smiled on. Dementia was exactly what I had been seeing and yet not seeing. My father's present behavior was familiar to my lifelong experience, just more extreme. Sometimes he was wildly incoherent. Sometimes he saw huge balloons floating or imagined people in the room. He pointed his finger and loudly fussed, "What are you doing *here*? Get out of here! You don't belong here!"

I had always loosely thought of Dad as "crazy." Now, it was official.

Nonetheless, in the days that followed, we had the best conversations of our lives. One morning, as I sat at his side, he awoke and announced to me, "Oh, I'm so happy to see you. It's a miracle that I found you. A miracle. You're a lucky man. You know, I was just at your mother's restaurant, and there are a lot of problems down there, they're all stealing from her. Here's what you need to do . . ."

There were more coherent moments when Dad was his old self, talking about the old days on Rampart Street, about meeting Dalí and running for mayor, and about the untrustworthiness of women. But I also learned of a woman with whom he lived in Taiwan for some time. While he was not the most reliable witness, the twinkle in his eye was enough to convince me that he remembered her fondly; it was neither a dream nor a boast. It was nice making the acquaintance of a man I had not known, one who could love rather than hate women.

And lots of talk about money. He wanted the doctor's advice about *those stocks*. He wanted me to buy ten thousand shares. No stock was mentioned by name. You could almost date the onset of his dementia: after the dot.com bubble and before its bursting. How this "craziness" differed from what I had long experienced seemed only a matter of degree.

But the biggest difference in the room was not in Dad, but in me. For the first time, I wasn't there to argue. I didn't need Dad to be a dad. I didn't need him to be responsible and presentable. Trying to argue my father into sanity had never worked. Now I found I no longer needed to try.

I didn't come to Las Vegas needing a father as I once had, but I did need to see the truth. Dad was truly himself always. In that regard he was not a dissembler. Yet, he had never lived in the truth. He felt no obligation to it. Sometimes his con was charming, sometimes ugly. His many contradictions now resulted, in part, from the neuron storm that raged in his head. In his present state, there was a childlike transparency to his lying. This was the Rodney who had adapted to the conditions of his early years on South Rampart and South Robert streets.

I had the turnabout experience many of us are destined for, of feeding a parent and helping to change him. I also got Dad talking. I took him back to his childhood, his family, and his romance with my mother. He seemed to come round more and more. Perhaps it was an illusion produced by happenstance, but I imagined this kind of talking cure was, like Lear's sleep, reknitting his addled brain.

More than once, Dad asked, *How do you remember all those things?* I told him I was writing a book. I was going to call it *The Gorilla Man and the Empress of Steak.*

Smiling, he hid his pleasure behind his gruffness. *You can call it anything you want.*

He confirmed much of what I had written and I learned a few new things. His grandfather Sam Fertel had been a *sweet man.* Julia was *brilliant.* Though there was no record of good feelings between Dad and his mother, he remembered her fondly. *She was a clever woman. Full of fun.* He remembered that Annie loved the races. She kept betting slips tucked in her rolled stockings. *She could really pick 'em.*

His old obsessions emerged. His brain was truly a cabinet of curiosities, more jumbled now, but much the same as when we traveled through Mexico, Europe, and around the world. And Hot Springs—if only he could get there now, he would be *fine in no time.* Cell shots wouldn't hurt either. *You owe it to yourself.*

I heard about Paul Stern the handicapper—*no one was as good with numbers.* And Dalí—*he was really famous.* Cuba? Sure, he saw Fidel on the street. Never Hemingway, though he'd eaten at La Floridita, Hemingway's favorite. How many times had he gone round the world? *Five!* How had he stayed out of the army during the war? A sidewise, uncomfortable grin: *That's my secret.* Another time, boasting: *I knew the right people.*

And, of course, gorillas. *You can learn a lot from gorillas. They're the smartest animals.* I played the story about his Gorilla Man campaign that I had read as a commentator on National Public Radio. He listened intently. *It's good,* he said proudly. *Do you know why it's good? Because it's all true.*

He told more details about the gorilla-buying trip, although the details changed in repeated tellings. Sometimes the gorillas cost $250 each, sometimes $6,000. In one story, he bought them from a ship's captain, Harrison Lane. In another story, he and the Black Cat had a ball traipsing across the globe to Singapore to pick them up.

—*Singapore? Sure, Rodney, I'll go. Where's Singapore?*

—*Black Cat, I think you go to Hong Kong then turn left.*

I reminded him of the plaque I'd had the Audubon Zoo put up acknowledging his gift. The zoo had taken down the original plaque after Dad complained ceaselessly about the gorillas' television not being repaired. He had

17.2 The Audubon Zoo gorilla habitat.

donated the television when he saw how bored the gorillas were. A few years later, I wrote to the director and managed to have the plaque replaced. The director, Ron Forman, allowed me to write the copy on the plaque that now stands before the habitat. I showed Dad a picture. He beamed.

> ON NOVEMBER 1, 1970,
> RODNEY FERTEL
> GAVE THE GIFT OF WONDER
> TO THE CHILDREN OF NEW ORLEANS:
> TWO LOWLAND GORILLAS NAMED
> MOLLY AND SCOTTY.

If he saw Red Beans and Rice today, Dad said, *they would remember him. They loved him. They would come right up to him. That's why he always wore his pith helmet, so they would recognize him. And yes, he had indeed climbed the fence at Audubon Park in the dead of night to see his buddies.*

"Why?"

"To feed them. Potato chips, not bananas. They don't eat bananas, people don't realize."

"Dad, why did you run for mayor?"

"Well, I didn't like the way the city was being run."

"What about Judge Gertler?"

"That Gertler," he spat out, "he was a bad man."

And Ruth? They had met at LSU. In one version, she was watching him at swim practice. In another they met at his stables. They married in Baton Rouge and honeymooned on a trip around the world. "Watch out for those huge snakes in the ocean and the sharks. They'll get you if you don't watch it."

Yes, they went to Africa, had braved the long flight from Buenos Aires to Dakar on a plane he wasn't sure had enough engines. "They said I was crazy to try it. You need four engines for that long ocean crossing." No, they hadn't fought on the trip. "Ruth loved to travel."

I learned of his favorite picture, a photo taken on Central Avenue in Hot Springs when they were first married. He liked it so much that thirty years after the divorce he had a photographer friend blow it up to poster size. He couldn't remember what he had done with that photo.

17.4 The author, c. 1970, with Scotty, who sports the better haircut but the less revealing shadow.

"Why did you get divorced?"

He asked me if I "really wanted to know." It was the most care he ever showed regarding my feelings.

"Well, that cop, Joe DeMatteo. I came back to town and a guy said, 'Your wife's going out with that Joe DeMatteo.' Yeah, I knew him. I had just given him a horse. A good horse. Yeah, and he had a gun. What could I do?"

"Gee, Dad, that must have really hurt."

"Yeah," he said.

"Was Ruth good at picking horses?" I asked.

With one eyeless socket closed and the other eye barely open, Dad's face was filled with a look of half-grudging admiration. It was a look suffused with the warm regard of that picture from 1948 on Central Avenue in Hot Springs. He was young again.

"Ruth," he said. "She was good at everything she touched."

The day I finished a draft of this manuscript, about eighteen months after Dad's death, I received an auspicious phone call. It was Dan Maloney, general curator of the Audubon Zoo. He called to break the sad news: Scotty the gorilla (aka Grandeza, aka Red Beans) had died in the Denver Zoo. He and Molly (aka Boneca, aka Rice) had never hit it off. They had been sent to other zoos for more productive relationships.

Dan made a point of saying—as if this were a condolence call for a family member—that Scotty had died in his sleep. He had a favorite plastic tub he liked to sleep in and it was there where they had found him this morning. Best of all, Scotty went out as any red-blooded gorilla could wish: he had spent the morning enjoying the she-gorillas. His life was what the *Times-Picayune* called "a triumph of preservation."

CHAPTER EIGHTEEN

THE EMPRESS'S LAST LEVÉE

DAD'S EVERY MOMENT HAD BEEN GIVEN TO PROLONGING HIS LIFE AND Mom's every moment was lived as if she were immortal. Fetal lamb cells on his side and slabs of richly marbled meat on hers; a few years of cigars versus a lifetime of cigarettes; daily exercise versus a largely sedentary life (except when the helicopter flew her to the duck blind): the scales leaned his way and Mom died a year and a half before Dad. In Dad's passing I found myself reconciled to him in ways I had not anticipated. Mom proved a bigger challenge.

There was much to admire, first and foremost her presence, her ability to be present. There is no road ahead, it has been said, we make the road as we go. Always here, now, my mother lived this wisdom in her business career. Ruth Fertel had no foresight, no master plan. But she had presence and she had guts. She built her empire by accident, always responding to the present moment, improvising like Huck Finn on his raft. Like Huck she went "a good deal on instinct." A fire closed her first restaurant and in one week, she turned her catering hall four blocks away into a restaurant twice the size. A good customer proposes that he open a franchise near Baton Rouge and by 1999, when the company was sold, Mom had opened restaurants from Manhattan to Hong Kong, and from Cancún to Seattle— more than eighty-five restaurants selling millions of pound-size steaks and annual sales topping a third of a billion dollars.

Mom managed to turn her lack of foresight into a strength. Most impressive of all, needing $18,000 Mom was talked into borrowing $22,000 and bought a restaurant and had the working capital to make a go of it. Thirty-four years later she sold her company for a low nine figures. My mother seized every opportunity as they came or as they were put before her and cobbled them into a large life.

Much to her credit, she achieved it with a commitment to equality. She rarely pulled rank in the dining room or kitchen, a signal achievement for someone who was raised by a father who told her that she "hung the moon."

In 1997, when Mom turned seventy, she visited forty-two of her restaurants *to smell out how they're doing*. True to form, when Mom saw folks working hard in one of her kitchens and needing help, she rolled up her sleeves and started peeling shrimp.

Mom's assumption of equality was real, but it was also a generous sleight of hand. Behind the corporate scenes, she shone for herself alone. For all the abundance at Ruth's Chris tables, the corporate culture, like the family culture, was one of scarcity. Mom reserved the glory for herself. After quitting, Ralph bitterly made this point in a letter to my mother. He wondered about all of the people who helped make her the national figure she took great pride in becoming. They were now all on the outside looking in, wondering why she never acknowledged their contributions, and why she abandoned their friendship. Ralph felt it was he who had taken the business from "a Mom operation," as he called it, to the nation's largest upscale restaurant. From his point of view, he had always stayed in the background and let her accept the accolades. It galled him that, receiving every possible award they could possibly win, he had yet to hear her mention his name publicly. Even ever-placid Uncle Sig had been driven into a rage when his sister passed him over for the second New Orleans Ruth's Chris, just up the road from Happy Jack. "Why did they have to compete so hard?" Aunt Helen had wondered aloud.

Mom's glee at winning was so infectious she could almost charm you into forgetting that you'd just been beaten in her zero-sum game. This five foot two blond exulted in being top gun on the duck or dove hunt, top rod on the fishing trip, and top hand at the card table—and left you feeling charmed, for a while.

True, it got a bit old when she insisted on beating you (and later your toddlers) at Go Fish! When I would suggest that maybe she should let my five-year-old—who could barely hold the cards—win a game or two, she'd say, *He needs to learn to lose,* and look at him with disdain if he couldn't take an honest licking. *You don't want to spoil them.* I spared my second son this rite of passage.

Mom had plenty of feed corn for people who weren't close. The stories are legion and legendary. She counseled young women starting up in business, explaining how to calculate food costs and what to charge. She paid the tuition for who knows how many kids (including those of a franchisee who later sued her for millions) and was the last-minute angel who kept a Catholic grammar school in New Orleans from going belly up.

But Mom was a one-woman show. Once in the mid-1970s, at Jimmy Moran's Riverside restaurant, a fortune-teller was going from table to table, picking up each person's "vibe" and giving them a reading of their character. When he came to my mother, he described a self-starter: *she was self-satisfied, and nothing made her happier than being by herself. And the best marriage you could possibly make is if you could marry yourself.* We all cringed at the thought of her response.

Mom slapped the flat of her hand gleefully on the table, *Oh, yes!*

The Empress's throne, there at the beginning of her illustrious career, awaited her. She would sell the first franchise in 1976. She would sit the throne largely alone.

Certainly her competitiveness was an element in the circle of friends and key employees she chose. There was little danger of any holding a candle to her. The strength of the Ruth's Chris product can be seen in this: her commitment to superlative quality in food trumped the mediocrity of the key personnel she chose to help deliver it. Even Ralph, who never ate a mouthful he didn't relish, couldn't manage to screw it up.

But her reactiveness, her lack of foresight, was another element in her inability to see through Ralph, Lana, Phil, and their ilk. One paradox about my woman-of-action mother was a well-hidden, little-known passive element in her makeup. She had the money, business clout, charisma, and willingness to stake everything on the next roll of the dice. But she needed the Ralphs and Lanas to bring her the deals, to set the dice before her, to give her the first push and to be her audience. For Mom, like many gamblers, it was being in the game that counted. They brought her games to play. Win or lose, Mom was happy. It didn't matter that they always made out fine as the bets flew, before the long shot came up short and the venture came crashing down on her head alone, seven and out.

RUTH U. FERTEL
CULINARY ARTS BUILDING

CHEF JOHN FOLSE CULINARY INSTITUTE
NICHOLLS STATE UNIVERSITY
THIBODAUX, LOUISIANA

WEIMER & BOUDREAUX
ARCHITECTS, AIA-LLP

18.1 The Ruth U. Fertel Culinary Arts Building plans for the John Folse Culinary Institute.

Mom's sale of the company in late 1999 was an expression of her utter self-sufficiency. No one in the family, nor any who had helped her build her empire, was worthy to carry on her legacy. Better to cash out to anonymous strangers. The company would keep her name and she assumed the Chicago financial group Madison-Dearborn would do her bidding. Everyone else always had.

When they didn't, Mom's response was to retreat. Her lung cancer, diagnosed soon after the sale, reinforced her impulse to isolate herself.

During one of Mom's remissions, I teamed up with her friend Cajun chef John Folse to hold a tribute dinner. The tribute was something Ruth's Chris Steak House's new owners had not thought to do, and most of her former henchmen were long out of the picture—terminated, paid off, or suing, in any case, angry. But Mom had touched many lives. She deserved a salute.

Soon after she had been diagnosed, I asked her, *If I were to endow something in your name, where should I do it?* I imagined that she would choose Tulane University, where I then taught English, and where she had once worked in the lab of renowned cardiologist Dr. Burch, or the University of New Orleans's hotel and restaurant school where she sometimes spoke. Much to my surprise, she selected the John Folse Culinary Institute at Nicholls State University, seventy-five miles away. Chef John was her good friend, a famous and charming Cajun chef from upriver in Donaldson-ville, and like her a hard driver who was building a culinary empire. Ne-gotiations with John quickly escalated from a scholarship program which, because of low state tuition they didn't need, to a desperately needed culi-nary arts building. I would provide the seed money, and the tribute dinner would launch the fund-raising program. My brother, Jerry, agreed to match the seed money I pledged.

For Christmas of 2000, I gave Mom a framed sketch of the future Ruth U. Fertel Culinary Arts Building. The tribute/fund-raising dinner was put on hold when she was rediagnosed with cancer, and then again when the events of September 11 made the prospect of festivities unseemly. Finally in December of 2001, Mom's X-ray was clean again and we set April 24, 2002, as the date. But soon after, her cancer returned once again. The race was on. She had always been a Thoroughbred. Maybe with her competitive juices, she would make it.

The call came at five in the morning. As I drove to the hospital it was fully light out. Mom was in ICU. She was on a ventilator. There was no measur-able brain function.

Family and friends began to gather. Earner. Little Sig. Lana and her son David. Jerry's son Rien. Soon, with all her retainers arrayed around her bed, it began to look like the Empress's last levée. Finally Aunt Helen swept in, having driven from Buras at the river's mouth, a breath of simple grace and finally some sanity in that room so full of enmeshed emotions.

Mom was propped up in the bed. She still wore the Ruth's Chris Steak House ball cap. Every minute or so a nerve storm seized her and an invol-untary twitch racked her for five long seconds. Her eyes, rolled back in her forehead, had that look health providers refer to as "circling the drain."

The ICU was brand new and spacious, far less antiseptic than it could have been, with oak paneling and a window seat for the family. It was the Goldring ICU wing, named for a family who for generations has made a fortune in New Orleans selling liquor and fine wine, much of it for the last thirty-five years to Ruth's Chris. The Goldrings' philanthropy provided care for the illnesses the City that Care Forgot got drinking the Goldrings' beverages and eating the Empress's steaks. So here we were. The nursing staff was of the highest caliber. In a quiet moment, a nurse approached me and explained that when not working ICU she was pursuing a degree at the John Folse Culinary Institute. She planned to change careers. She wanted to thank the family for their commitment to the Fertel Culinary Arts Building. *They need the building so bad and Miz Ruth is such an inspiration.*

The ventilator continued its rhythmic hum. As the Empress's retainers watched this sad spectacle, I began to work on the doctors to have the ventilator removed. *No,* I had to reply, *there is no power of attorney. No, there is no living will. Yes, there is another sibling.* And it became clear that Jerry's wishes were the key. They would not commit to removing the ventilator—you could almost hear the lawyers whispering in their ears, or was that the whoosh of the ventilator?—but they would not even consider it until Jerry weighed in.

So, after much begging, I convinced Jerry to join the retainers. Just as he would become during my father's last crises, Jerry seemed paralyzed, as if on overload. But finally Jerry came and finally we spoke to the doctors. *No machines.* While they caucused for what seemed an eternity, we, faithful retainers, gathered closer to her deathbed, the ventilator heaving, the eyes rolled back, the nerve storms having their way with her.

Jerry stood at her left shoulder, rubbing it with his finger in tiny circles. Had she lasted longer he might have worn a hole in her gown. When the nerve storms seized her he would fuss: *stop it Mom, stop it Mom, stop it Mom,* as if it was in her power to stop, as if there was a her.

I sat down and waited for the doctors to come.

Mom died on April 16, 2002, missing her tribute dinner by one week. Hoping to surprise her with a tribute video we made for her, I did not play it for her. She did not hear the many marks of love and respect from employees, customers, and colleagues. She did not hear Ella Brennan's generous tribute: "I've always admired Ruth's 'get up and go.' I can just imagine the obstacles that Ruth came up against over the years—real obstacles—serious problems. Things that will keep you up all night—night after night. Once you attain a certain level of success people forget all that—most people never knew. Well, Ruth, I haven't forgotten. And I always respected that you knew your business, that you knew your customer and that you treated your team, your people so well. It always inspired me to know that you were across town from me working your heart out. And I always knew you were smarter than me 'cause you only had to perfect that one thing—that steak. Oh! If you only knew how many nights I felt stupid thinking about that. And oh what a steak it is! Well, old friend—you did it! You did it with

A Tribute to *Ruth Fertel*

"I MORTGAGED MY HOME TO START A STEAK HOUSE I THOUGHT YOU'D LIKE."
Ruth's Chris Steak House

18.2 Ruth's tribute dinner invitation.

an old-fashioned work ethic and dignity that this world could use a lot more of. Ruth, I take off my hat to you!"

Paul Prudhomme paid her one of the most resounding compliments, saying, "To have fifty, sixty, seventy restaurants is almost impossible. I've been in the restaurant business for over fifty years and I'll never try it. We'll probably never match what you did in your lifetime. So when I say thank you I mean it for the whole industry."

Actually there were over 90 at the time. Now there are over 130 worldwide, the largest upscale restaurant group in the world.

We played the video on a loop at her funeral on a TV surrounded—in-undated—by flower arrangements that had come from all over the country. It looked like a Mafia funeral. Franchisees vied to see who loved their friend and benefactor the most—Marcel Taylor, the Las Vegas franchisee, won hands down with an arrangement of purple orchids at least six feet tall and four feet across. The chapel at Lakelawn cemetery held four hundred at least and it was SRO and overflow into the adjoining rooms where sound was piped in. Lilian Boutte sang the hymn "In a Garden" and wept, channeling the recent loss of her own mother. I adapted my eulogy from the speech I had written to deliver at her tribute dinner—sadly, all I'd had to do was change the tenses. In her absence I celebrated her gift of presence—to resounding applause and a standing ovation like I had never witnessed at a funeral. I'm not boasting. It was a great life and the public, iconic Ruth Fertel went out beloved. The Olympia Brass Band played her last ramble.

A week later, five hundred people honored Mom's memory. A yellow rose, her lifelong favorite, marked her vacant spot at the head table. We raised half a million dollars for the Ruth U. Fertel Culinary Arts Building.

And now I know a bit better the forces that shaped my parents and, through them, me.

By the end of his life, I had managed to cut Dad some slack. But Mom, whom I admired in so many ways, was the greater challenge. Though I set out here to find forgiveness—which doesn't really seem the right word—I continue to be conflicted. I feel a need to accept my mother for who she was. I also want to reconcile that with my awareness that she often wasn't what I most needed. She seemed to believe I never had a right to need her. But I did need her; I had that right.

Neither of my parents was much good at seeing me as a being apart, someone separate from themselves that they had, at least for a time, some responsibility to nurture.

Other than money, Dad had so little going for him. And the money poisoned his one great gift, his passion for coaching. Instead of mentoring kids, he spent his life telling us all what to do. Being on the receiving end of his hectoring aggravated me all my life. But now I see better where it came from. He grew up in a family not blessed with the gift of cupboard love, perhaps without the gift of love itself. Dad seemed to have fewer personal gifts than Mom to deploy in overcoming traumas. Eventually I managed, at least somewhat, to overcome my need for a normal father. I understood better that "normal" just wasn't in the cards he was dealt.

Mom, on the other hand, was rich in gifts: intelligence, charisma, presence, a family that adored her. The cupboard love she enjoyed growing up was unrivaled, incomparable. I mostly tried to understand the world through my brain, my intelligence. That blinded me to the fact that emotional intelligence is a different kind of gift, and one that my mother was *not* granted. *You're better at feelings*, she admitted, then made no effort to grow. Feelings had so little role in a success that was all-important to her. Why should she change? Why couldn't I accept that? I still wrestle with the conflicts.

When you've survived a drought, it's hard to find sympathy for those who grew up awash—to a fault—in love. I was so thirsty for love, I felt there was something wrong with me—that the well of love was dry only for me. No, it was just dry. And yet it was I who felt ashamed. Shame can be hard to shake.

Mom was widely beloved, but the closer you got, the dryer the well. She had a huge circle of acquaintances and a gigantic group of business associates that admired, even worshiped her. If she made some mistakes, she had a ball doing it. It is also true that grandiosity, her need to be right, isolated my mother. As angry as I am for living a lifetime beneath her cool gaze, I feel pity for her isolation, which grew greater and greater in her last years and seemed complete on her deathbed. Insofar as it was not her choice but one created by a family legacy, she should be the object of pity rather than anger. I do my best.

KATRINA'S AFTERMATH

Didn't he ramble . . . he rambled
Rambled all around . . . in and out of town
Didn't he ramble . . . didn't he ramble
He rambled till the butcher cut him down.
TRADITIONAL

I AM GRATEFUL THAT BOTH MY PARENTS, WHO EVEN IN DEATH REMAIN iconic figures locally, missed the destruction of the city that they loved. Most of all I am glad that Mom missed the departure of the Ruth's Chris corporate offices from New Orleans. Craig Miller, CEO, announced within a week of Hurricane Katrina that he was moving the corporate offices to Orlando. He explained that only weeks before they had taken the company public—the NASDAQ symbol was RUTH—and they needed to show their shareholders and customers that Ruth's Chris was viable. *It's what Ruth would have done,* Miller claimed. He wasn't sure if they would ever re-open the flagship. Sitting at an intersection that flooded and left customers stranded even in a hard rain, the Broad Street restaurant took on five feet of Katrina's floodwaters.

"No, that's certainly not what Ruth would have done. And if she had, she would have added, 'We'll be back soon.'" That's what I told an audience less than two months later at the Southern Foodways Alliance Symposium in

270

Oxford, Mississippi, where I sponsor the Ruth Fertel Keeper of the Flame Award, which honors an unsung hero or heroine, a foodways tradition bearer of note. Most of all, I argued, they had no right to appropriate her voice in defending their corporate decision. R. W. Apple Jr. of the *New York Times* was in the audience and published my remarks.

Miller called me, urging me to back off. "You're hurting the value of your stock."

"Between my stock and my mother's legacy," I replied, "it's an easy choice." We never spoke again. He was eventually replaced.

Many in New Orleans announced they would never dine at Ruth's Chris again. But Mom had created the Ruth U. Fertel Foundation in her will and it was devoted to education in the New Orleans area. She had made me president, her parting gift. This was a legacy I could help steward. There was much work to do.

I was teaching the Literature of Exile at the New School for Social Research in New York, never imagining my own narrative would suddenly become part of the syllabus.

On my first trip back, I found New Orleans unspeakably lonely. The devastation wrought by the levee breaks went on and on, block after block at the lakefront (where I grew up), Mid-City (where Mom had lived), the Lower Ninth Ward, and St. Bernard Parish—areas once shimmering with funky life, now lifeless and forlorn.

Everywhere dump trucks trolled—FEMA paid by the load. Men with masks directed traffic, sometimes in Hazmat gear. I passed huge dumping areas piling ever higher, flooded cars, blocks and blocks boarded up. I negotiated one surprise detour after another. Refrigerators taped shut against their stench littered the sidewalks. All the grass and many trees were dead—drowned. Everywhere I looked for the high water line still visible on homes—dubbed the bathtub ring—sometimes feet from the ground, sometimes over my head.

Grey dust covered everything. It was like being in an old sepia photograph, but with blue sky. In Audubon Park and on St. Charles Avenue there was too much sky: huge holes where live oaks once stood.

Seville Drive saw nine feet. Our one-time home's foundation had cracked and its brick façade was tumbling down. The pine trees Paw-Paw had planted were cut and piled amidst the last owner's detritus. The house has since been demolished.

Coda.1 Seville Drive after Katrina.

Birds, too, were gone. In "Do You Know What it Means to Miss New Orleans" Louis Armstrong laments "the tall sugar pines / Where mockin' birds used to sing." Who knew it could mean this?

For many years, I had proudly given my "Fertel Funky Tour" to friends visiting New Orleans, emphasizing sites that the tour busses missed. We would lunch at Uglesich's or Willie Mae's Scotch House. I would take them by the flagship Ruth's Chris. Broad and Orleans is not the safest corner in New Orleans but it is one of the most interesting, a crossroads Eshu must have had a hand in creating. It lies on an axis that passes from the St. Louis Cathedral through Congo Square and then on to the headwaters of Bayou St. John. The corner is an unheralded New Orleans power nexus. Catty-corner from the flagship Ruth's Chris, with its one-time power lunch, stands the Zulu Social Aid and Pleasure Club, the black Mardi Gras krewe which Louis Armstrong once proudly ruled as king. Across the street lies F&F Candle and Botanical, the voodoo supply shop where Earner got her gris-gris, the hoodoo amulets of her youth. Across the street the other way, flashy light-heavyweight champion Willie Pastrano, who fought for the Mob, had his gym. Jerry owns it now; it's a plumbing warehouse. Broad and Orleans was to the city what the Dockery Plantation crossroads was to Robert Johnson and the blues.

Rampart Street with its jazz history was another important stop. I would always take my guests by the corner where the Fertel Loan Office once stood and then take them two blocks up to Perdido and Rampart where a young Louis Armstrong got his first cornet from Jake Fink, our relative by marriage. At that corner Little Louis was lost and found: arrested for firing a weapon and sent to the Colored Waifs Home where he got his first musical instruction. American and world culture would never be the same.

Would New Orleans ever be the same?

Now, in Katrina's floods, Perdido Street was lost again. Just two blocks from the now infamous Superdome—with its storm-tossed refugees and its peeled-back roof—Perdido saw nearly three feet of water.

Once, my Parisian guests, who were in town for a conference on Hermes the Trickster, politely asked, *What ees thees 'funky'?* I explained that "funky" first of all means smelly—*puant*. Buddy Bolden, arguably the first jazzman of them all, played at a club near Rampart Street called the Funky Butt, named for the song, which begs someone to "open up the windows and let the bad air out." But in New Orleans we have another type of "funk," a kind of soul music, like that played by the Funky Meters. The word's probable roots reflect the two meanings. According to African art historian Robert Farris Thompson, "The black nuance seems to derive from the Ki-Kongo *lu-fuki*, 'bad body odor,'" but "both jazzmen and Bakongo use 'funky' and *lu-fuki*, to praise persons for the integrity of their art."[20] So, funk calls up the roots of jazz and its offspring, with a syncopated, heavy backbeat. It's the kind of music, to paraphrase jazz great Danny Barker, you gotta dance to unless there's something wrong with you.

In the first months following Katrina, the common meaning of "funk" could no longer be escaped. People speculated about the source: was it the smell of those still entombed beneath their roofs? the smell of fifty thousand refrigerators now on the street after weeks without electricity? or the smell of sludge the floodwaters left behind?

Commercial "disaster tours" covered much of the territory that once delighted my guests. But that territory had shrunk. Overnight, Katrina washed away twenty-five more square miles of the marsh that characterized my mother's home parish of Plaquemines. "The wettest place in the world" was now again wetter.

Coda.2 Boat on levee in Empire.

Aunt Helen wisely fled Buras before the storm. Katrina just plain flattened Plaquemines Parish. The hurricane's eye passed directly across the toe of Louisiana's boot—officially making landfall at Pointe à la Hache, five miles above Happy Jack—before moving on to the Gulf Coast. Where New Orleans experienced Category 2 winds, and the Gulf Coast Category 4, Plaquemines suffered Category 5: sustained winds of 140 miles per hour with gusts up to 190. As with Hurricane Betsy, Buras once again was gone, huge shrimp and menhaden boats tossed upon the levee and beyond.

But even in Plaquemines, Katrina's worst winds were just her love pats. The storm surge swept across the east bank and across the east bank levee, then across the broad Mississippi (two miles wide at that point) and then across the west levee. Starting in Happy Jack and stretching to the end of the road in Venice, the back levee was meant to protect the area from a storm surge coming in from the west as it had in 1915. This time it held the water in, sloshing back and forth between the levees, and floating homes off their foundations helter-skelter. Instead of New Orleans's ubiquitous X markings and the shorthand for when and who had searched a property and what they had found (live or dead people or animals), in Plaquemines floaters were marked with their address to show where they had floated

Coda.3 Sig and Helen's restaurant with the "floater" on the right.

from. The destruction was as complete as it was in the now-infamous Lower Ninth Ward. The land was rural so the population was not as dense. But it went on for twenty-five miles. The salt water drowned five hundred of the one thousand acres of Louisiana navels, the best oranges in America. Muck from the lost marshland smothered 60 percent of the nation's largest oyster beds, 2 million acres of public and private grounds yielding 250 million pounds of shucked oysters annually. The Fertels did not enjoy oyster dressing the year of Katrina.

Tired of fleeing hurricanes, Helen moved once and for all to Beaumont, Texas, to live near her sister. Within weeks she was fleeing Hurricane Gustav.

Two months after Katrina, I went to Happy Jack to see how Sig's Antique Restaurant, the first restaurant in our family, had fared. Made of old brick scrounged from old plantation foundations and dating from the late 1950s, perhaps it had withstood the winds and waters. I stopped to photograph one of the houses that had floated up to Highway 23, the parish's main artery. Just as I was driving away, a second glance revealed behind it the wreck of Sig's Antique Restaurant, its old-brick arches outside and its huge hand-hewn cypress beams inside collapsed. I drove on.

It was disconcerting to come to the end of the road in Venice. Everything beyond is river and marshland. I had not seen it since fishing trips in the 1960s and so was not prepared for the dystopian world of machinery and vessels built up since then by Halliburton and Bechtel and their kind. The world that had been mostly water was now blue and gray with steel. In Plaquemines Parish, Katrina swept away 250 years of Alsatian, Dalmatian, Isleño, and African American culture. Here alone in the parish, men were hard at work on something besides cleanup. Somehow, it seemed connected to that other world—Iraq—where, in the midst of devastation and chaos, the same kind of men manage to prosper.

• • •

Got my red beans cookin'
Got my red beans cookin'?
Yea my red beans is cookin'?
When they get done?
I'm gon' give you some
MUDDY WATERS

Back in the city, I would suddenly think of a restaurant or shop and realize I didn't know its fate. Or, on automatic pilot, I'd head for a favorite hamburger joint, drive through several miles of devastation and then find Bud's Broiler's door closed, with the bathtub ring at five feet eloquent testimony they wouldn't be opening anytime soon.

One by one, restaurant reopenings were big news locally, each a salve to the city's bruised collective soul. Cuvée, Restaurant August, Upperline, K-Paul, Bayona, Emeril's, then the traditional Creole mainline restaurants, Antoine's and Galatoire's—each in that order helped us imagine that New Orleans might again become livable. Tasting crabmeat maison again at Galatoire's made everything momentarily whole: a mound of jumbo lump crabmeat in mayonnaise, lemon, green onions, and I'm not sure what. But I do know that it is sweet beyond sweet and rich beyond rich.

Basse cuisine was there alongside its *hautes cousines*: when Faubourg St. John's Parkway Bakery—just blocks from Ruth's Chris—held a gala reopening in late December, a thousand people showed up, looking, according to *Times-Picayune* food critic Brett Anderson, "like the wedding party of a Mafia prince." Most came for the famous roast beef poor boy, which serves New Orleans as a kind of terrestrial ambrosia. Best of all was the first taste

Coda.4 Earner visits with Willie Mae
Seaton after the storm.

of a Louisiana navel orange, picked that morning on Johnny Becnel's family farm, now in its eighth generation, high and dry in Jesuit Bend in upper Plaquemines.

Like many in the New Orleans diaspora, I longed for the proper ingredients to re-create our food. I returned to New York from New Orleans with my suitcase filed with Camellia Brand red beans, green baby lima beans, crawfish tails, ham seasonings and smoked sausage (or, as we say, "smoke' sausage"). I cooked for my friends in New York in an effort to believe that New Orleans was still alive.

"Honey, I lost everything," Willie Mae Seaton told me on my next trip back, sitting out front while the Southern Foodways Alliance gutted and restored her Scotch House Restaurant. In 2005, at age eighty-nine, Willie Mae Seaton received a James Beard Award for more than three decades of heavenly fried chicken and "bread pudding that limns the platonic ideal." Once, if the black power elite wasn't doing deals at Ruth's Chris, they were doing them at Willie Mae's. Four months after the awards ceremony, five feet of water left behind a pudding of silt. The flagship Ruth's Chris four blocks away at Broad and Orleans saw the same five feet of water and was still untouched.

In early December, I attended the gala reopening of Ruth's Chris in Metairie, our suburban store since the early 1970s. Joe Bruno, an old friend from Mid-City who had owned a string of Tastee Donuts shops and hunted with us in Mexico, expressed his relief: "Randy, I'm so glad they opened. I was SOOOO hungry." Some New Orleanians were slowly relenting.

But most New Orleanians were not in a position to worry about Ruth's Chris. Even Earner, who no longer had Miz Ruth to tend to.

Earner, who grew up on the banks of the Mississippi, feared water. She would not drive herself over any large bridge. For most of her life this confined her to what was once known as the Ile de la Nouvelle Orleans: the island city surrounded by swamps to the east and west, lake to the north and river embracing the Crescent City on three sides.

Earner rode out the storm in the home Miz Ruth helped her buy, itself suddenly an island, on Arts and Dorgenois in the Upper Ninth Ward. A neighbor rescued her by boat and took her to the Superdome. Her daughter, Connie, rode out the storm nearby on Pauger Street. Connie had worked at Ruth's Chris for thirty-two years, first as a busser and later as a much-loved waitress. She had many "call parties," regulars who asked for her by name. I had promoted her from busgirl to waitress and she long ago proved my faith in her.

Connie couldn't say much about the storm because she was so frightened that she hid. The wind was "howling like the evil one." When the levees broke, she walked amidst floating bodies toward the Superdome with water up to her chin. She is four foot eleven.

There Connie found her mother. They spent five or six days in the Dome, at the forty-yard line down by the field. "It was nothing nice," Connie related, the story pouring out of her. She spoke of the smell and of rumored rapes in dark bathrooms. "People were dropping around you like flies." Refusing Meals Ready to Eat—imagine New Orleanians reduced to MREs—she survived on potato chips and water. Finally, in frustration, they walked to the Convention Center where busses were accepting children and the elderly. Connie pleaded her mother's Alzheimer's.

On the way to Houston's Astrodome, Connie couldn't take any more of her mother's "Alzheimer tantrums." Leaving Earner with her sister, Connie got off the bus in the middle of the night in Franklin, near Lafayette in the heart of Cajun country, and started walking. She stayed many months in Franklin, lost among country cousins she could not fathom and longing to return to New Orleans and Ruth's Chris where there was a job waiting but no place to live. Connie doesn't drive.

Ruth's Chris, to give them their due, did right by their employees. They lost three restaurants at one blow. The one in the Hard Rock Hotel and Casino in Biloxi had just that weekend held its opening parties for VIPs. The restaurant had yet to sell its first steak before a barge slipped through their second-floor windows into the dining room. Despite these corporate losses, Ruth's Chris made money available to those who needed it and promised a job to anyone who could find their way to another restaurant. Some from Broad Street went to Metairie; others were flung far and wide.

Earner ended up in Fort Worth in a Best Western hotel room paid for by FEMA. I sent money. Jerry tracked Earner down and drove her to Hot Springs. Earner couldn't remember anyone but Connie and her grandson Pie, Jerry, and me. She would call Connie to come get her in a cab and take her home. When Connie reminded her where they were, three hundred miles apart, and with no home in New Orleans, Earner would slam the phone down.

Jerry was in Hot Springs for the storm. Afterwards he went out and bought a dump truck to help clean up New Orleans. Then he learned he had to get a license to drive it. The building he owned in the Warehouse District, where his son Rien managed a grocery store and lived upstairs, was hit doubly, ransacked up and down. It was two blocks from the now infamous Convention Center. Rien moved to New York where he took classes in food writing and history at the New School for Social Research where I was teaching. Now he is finishing a PhD in history at Tulane, writing a dissertation on the history of New Orleans white Creoles. He seems more my son than Jerry's.

Jerry lived for a while in Rien's place with the crew he brought from Hot Springs, hard workers who seemed to know what they were doing. Jerry, whose love for New Orleans is unmatched, worked at their side. Jerry has now fully adopted the family totem. His work truck sports a GET THE GO-RILLA decal and his several portable generators were identified GORILLA. His voice mail—Jerry himself never answers—baldly intones, *Jerry Gorilla*. His mailbox is constantly full. He doesn't return calls. Concerned, his friends all remark, *Jerry's more and more like your dad every day.*

Together they restored Earner's house and moved her back. I paid for her new AC and hot water heater.

Coda.5 Jerry's GET THE GORILLA Truck.

Some eighteen hundred people died in Hurricane Katrina and the ensuing federal flood when the poorly designed levees fell. However, it can take a long time to total up luck or loss. In the catastrophe's wake, how many more fell victim to the stresses and the heartbreak?

Earner died in her sleep on May 27, 2008.

We gathered in the church where Earner's mother, Pearl's, funeral had been held, Our Lady of the Sea Church near the famous St. Roch chapel. The church is now graced with an altar mural that must have been painted by a follower of *Playboy*'s Alberto Vargas who imagined the heavenly host as so many vixens, or perhaps by Eshu himself, stirring it up, determined to keep us from our prayers.

I sat with Earner's family. I am sorry Jerry did not attend. I have never felt so embraced by a family as by the Sylvains that morning. The church was full. Earner's legendary posse, all those folks she'd say hello to whenever we ran the city together, had turned out. I sat next to a cousin Cookie who told me she, too, had been raised by Earner, and who took my hand and held it for long passages and told me she knew all about me, that Earner had told the story of her *other* sons many times. She pointed out who was who. She cried with me when they closed the coffin. She took communion with me. It was this sense of community that I had experienced the last time I had come to this church, for Earner's mother's funeral right after the family business debacle. This time I was on the receiving end of those feelings of community I had admired and envied. I was part of it, I was embraced. Connie had for years called me her brother. Now she listed Jerry and me in the program as Earner's stepsons, and we were so recognized from the pulpit. Everyone I spoke to knew the story of Earner's raising us. I thought of Thoreau's question: "But are they not indeed distinguished who are conscious that they are regarded at all?"

The sermon was eloquent and the singing angelic, that near falsetto blacks command that sends you with the song itself up to the peak of the nave. I'm sorry Jerry missed it. He seems to share Mom's discomfort with finality.

After the service, just as the Sylvains had, the Ruth's Chris posse embraced me, all the servers and back-house staff that had been with us, some since the 1960s.

Ralph was a less gracious presence. He threw out his hand and commanded, *here, boy.* Nonplussed by his gruffness, I regret that I shook it.

The drive to Edgard for the burial took us through Boutte, where Louis Armstrong's mother had worked the plantation before moving to New Orleans, then past field after field of young sugar cane. St. John Church was lovely, just down from the levee, the cemetery full of French surnames. There Earner Thelma Sylvain, the family's chief pot stirrer and my "hired mother," as my poet friend Ronnie put it, was laid to rest.

After the graveside service, I ran up River Road and sought out Chef John Folse at his Donaldsonville restaurant, Bittersweet Plantation. There he served me the crawfish bisque La Côte Allemande is famous for. It was a dead ringer for Pearl and Earner's, though theirs was better.

• • •

I went on down to the Audubon Zoo
And they all axed for you.
The monkeys axed, the tigers axed
And the elephants axed me too.

THE METERS

Animals, too, were part of the Katrina story. Many New Orleanians refused to evacuate after the water rose because they knew their pets would have to be left behind to starve or be destroyed. Extraordinary efforts—both personal and official—were made to rescue animals. The Louisiana SPCA and the Humane Society of the U.S. went house to house. *The New Yorker* reported that for a while the animal rescue workers outnumbered FEMA representatives.

The Audubon Zoo was in some ways a microcosm of the city.

Unlike much of the city, the zoo was well prepared with generators and enough fuel, food, and water for keepers and animals to last ten days. Dan Maloney and his skeleton crew hunkered down in the Reptile House to wait out the storm. Afterwards they found the zoo had lost only four animals, less than half a percent of fifteen hundred animals in the zoo, almost exactly the percentage of New Orleanians lost.

But the most significant loss was the people—locals and tourists—that had made the Audubon Zoo, like the city itself, one of the most vibrant destinations in the world. Dan wrote me: "This was never more evident than in the quiet, lonely months just after the storm. Many of us lived at the zoo throughout the ordeal, and the abnormal stillness began to take a toll on the people and the animals. It became exceedingly clear just how important guests are to defining the true essence of a zoo. Without our visitors enjoying and learning about wildlife in a beautiful and secure setting, we are only a pretty place holding and breeding endangered species."

Which sounded a lot like the new New Orleans. But, rescued from the waves, the new New Orleans was Protean in another sense: it was constantly shifting. Returning to New Orleans intermittently gave me snapshots of the city in its progress to return. One visit everyone would seem clinically depressed, the next visit everyone seemed burning with optimism.

At an early benefit concert at the House of Blues I met a man who recounted his experience of rebuilding his house in Lakeview. "I see the same group of folks every morning at Home Depot," he explained, "where we've all come for building supplies. I haven't felt so much a part of a community since the sixties." With the city abandoned by leadership at the local, state, and federal levels, community spirit slowly rebuilt New Orleans, the perfect Horatio Alger story as it pulled itself up by its own bootstraps. We had outside help, and it came largely from volunteers from across America and from the young folks who have been flocking to New Orleans: the Young Urban Rebuilding Professionals (YURP), over five hundred Teach for America Fellows, and the entrepreneurs at the Idea Village. Our decades of brain drain have turned into brain gain. New Orleans personifies the spirit of a new sixties, a place where people come to make a difference. Many think the city, washed clean by Hurricane Katrina, is now incubating the future of American education and entrepreneurship.

In another way, New Orleans is the canary in the coal mine, a warning—I hope not from Cassandra—to other cities. The "federal flood"—as we insist on calling it—was caused not by nature's forces—a mere Category 2 hurricane in New Orleans—but by the collapse of the infrastructure, fecklessly built and maintained by the U.S. Army Corps of Engineers. This is a problem that will haunt many of us in coming decades as the impending effects of violent climate change test decaying infrastructures worldwide. Ultimately the city's and the populace's tribulations came from the same surge in deregulation and government-at-arm's-length policies that power the economic tsunamis that in 2007 threatened to submerge families and businesses across the globe.

Cassandra's curse was that her countrymen refused to listen to her oh-so-accurate prophecies. We must see and hear the Cassandra-city or America's walls will tumble as surely as our levees did.

New Orleans is also a model of rebirth—if I don't speak too soon—the canary as Phoenix.

Eventually Ruth's Chris corporate, with a new CEO at the helm, reopened a New Orleans location near the Convention Center. Mom had always resisted a location so near her flagship but that conflict had been washed away. The new location flourished, rivaling Manhattan in sales, I am told. More New Orleanians had let go their grudge, or at least could no longer forgo the sizzle. Many were further appeased when the corporation finally donated the flagship to Tulane University for a community health center to help anchor the neighborhood. It was the vision of community health whiz Dr. Karen DeSalvo, whose earthy good sense and love of hunting and fishing would have recommended her to Mom. It was a good fit in every way (except the lack of a steak house) and I supported it by giving a speech at the donation ceremony held in the Tulane Medical Center where Mom once worked and where a bust memorialized her boss, Dr. George Burch. More circles turned full. The Broads from Broad Street—Connie, Lainey, Robin, and others—came in force and we laughed and cried together.

Jerry so far has resisted my recommendation that he donate Mom's house that sat across the parking lot, still suffering from Katrina's waters, to add a mental health clinic for New Orleans musicians. Jerry gutted it and then it was vandalized. He seems to have given up on it.

In January 2006, just months after the storm, the Ruth U. Fertel Foundation held a press conference to announce $1.1 million in grants to New Orleans schools. With its school board washed away, New Orleans has become a hotbed of educational reform. I am glad Mom's gift has given me a small part in its rebirth. Jerry has expressed no interest.

In March 2007, Alice Waters, famed chef and founder of the Chez Panisse restaurant in Berkeley, California, sat at a first-grade desk in the Samuel J. Green Charter Elementary School in New Orleans.

I had met Alice at the Nation Institute annual dinner shortly after Katrina and she told me of her lifelong love for our city. She wanted to do something because Chef Paul Prudhomme had once helped her. I knew about her Edible Schoolyard project in Berkeley, which introduces students and faculty to seasonal growing, eating and learning. Would she be interested, I wondered, in bringing her Edible Schoolyard to the Crescent City?

For a long time, I've been a big fan of Samuel J. Green Charter and its principal, Tony Recasner. The school had suffered several feet of water, but Tony had managed to stitch the building, and a reduced faculty and student body, back together by January 2006, making it one of the first schools to open after Hurricane Katrina. Starting from scratch more than ten years before, Tony had made a success of a charter school where 99 percent of the students were African American and 90 percent qualified for the federal assisted-lunch program. After Katrina, most of them were living in trailers and relatives' homes.

Just as I anticipated, Tony became an avid supporter of Alice's ideas about weaving food throughout the learning experience and curriculum. His hope was "to renew New Orleans one okra plant and one child at a time." By March 2006, Tony and I visited the Berkeley program. In April, Alice came to New Orleans to meet with the Green Charter School teachers and a superb local task force.

The Edible Schoolyard of New Orleans quickly became a reality. Less than three years after Green School's reopening, the half-acre garden, filled with cabbages, parsley, broccoli, and other herbs and vegetables as well as flowering plants, was completed and a full-scale teaching kitchen was built. More than $2 million was raised, spearheaded by the Ruth U. Fertel Foundation with major support from the Viking Range Corporation, the Emeril Lagasse Foundation, the Zemurray Foundation, the Octavia

Coda.6 Alice Waters at Edible Schoolyard.

Foundation, and others. If Ruth's Chris had been clogging arteries for forty years with ecologically unfriendly corn-fed beef, it seemed karmic justice that the foundation Ruth established should help a new generation learn how to eat better and how to steward the land. The community embraced the program. Our first benefit party—with Alice in attendance—sold 609 tickets and raised $60,000.

Because of the Edible Schoolyard, the multinational food provider Sodexho—normally glacial in its willingness to change—was cooking lunch on the premises with whole grains and fresh, local fruit and vegetables. They were planning to make the alternative menu available to other schools. The Ruth U. Fertel Foundation joined with the Emeril Lagasse Foundation to hire a master's of public health–trained coordinator to work with the many charter schools that sought a better lunch program. The thriving Green Charter School's parent organization opened a second school, eventually to be housed at Bienville School, half a block from where the Empress of Steak did what she could to raise her two sons alone.

Now Alice Waters had come to visit the first satellite of her Edible Schoolyard program. A banner—"Welcome Ms. Alice"—decorated with flowers and butterflies greeted her arrival on the school's beautifully planted front porch. The children had escorted her on a tour of the Edible Garden.

I welcomed Ms. Alice, too. Alice was a visionary like my mother. Both women transformed American restaurants, but Alice did so not just by her commitment to quality, but also by honoring and respecting her chefs. At Chez Panisse two chefs share the top position, rotating six months on and six months off (though paid for the whole year). Alice understands that renewing yourself—and your family—is good business. Her empire is not extensive but intensive, growing not out but down, into the way we live and experience life. Ruth put more food in front of more people, but no one has done more than Alice to change the way Americans eat.

We sat together at classroom desks, just a few blocks from the Robert Street home where my father spent his teen years. Alice wore a hand-painted apron, a gift from the first graders. Sitting in her diminutive chair, the guest of honor opened a card decorated with a child's version of an orange tree. She read aloud, "I love being in the garden because it feels like heaven. The birds are singing over my head." And from another: "I want to be a chef."

ACKNOWLEDGMENTS

THIS PROJECT HAS BEEN BLESSED WITH THREE ANGELS THOUGH I PREFER to think of them as my Fates: Rebecca McClanahan, who helped me to spin, Diana Pinckley, who helped me to weave, and Didi Goldenhaar, who helped with the hardest task, cutting.

Additional thanks go to Ronni Lundy for a bottom-of-the-ninth game-winning idea about structure, and to Judy Long for last-minute shaping and refining and for effort well beyond the call of duty. Special thanks to Leila Salisbury and the staff of the University Press of Mississippi for "getting" the project from the start and helping me make it as good as possible.

I have many friends, many in the writing game, to thank for advice, counsel, and encouragement: Christina Adams, Fred Anderson, David "Jellyroll Justice" Averback, Darren Bagert, Lynn Bell, Michelle Benoit, Phil Caputo, Mark Childress, Elizabeth Cooper, Jack Davis, Stephanie Samuel Durant, John T. Edge, Lolis Eric Elie, the late Gloria Emerson, Ham Fish, Tom Fitzmorris, Greg Fleeman, Betty Fussell, Carol Gelderman, Tony Gentry, Paul Goldberger, Ron Grant, Annette Harper, Jessica Harris, Paul Hendrickson, Ellis Hennican, Tom and Dorothy Howorth, Rosemary James, Wayne Karlin, Richard Katrovas, Sally Knight, Daniel Kornstein, Karen Kudej, Mayor Mitch Landrieu, Jack Langguth, Virginia LaPlante, Susan Larson, Nancy Lemann, Cynthia Lewis, David Lynn, Bobbie Malone, Martha Nelson, Tim O'Brien, Pat O'Hara, Molly O'Neill, Susan Palo, Ellen Morris Prewitt, Sue Ribnor, Ted Sann, Margaret Sartor, Jonathan Schell,

Eric Schroeder, John Simonson, Frances Smith, Julie Smith, Suzanne Farrell Smith, Ben Sontheimer, Susan Spicer, Pavlina Sudrich, Ben Fong Torres, Justin Vogt, and Chris Wiltz. Judge Jacob Karno (Louis Karnofsky's grandson) helped with genealogy. James Hillman, James Silberman and Tracy Kidder were kind long before my manuscript deserved kid gloves. Special thanks to the members of Rebecca McClanahan's *Kenyon Review* summer writing workshops, who convinced me my wacky stories added up to a book, and to Peter White, who dragged me there. Thanks go also to Patricia Hampl, who allowed me to sit in on her class at the Prague Summer Writing Program.

Many others helped in recovering the memories that make up this book: my aunt Helen Garma Udstad Tarter and her son, my cousin Sig; cousins JoAnn Purcell Levert, the late Audrey Jacomine Cascio, the late Stanley Fink, Sydney Fertel, and the late Bluma Fertel Wolfson; my nephew Rien Fertel and his mother, Rosemary Parisi; Terry Bowers Gerosa; the late Marjorie Troxler and her son Dr. William Troxler; Rosemary James and the late Iris Kelso; the late Earner Sylvain and her daughter, Connie; my father's school chums Lenny Ferrara, Jan Pedersen, and Frank Zito; and mine: Rick Permutt and his wife, Jill, ron caron and his wife, Maury Strong, Susan McLean Welsh, Judy Agular, Elissa Zengel, and Max Begué. Many others told tales of the early days of Chris Steak House, too many to list; special thanks to Lolis Edward Elie, who integrated Chris Steak House, to Jim Polster and to James Quaid, whose father offered my mother the key advice to borrow some working capital. Bill Betcher, Charlotte Mathes, Pia Melody, Terry Real, and Jan Rieveshl for many long years helped me dig deep and to make sense of the muck I found there. Thanks to former head curator of the Audubon Zoo Dan Maloney for his account of the aftermath of Katrina and to Ron Forman for his memories of the aftermath of the Gorilla Campaign (and for remembering Dad so fondly). Thanks to John Sylvest for his expert and energetic curatorship of Port Sulphur memories, and to Ron Swoboda and Garland Robinette for memories of my mom and dad. Thanks to John Pope for his expert help in the TP morgue.

My wife, Bernadette, asked the hardest, most incisive, and therefore the most helpful questions. She put up with my navel gazing long past the point of decency. My love and thanks.

I wish to thank Adam Fulk, Stephanie Moss, Susan Burke, Marion White, Elizabeth Mitchell, and all the hard workers at Free Gulliver who helped not only in research but also in giving me the essential gift: time *non fare niente* and therefore to create. Thanks to Tripp Friedler and Steve Kupperman, together the project's most industrious readers and advocates.

My gratitude goes to George Schmidt for permission to use his gorgeous painting of a young Pops and the moment that changed world culture. Thanks to Chris Harris and Bunny Matthews for permission to publish their art and to ron caron for permission to publish his poem.

Finally, I wish with love to thank my sons, Matt and Owen, who know all too well how weak my memory can be and for whom I was not always present while I was busy recovering memories with which to celebrate (and mourn) my parents' presence (and absence).

NOTES

1. Betty Fussell, *Raising Steaks: The Life and Times of American Beef* (New York: Houghton Mifflin, 2008), 287.

2. John Berger, *About Looking* (New York: Pantheon Books, 1980), 15.

3. Terry Teachout, *Pops: A Life of Louis Armstrong* (New York: Houghton Mifflin Harcourt, 2009).

4. A. J. Liebling, *The Earl of Louisiana* (New York: Simon and Shuster, 1961), 17. Long got out of Mandeville by firing the director of hospitals and hiring another who would do his bidding.

5. Louis Armstrong, *Satchmo: My Life in New Orleans* (Rpt., New York: Da Capo Press, 1986), 8.

6. Alan Lomax, *Mister Jelly Roll: The Fortunes of Jelly Roll Morton, New Orleans Creole and "Inventor of Jazz"* (New York: Duell, Sloan and Pearce, 1950), 25.

7. Quoted in Laurence Bergreen, *Louis Armstrong: An Extravagant Life* (New York: Broadway Books, 1997), 14.

8. Michael Ondaatje, *Coming Through Slaughter* (New York: Vintage, 1996), 2.

9. Armstrong, *Satchmo*, 8.

10. "Louis Armstrong + The Jewish Family in New Orleans, LA, The Year of 1907," in *Louis Armstrong in His Own Words: Selected Writings*, ed. Thomas Brothers (New York: Oxford University Press, 1999), 16.

11. In "Louis Armstrong + The Jewish Family. . . ," he writes, "One day when I was on the wagon with Morris Karnofsky—we were on Rampart and Perdido Streets and we passed a Pawn Shop which had in its Window—an old tarnished beat up 'B' Flat Cornet. It only cost *Five* Dollars," 15. In *Satchmo*, Armstrong writes, "The first time I heard Sidney Bechet play that clarinet he stood me on my ear. . . . [Red] Allen must have known Bechet could play a lot of cornet, for he sent him into Jake Fink's to

borrow a cornet from Bob Lyons, the famous bass player. Bechet joined the band and he made the whole parade, blowing like crazy," 134.

12. "Louis Armstrong + The Jewish Family...," 13, 18.

13. Letter from Harry Latter to William Zechendorf, May 1948. Latter & Blum archive.

14. Harnett Kane, *Deep Delta Country* (New York: Duell, Sloan and Pearce, 1944), 86.

15. Robert Farris Thompson, *Flash of the Spirit: African and Afro-American Art and Philosophy* (New York: Vintage, 1984).

16. Myldred Masson Costa, trans., *The Letters of Marie Madeleine Hachard, 1727–28* (New Orleans: Laborde Printing, 1974), 43, 57.

17. William R. Stringfield, *Le Pays des Fleurs Orangiers: A Genealogical Study of Creole Families of Plaquemines Parish, Louisiana*, 2nd ed. (Baltimore: Gateway Press, 2010), passim.

18. Liebling, *Earl of Louisiana*, 167.

19. Ibid., 165.

20. Glen Jeansonne, *Leander Perez: Boss of the Delta* (Jackson: University Press of Mississippi, 2006), 108.

SOURCES

One of the treasures I discovered in researching this book is what I learned about jazz and its birth and Louis Armstrong's particular role in it. Thanks to Bruce Raeburn of the William R. Hogan Jazz Archive at Tulane University for his guidance, and to Jack Stewart for his help with Jake and Max Fink's role in jazz history.

New Orleans counts among its many blessings a number of wonderful native story-tellers. Louis Armstrong, Sidney Bechet, Jelly Roll Morton, and Danny Barker all bring the early years of jazz to life in prose that riffs and expands just the way their music does. For further reading, see Louis Armstrong, *Satchmo: My Life in New Orleans* (New York: Prentice-Hall, 1954) and *Louis Armstrong in His Own Words: Selected Writings*, ed. Thomas Brothers (New York: Oxford University Press, 1999); Danny Barker, *A Life in Jazz*, ed. Alyn Shipton (New York: Oxford University Press, 1986), and Danny Barker, *Buddy Bolden and the Last Days of Storyville*, ed. Alyn Shipton (New York: Continuum, 2001); Sidney Bechet, *Treat It Gentle: An Autobiography* (2nd ed.; New York: Da Capo Press, 2002); Alan Lomax, *Mister Jelly Roll: The Fortunes of Jelly Roll Morton, New Orleans Creole and "Inventor of Jazz"* (New York: Duell, Sloan and Pearce, 1950). I also benefited greatly from New Orleans scholars: Harnett Kane, *Deep Delta Country* (New York: Duell, Sloan and Pearce, 1944) and his *Queen New Orleans* (New York: William Morrow, 1949); and Barbara S. Malone, *Rabbi Max Heller: Reformer, Zionist, Southerner, 1860–1929* (Tuscaloosa: University of Alabama Press, 1997).

Many nonnatives, too, write brilliantly about jazz history. On Louis Armstrong, see Thomas Brothers, *Louis Armstrong's New Orleans* (New York: Norton, 2007); Gary Giddens, *Satchmo: The Genius of Louis Armstrong* (New York: Da Capo Press, 2001); and Terry Teachout, *Pops: A Life of Louis Armstrong* (New York: Houghton Mifflin Harcourt, 2009). For an account of the world into which Armstrong was born, see Donald Marquis, *In Search of Buddy Bolden: First Man of Jazz* (Baton Rouge: Louisiana

State University Press, 2005), and for a fictional account of that world, see Michael Ondaatje, *Coming Through Slaughter* (New York: Vintage, 1976).

On other aspects of New Orleans, see Roy Blount, Jr., *Feet on the Street: Rambles Around New Orleans* (New York: Crown, 2005); John Churchill Chase, *Frenchmen, Desire, Good Children: . . . and Other Streets of New Orleans!* (New Orleans: Pelican Publishing, 2001); John Davis, *Mafia Kingfish: Carlos Marcello and the Assassination of John F. Kennedy* (New York: McGraw-Hill, 1989); James Gill, *Lords of Misrule: Mardi Gras and the Politics of Race in New Orleans* (Jackson: University Press of Mississippi, 1997); Arnold R. Hirsch and Joseph Logsdon, *Creole New Orleans: Race and Americanization* (Baton Rouge: Louisiana State University Press, 1992); Glen Jeansonne, *Leander Perez: Boss of the Delta* (Jackson: University Press of Mississippi, 2006); A. J. Liebling, *The Earl of Louisiana* (Baton Rouge: Louisiana State University Press, 1960); Bob Roesler, *Fair Grounds: Big Shots & Long Shots* (New Orleans: Arthur Hardy & Associates, 1998); William R. Stringfield, *Le Pays des Fleurs Orangiers: A Genealogical Study of Creole Families of Plaquemines Parish, Louisiana* (2nd ed.; Baltimore: Gateway Press, 2001); and Chris Wiltz, *The Last Madam: A Life in the New Orleans Underworld* (New York: Da Capo Press, 2001).

Special thanks to Richard Campanella for his work on New Orleans geography and history, especially *New Orleans Then and Now* (New Orleans: Pelican Publishing, 1999), where I first discovered the photograph of the Fertel Building on Rampart, and for the maps which grace this book's inside covers.